# A MATHEMATICAL MYSTERY TOUR:

## HIGHER-THINKING MATH TASKS

MARK WAHL

Designed and Illustrated by Pam Horbett

**ZEPHYR PRESS**
**TUCSON, AZ**

# ACKNOWLEDGMENTS

Much applause goes to Pam Horbett for her dedication to making this book a superior visual product, above and beyond her job description and remuneration.

Much gratitude to Joey Tanner of Zephyr Press for believing in this book and desiring a quality product, and to the editors who put up with my writing quirks.

Much love to my wife, Flay, and daughter, Hanna, for sacrificing many family evenings and weekends to me and my computer, as well as for sharing the excitement about this unique learning product with me.

Many thanks to the teachers who tried out prototype lessons in the Bellevue School District—especially to Linda Oman's 6th-grade class whose frank and insightful comments created many changes for the better in this Tour.

And finally, thanks to Peter Thompkins, whose book **Secrets of the Great Pyramid** jolted me into pursuing a whole new level of mysterious mathematical exploration.

Mark Wahl
January, 1988
Seattle, Washington

---

Cover design and book production by Kathleen Koopman.

# Contents

# ORIENTATION FOR THE TEACHER

(Please Read before Using this Book)

Your students are about to journey into a mathematical world that is largely unknown to them. Perhaps even to you. This journey has not been part of the traditional math curriculum.

The **Mathematical Mystery Tour** contained in this book takes you through thought landscapes I discovered years ago and still continue to explore. You might say I pursued them as a hobby while I was teaching. Now I bring my hobby into what I teach.

These concepts create great interest in young people. Adults, too, are intrigued by the ideas. I'm eager to share them with you and your students!

As you proceed you will encounter mystery and historical depth in a subject you may have previously found stripped of flesh, blood, color, wonder, and relation to life. While my activities require and develop many of the "usual" math skills, you needn't be an "expert" in the special concepts to understand or teach them. You'll be learning many ideas at the same time your students do, though you'll have the advantage of detailed teaching notes and discussions in the "Teacher's Guide to Student Pages" following the activities. Your best "compass" on the journey, however, will be a sense of curiosity and a desire to explore amazing number "coincidences."

I've taught a lot of teacher workshops, and found varying levels of math discomfort or anxiety in a sizable percentage of elementary-level teachers. If you're in this category, you have a lot to gain from these activities. They're meant to motivate math avoiders and lead them to a more intuitive appreciation of mathematics.

## ORGANIZATION OF THE BOOK

Early in the trip (at the end of Unit I) you'll see a full map of the **Mystery Tour** displayed. Though its full complexity can be appreciated only as the **Tour** proceeds, a glance at it will give you some idea of the richness of interconnecting ideas available in this **Tour**.

This book is a mosaic; it doesn't unfold in the strictly linear fashion of most math instruction. You'll find each idea relating to several others, and you'll see new concepts suddenly connecting to much earlier ones. Seemingly unrelated pieces will begin to fit together more as the student's repertory of experiences and discoveries broadens. Later in the **Tour** the mosaic emerges with rich synergy, giving new power and insight to earlier adventures. My goal is to give both you and your students a changed conception of mathematics and its relationship to the world.

Generally speaking, the students should encounter the activities in order, but some reorganization is possible. Unit I and the beginning of Unit III introduce the pivotal concepts of the book. These are the **Fibonacci Numbers** and the **Golden Ratio**. Once these are grasped, it's possible to shop among the units for material that relates to student interest and your current curriculum. After several activities have been done, in or out of order, the mosaic will begin to emerge.

## UNIQUE FEATURES OF THIS BOOK

This book is unique among math learning materials. Here are some of its uncommon features:

• An interesting union of higher thinking skills with a wide selection of new concepts and a good helping of calculation practice.

• An integration of several different subject areas with math as the focus.

• Helpful teaching notes following each activity.

• A visual map ("mind map") at the end of each unit showing how the concepts relate to each other and to the rest of the book. All units also merge into a single map so you and your students can see your whole itinerary at a glance.

• Extensions and home tasks for many activities.

• Bibliographical references in the teacher material; complete bibliograhy appears on page 256.

• "Learning Inventories" at the end of each unit after Unit I.

• Optional Activities for teachers to use at their discretion.

• A potpourri of activity modes, from imaginative flat work to paper constructions to debate and art.

• A personalized, first-person tone throughout.

• An attractive visual layout with numerous illustrations.

• A *Tour Guide* newspaper providing historical and scientific background for the activities.

• Questions for thought and comprehension sprinkled into the text of the reading selections in the newspaper.

## EDUCATIONAL OBJECTIVES OF THE BOOK AND *TOUR GUIDE* NEWSPAPER

1. To motivate students who may not be attracted to math. The material integrates history, design, writing, geometrical constructions, botany, zoology, astronomy, and philosophy, which, like musical notes, are harmonized with mathematical concepts.

2. To introduce and give meaningful practice in computational skills.

3. To encourage intuitive use of these skills for problem solving and investigation.

4. To develop thinking skills by encouraging

| | |
|---|---|
| • planning | • research |
| • new applications | • formulation of results |
| • problem solving | • spatial visualization |
| • inferences | • pattern recognition |
| • estimation | • analogical thinking |

5. To foster surprise in mathematics—yes, even joy!

## HOW TO USE THESE MATERIALS

These materials are best used with a teacher as a resource and guide and with students working on projects in small groups. You need to encourage the following higher-level thinking processes at every possible opportunity. (You will be periodically reminded to do this in your teaching instructions.)

## ORIENTATION FOR THE TEACHER

- Formulating patterns and results into words and symbols.
- Fitting new ideas and discoveries into the context of the rest of the **Tour**.
- Researching events, concepts, and persons encountered on the **Tour**.
- Discussing with peers the methods used and results obtained with each activity.
- Trying suggested extensions of activities as well as inventing their own.

Photocopy the activity pages from the book in order and give them to the students one-by-one. (Occasionally two or three sheets are required in connection with a task.) Prepare for an activity by reading the teacher notes following it, as well as by reading through the activity and its answers. You will often have to supply materials, listed in the **Toolbox** on top of the student page, so be sure you have them on hand before starting an activity.

I recommend that students keep their work in a folder or notebook so they can refer back to all papers throughout the Tour. There will be times when this back-reference will be part of their work. (Again, you will learn that this book is best understood as a knitted whole rather than a sequence of skill-developments.)

## COOPERATIVE LEARNING WITH THESE ACTIVITIES

You may have many of your own ways to organize your class to work on these materials, but it's worth describing at length the use of groups and the Cooperative Learning Model.

These materials are well suited to small groups. Group members may exchange methods and answers, discuss results, and work together on the projects in pairs, threes, or, when they are more experienced cooperators, in fours. This can cut down considerably on the amount of photocopying required because students can cooperatively complete pages and read some introductory pages aloud to group members.

It's important to stress to the students at the beginning the importance of cooperative work in society. Also there are many skills of cooperation to be taught—ranging from no *put-downs* to summarizing results for the group to asking thoughtful questions. Each skill, as you perceive the need and readiness for it in the class, should be described and discussed, then assigned for practice in the groups as activities are being done. Afterwards, students should reflect on the successful use of the cooperation skill and on the effectiveness of the methods used to solve problems in the activity.

In this model you become an observer, a resource person, a motivator, and a troubleshooter when a group gets very stuck. Your role is not to rescue students from temporary setbacks in the work, or temporary confusion, as this will weaken their problem-solving abilities. The standard rule is **Students may ask for help from the teacher only when all group members have the same question.** Occasionally, though, you may need to intervene when a group is simply bogging down and doesn't know what question to ask.

Discussion questions are included in the activities, and students are often asked to discuss and work with each other while exploring "new territory." Many other optional suggestions of this type appear in the teacher notes following the activities.

In this cooperative model you evaluate products of an activity for a group grade. Further group grade points are accumulated for collaborative skills. Individual accountability can be monitored by
- Creating student feedback sheets on which students rate each other's participation and contributions.
- Assigning the Learning Inventory at the end of each unit.
- Asking for individual written discussion of the results of an activity.

A combination of group grade and individual grade becomes each student's mark for the activity.

(More variations and suggestions for cooperative learning can be found in the book **Circles of Learning** by Johnson and Johnson.)

## THE *TOUR GUIDE* NEWSPAPER

Students are given their *Tour Guide* newspapers at the beginning, and these must be saved to continue as a resource throughout the journey. (The journey can be done all at once in three to seven weeks or spread unit-by-unit or even activity-by-activity throughout the year. In the latter case, the extension activities can be done in more detail to integrate the material with the regular curriculum.)

The activity sheets indicate which articles in the *Tour Guide* newspaper should be read to give necessary and helpful background on the activity underway. Articles are marked with the unit number they belong with. There are other articles that are not directly required by an activity, but give more information of interest. There are also games, trivia, and other entertaining features. You may also wish to assign articles in the newspaper for research projects, reports, or extra reading on activities underway.

Now you are ready to start the **Tour**. May this truly be a journey on many levels for you and your students!

Mark Wahl

## INTRODUCTION TO THE STUDENT

Dear Student Friend,

Congratulations on your arrival at the starting point of this **Mathematical Mystery Tour!** It will take you to some ancient locations, some secrets of Nature, and some new places in your mind. You'll study a lot of non-boring math and some other subjects like geography and astronomy all at once.

I've played with these number ideas for about 15 years now. They still give me thrills and boggle my mind as I go back through my old notes to write this book. I imagine you'll feel a bit like this at times, too.

Your teacher will give you your very own *Tour Guide* newspaper. The activity sheets will ask you to read articles from it as you go along on the **Tour**. As you read you'll find questions tucked into the paragraphs. Answer these right away—they'll keep you thinking about what you're reading. There are also activities in your newspaper you can read anytime you want.

So let's hop on board. And please don't forget to have some patience as the **Tour** unfolds. You can't know everything all at once, but it will all stick together in your mind by the time you return.

Bon voyage!
Professor Mark

P.S. Our first stop is the simple pinecone . . .

# UNIT I: LIVING THINGS COUNT

## THE PINECONE NUMBERS

**Toolbox:** Scissors; crayons or colored pens; pinecones pre-soaked in water to close them up (one pinecone for each group)

A wise person once said that a journey of 1000 miles starts with a single step. We are about to take our first step. Up to now you may have thought that numbers are just little squiggles on paper. Or you may have found them a threat when they don't seem to work out right. Now you have an opportunity to make friends with them and get involved in their mystery.

Your whole **Mystery Tour** starts when you gaze at a pinecone with a careful eye. Whether or not you have a real pinecone, continue with this exercise using the pictures. As soon as you get a pinecone, check to see that what is true here is true on your cone.

Here is a drawing of a pinecone (Figure 1). You may notice that its scales are not arranged just any old way. Do you notice the pattern in their arrangement? What do you see? Look again. Do you notice a pattern going another way? What is it?

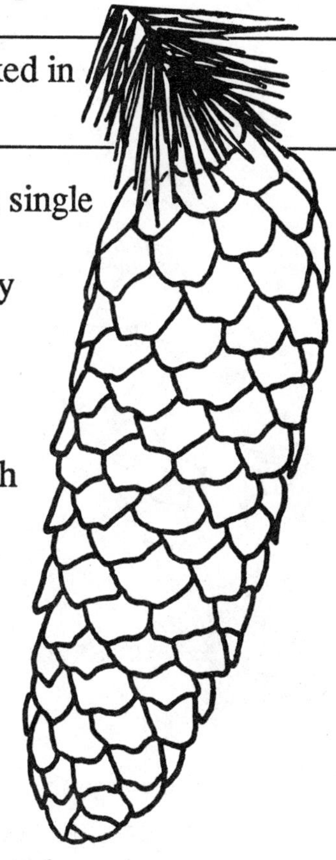

**Figure 1**

The scales are not really in straight lines but in curves called **helices,** pronounced "hee-lis-cees." (Just one is called a **helix.**) It's a kind of spiral in space. Figure 2 shows one helix of scales from the cone.

If you have trouble imagining a helix in real life, try cutting out the circle (Figure 3). Then cut along the curve and follow it to the center. It will produce a *snake* that stretches like a spring. Study this snake carefully. Notice that its spring is narrow at one end and wide at the other— just like on the pinecone.

Look at a real pinecone and see for yourself.

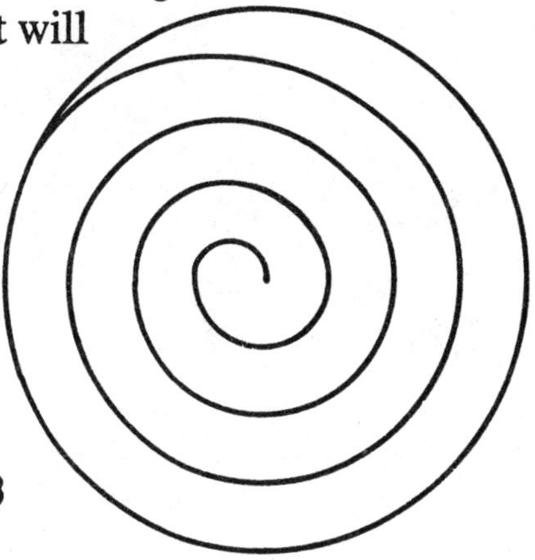

**Figure 3**

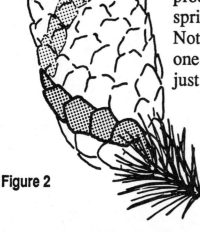

**Figure 2**

## THE PINECONE NUMBERS, continued

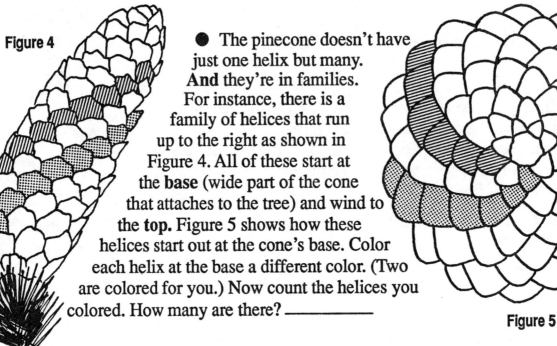

Figure 4

Figure 5

● The pinecone doesn't have just one helix but many. **And** they're in families. For instance, there is a family of helices that run up to the right as shown in Figure 4. All of these start at the **base** (wide part of the cone that attaches to the tree) and wind to the **top.** Figure 5 shows how these helices start out at the cone's base. Color each helix at the base a different color. (Two are colored for you.) Now count the helices you colored. How many are there? _____

Then use the **same colors** in the **same order** to color each helix you can see on the upright cone. (Two are colored for you.) This exercise will help your eye really see each helix.

● Some other helices also start at the base but they slant **slowly** to the right like the two colored ones in Figure 6. This means each of these helices wraps around the cone a few times. One helix is colored for you on the cone. Try coloring one more helix as it disappears around the back side of the cone and then reappears three times. Now that you have the hang of it, try coloring more until all are colored. How many are there on the cone? _____

In Figure 7 you can see how these helices look when they start out at the base. Two are colored. Carefully color the rest and count them. Do you get the same number?

Figure 6

Figure 7    2    _____

**THE PINECONE NUMBERS, continued**

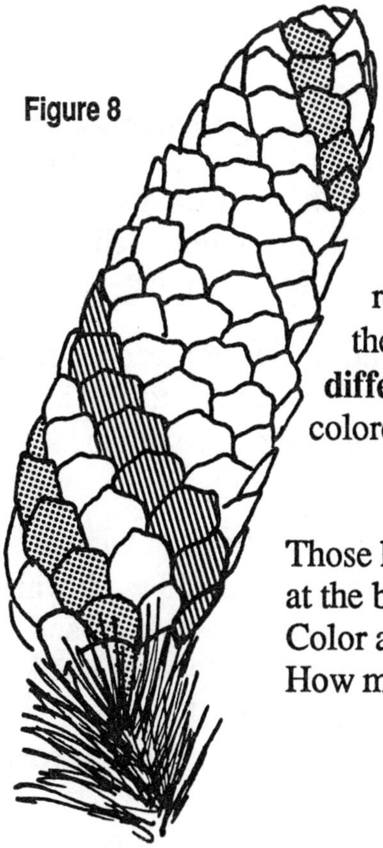

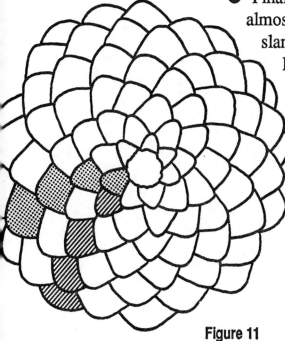

Figure 8

● There are also helices that slant more steeply to the left. See Figure 8. Two are colored for you. Color the rest in different colors and then count how many **different** helices you've colored. How many?

_____

Those helices start like this at the bottom as in Figure 9. Color and count as before. How many?

_____

Figure 9

● Finally, some helices are almost vertical (with no slant, Figure 10). Figure 11 shows how they look at the side and base of the cone. Two are colored. It's very difficult to color and count these. Estimate about how many of these you think there are:

_____

Figure 11

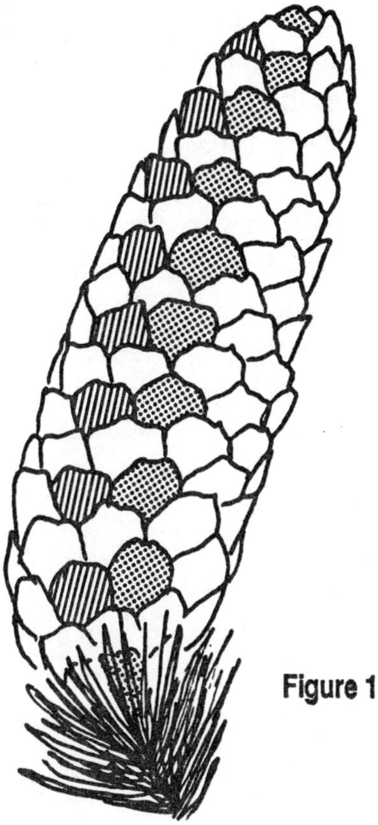

Figure 10

## THE PINECONE NUMBERS, continued

Figure 12

This would be a good time to start on a real pinecone and try to count at least three of the four families of helices. Be sure your cone has been soaked in water for about two hours so that the scales are not spread open. This makes it much easier to see the slanted helices.

You may have a different species of pinecone from the one in the drawings. You should still get at least two of your numbers to agree with the counts you made above.

Often it's very hard to keep track of what you have counted. I recommend that you work with someone else. Have your friend squat down and hold the cone above his head with base pointed down. He puts a finger on the first helix in the family you're counting, says "one," and then leaves his finger there (Figure 12).

You walk around your friend and the cone, reaching out and touching each helix on the fat *belly* of the cone. You count "two, three..." until all helices with the same slant are touched. (Be sure to stop at the helix before the one your friend is touching.) Something that may help you to count a very slanted family of helices is to use colored pens (Figure 13). Color the scales as you did in the exercises above, starting at the base.

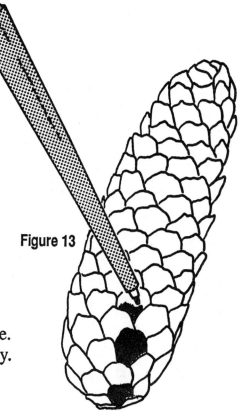

Figure 13

These numbers aren't just "any old numbers." They're clues to many mysteries of the universe. The next discussion will begin to show you why.

**THE PINECONE NUMBERS, continued**

The correct numbers of spirals on the pinecone pictures you've examined are **13, 5, 8,** and **21.** The real pinecones may have a number **3** and not **21,** along with **5, 8,** and **13.** (There are a few rare cones that don't have *any* of these numbers, but make sure you counted right before you jump to that conclusion!)

Let's take a look at these numbers, arranged in order. Say them and let them roll off your tongue:

# 3, 5, 8, 13, 21, . · ·

There's another number that wants to be said after **21.** Can you *hear* it? These numbers are all in a family and they have a **rule** that allows them to belong to the family. There are many, many more in this particular family.

What number comes next, and why? _____ _____

Now use your rule and list a few more numbers: _____

**If you don't see what's going on ask your friend or teacher to give you a hint. Remember, being told an answer helps make your brain flabby. It's more fun and better learning to get a slight hint and then find the answer yourself. So say, "A slight hint, please."**

What about the number before **3** in this family? _____ And the one before that? _____

Now, fill in all the blanks:

—,—,—,**3**,**5**,**8**,**13**,**21**,—,—,—,—,—,— · · ·

## THE PINECONE NUMBERS, continued

You can see that even though the pinecone has only four of these numbers, it *suggests* a whole family of numbers. Such a family, with a rule for making its members, is called a *sequence*. This particular sequence is called the **Fibonacci Sequence** for reasons you will soon learn. The correct pronunciation is *fee-bo-notch-ee*.

It turns out that this sequence is very famous, and it will be with us on much of our **Tour**. While wearing some of its disguises, it has **made history, helped Nature, and captured the attention of kings.** In fact, it is a real key to understanding the universe. But nobody even noticed that this powerful set of numbers was hiding out in the simple pinecone until about 1830. And it wasn't until after 1920 that it was found in other natural things.

Now let's really get you thinking. Try to come up with some interesting answers to the questions below. It's best to discuss them with a classmate before making any hasty conclusions.

**1.** Does this sequence have an end? Why or why not ? _____
_____
_____

**2.** How is this sequence **not** like the grains of sand on a huge beach?_____
_____
_____

**3.** What does this sequence have in common with the following sequence of fractions?
$$1/1, 1/2, 1/3, 1/4, 1/5, \ldots$$
_____
_____

**4.** What's one way that the two sequences are **not** alike?_____
_____
_____

OK. It's time for you to get the historical scoop on these critters, so get out your *Tour Guide* newspaper and read "Edouard Lucas Names Number Sequence after Fibonacci," "New Book by Leonardo Fibonacci Released!" and "Fibonacci Society Started!" Be sure to answer any questions as you go. When you're finished, return here to do a trick.

# THE REMAINDER TRICK

Pick any two numbers from the Fibonacci Sequence. It's more interesting if you choose two that are bigger than one digit and far away from each other. For example, I'll choose 233 and 13. I divide one by the other:

$$13\overline{)233} \quad 17R12$$

The **remainder** (12) is what I'm interested in here. Mathematicians have proved that **one of these two things** has to be true about the remainder:

- It's a Fibonacci Number. (Nope, not this time.)
- If you subtract it from the **divisor** (13) you get a Fibonacci Number. (Yes, indeed, 1 is a Fibonacci.)

Now you try this with at least six more pairs of Fibonaccis and make sure that one of the above is always true of your remainder. Save your work and let your teacher see it. You can also check to see if your classmates have found any pairs that don't work.

## A CALCULATOR CHALLENGE

Here's a good way to find remainders on your calculator when you calculate with big Fibonaccis. You'll need to know something about decimals to do it. You'll have a chance to learn more about decimals later if you need to.

In my example, I would push **233 ÷ 13** and get **17.923077**. This means that in **233** there are 17 **13**s, but the **.923077** means another (big) piece of a **13** is also in **233**. Now 17 **13**s make **221 (17 x 13 = 221)**. Subtracting **221** from **233** we get **12**, which means that **12** is left in the **233** after we remove 17 **13**s. That is, our remainder is **12.**

Now try the Remainder Trick by using your calculator on some big pairs of Fibonaccis.

7

# THE TRIPLES TRICK

Pick any three numbers from the Fibonacci Sequence, but make sure you take three in a row (these are called "consecutive numbers").

Multiply the first and last together: _____
Multiply the middle one times itself: _____

Notice how close your two answers are to each other.

```
      ┌───┐
      │ ? │
      └───┘
        =
      ┌───┐
      │ 3 │
      └───┘
        X
┌───┐ ┌───┐ ┌───┐
│ 2 │ │ 3 │ │ 5 │
└───┘ └───┘ └───┘
  └─ ─ ─ X ─ ─ ─┘
         =
      ┌───┐
      │ ? │
      └───┘
```

Try this with five more consecutive triplets of Fibonaccis. What do you notice? Carefully write your observations:

_____

_____

_____

_____

_____

_____

# UNIT I: LIVING THINGS COUNT

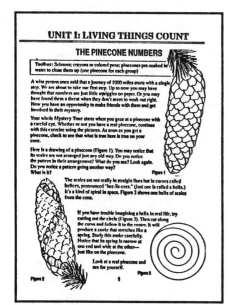

Student Page 1

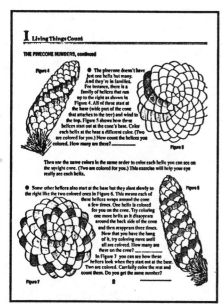

Student Page 2

## THE PINECONE NUMBERS

NOTE: For your convenience, some of the Student Pages are provided in the inside margins of the Teacher's Guide.

### HANDING OUT PAGES

I recommend that you hand pages for an activity to your students one-by-one rather than a few at a time or all at once. This helps students focus on one task; also, the answer to a question often appears on the next page. At times, though, I'll tell you to give them more than one. Be sure to always supply or have available to students plenty of loose-leaf notebook paper for answers and computations

### TIMING

The whole pinecone activity, including the resulting *number sequence*, may take students at least one hour and 15 minutes to do properly. If you have pinecones, include time to soak them in a bucket (two hours) to make the scales close.

The home projects on pp. 19 and 20 can be assigned any time after the pinecone activity.

### HELIX ACTIVITIES

• As they explore the helix shape, students may wish to use larger circles of colored paper with a similar spiral drawn freehand (but carefully) on it. They can make these helices (remind them this is the plural of helix) to create or adorn a mobile as part of an art project.

• List all the places where spirals or helices exist (galaxies, hair swirl at cowlick, climbing bean plant, the ear, barber pole, pin curl, and others). This could also be done as a class collage.

• Write a poem or song about spirals on a helix mobile.

## Teacher's Guide to Student Pages 1-8

• With the class in a circle holding hands, disconnect the circle at one place. One person at the break walks around the inside of the circle, bringing others in and around until all are wound in a spiral. Then reverse. Use music and repeat this in-out process.

• Do a drawing or design that uses spirals, helices.

• The book **The Mystic Spiral** by Jill Purce, is a beautiful paperback with numerous pictures and thoughtful text on the theme of spirals. It discusses their meaning in ancient art, philosophy, and architecture. Have students research the spiral and report to the class orally or by creating a chart, bulletin board, diorama or other creative expression.

### THE DNA MOLECULE

What I consider a profound science connection is this fact: the **DNA** that composes the genes in cells forms a *double helix* molecule. The double helix is like a springy *recording tape* on which even the smallest physical traits are *remembered* by the cell.

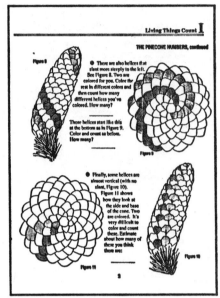

Student Page 3

For those of you who want more technical details to give your students, here they are. DNA is composed of two ribbons of sugar and phosphate molecules connected together by four types of complex molecular links. The whole thing is made of five kinds of atoms: carbon, hydrogen, oxygen, nitrogen, and phosphorus. Imagine the DNA ribbon like an ever-twisting ladder with rungs of four different types. The order of the rungs along the ladder forms a code that is translated into physical human traits.

This ribbon of DNA is only about 21 *ten-millionths* of a *millimeter* (Angstroms) in diameter. A length of it stretched from Earth to the sun would weigh only half as much as a paper clip! It makes a turn every 34 Angstroms. Note these numbers! They are shown on page 5 to be related intimately to the numbers found on the pinecone!

You may wish to encourage students to look this material up in an encyclopedia and report on how helices are at the very core of life. Incidentally, it seems that Nature prefers those that twist upward to the right. (Though this is called a *right-handed* helix, it has nothing to do with Nature's being right-handed; it simply means that Nature prefers one type of helix.)

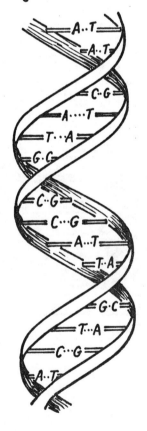

## Teacher's Guide to Student Pages 1-8

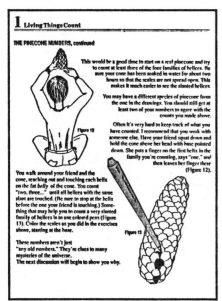

Student Page 4

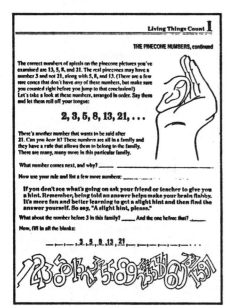

Student Page 5

### COUNTING SPIRALS ON THE PINECONE, PAGES 4-6

**NOTE:** If pinecones are not readily available in your area, check local arts and crafts and florists' supply stores.

Encourage students to visualize the parallel pinecone spirals arranged *around* the cone rather than *up* the cone.

This means that counting progresses in a circle *around* its *belly*, parallel to the cone's bottom.

Each curve starts at the base rather than at the place where it first appears on the visible side of the cone.

It's very rare to find a cone that doesn't follow the number pattern described on pp. 2 and 3, though some species may choose a few different numbers of the pattern. But it can happen. Perhaps students could be motivated by a search for one of these rare cones.

### THE WHOLE SEQUENCE

The numbers on the pinecone are given on page 5. The next number is 34 because each number is the sum of the two before it: $13 + 21 = 34$. The whole sequence can be filled in with this rule to give:

$$1, 1, 2, 3, 5, 8, 13, 21, 34, 55, 89, 144, 233, 377, \ldots$$

Notice that the 21 and 34 Angstroms of the DNA helix are in this sequence! There's more about this in the teacher notes for "The Golden Rectangle" activity of Unit III.

### ANSWERS TO QUESTIONS ON PAGE 6

**1.** The sequence has no end. It's called an **infinite sequence** because we can *always* add two members to get another one. Thus, there is never a last one, which is the mathematical meaning of infinite.

**2.** Perhaps nothing in the physical world is truly unending. The grains of sand on a huge beach could be counted (theoretically!). That's how they differ from this infinite sequence.

## Teacher's Guide to Student Pages 1-8

**3-4.** The sequence 1/1, 1/2, 1/3, 1/4, 1/5, . . . could go on forever, too. This makes it similar to the other sequence. However, each fraction is *smaller* than the one before it. In the other sequence each succeeding one is *larger*. This is how it differs from the other sequence.

### THE *TOUR GUIDE* NEWSPAPER ARTICLE

You can check to see if the students have meaningfully read the article by noting their answers to the questions implanted in it. All answers are found in the Key at the end of this book, on page 253.

### EXTENSIONS

• Space is one of the best examples of *going on forever*. It appears to be an example of the infinite in the physical world. But Einstein shot that down when he demonstrated that space-time is the fourth dimension, and that our universe is a finite *ball* in the fourth dimension. In other words, if you got a super-telescope that could see *far enough*, you could make out the back of your head!

Have students research and report on topics like infinity, Einstein, and Relativity (Einstein's Theory), in the encyclopedia and report. If they look up Zeno's Paradoxes, too, and Copernicus, they will get some dated views of infinity and space. Then have a panel of the three gentlemen discuss infinity from their points of view.

• A few students can research life in the Middle Ages, and a few can research life in the Moslem Empire. They can create costumes of those times and then present an improvised dialog between the groups across the Mediterranean. One group stands on a sketched map of Europe, and the other stands on a map of the Moslem Empire. They talk about their differences, their desires, and their accomplishments as the rest of the class listens.

• Students can find out why the Leaning Tower of Pisa leans. Its construction was started about the year Leonardo Fibonacci was born in that city. Students can construct a model of the tower with a paper tube and paints. It could become part of a class exhibit on Leonardo or on his numbers. (Note the article in the *Tour Guide* newspaper, "Tower in Pisa Leans 5°!")

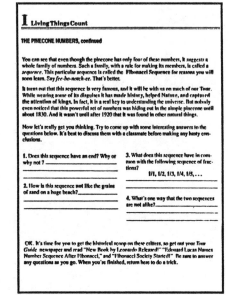

Student Page 6

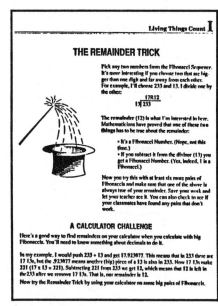

Student Page 7

## Teacher's Guide to Student Pages 1-8

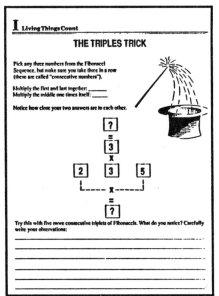

**I** Living Things Count

### THE TRIPLES TRICK

Pick any three numbers from the Fibonacci Sequence, but make sure you take three in a row (these are called "consecutive numbers").

Multiply the first and last together: _____
Multiply the middle one times itself: _____

Notice how close your two answers are to each other.

| ? |
| = |
| 3 |
| x |

| 2 | 3 | 5 |

| x |
| = |
| ? |

Try this with five more consecutive triplets of Fibonaccis. What do you notice? Carefully write your observations:

_____
_____
_____
_____
_____

Student Page 8

### THE REMAINDER TRICK

This is the first in a series of many number tricks that the Fibonacci Numbers can do. Many more of them are available in Unit II. Some students may wish to try some of those tricks right away because most can be understood at this point.

After the students have fully explored a trick it's always a good exercise to ask them to state precisely what the trick is, without reading from the paper. The ability to generalize experiences as a simple rule is key to mathematical thinking.

### THE TRIPLES TRICK

The answer to the trick is that any three consecutive Fibonacci Numbers will have a difference of **1** between the product of the first and last and the square of the middle (i.e., middle times itself).

Students who are very precise may notice that sometimes the middle squared is **1 greater** and sometimes it's **1 less.** There's even a pattern to this: every *other* group of three numbers along the sequence has **1 more,** and the alternates have **1 less.** Students should show evidence of trying several triples to see if the pattern continues to hold.

# COLORING SUNFLOWER SPIRALS

**Toolbox:** Red and blue pens or crayons

**Sunflowers** also join us in the Fibonacci adventure. Here's a diagram of how the seeds arrange themselves in a typical sunflower's center (called the *head*). Below is a drawing of a real sunflower so you can see how it looks with seeds. On the diagram to the right some curved spaces are labeled "1, 2, 3." Continue counting the spirals all the way around. These curves are called *clockwise curves* because they bend in the direction clock hands move. The number of clockwise curves is _____.
Now count on the diagram the number of *counterclockwise* (bending the other way) curves. They've been started with the words "one, two, three." The number is ____.

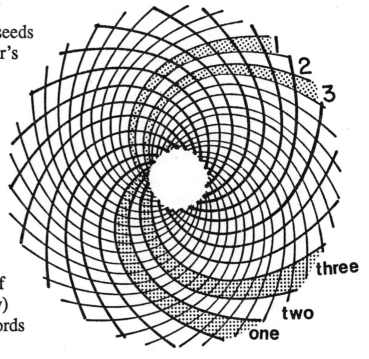

Your two counts should be Fibonacci Numbers that are consecutive in the sequence.

Sometimes sunflowers have much larger numbers of clockwise and counterclockwise spirals. These large numbers are Fibonacci Numbers too!

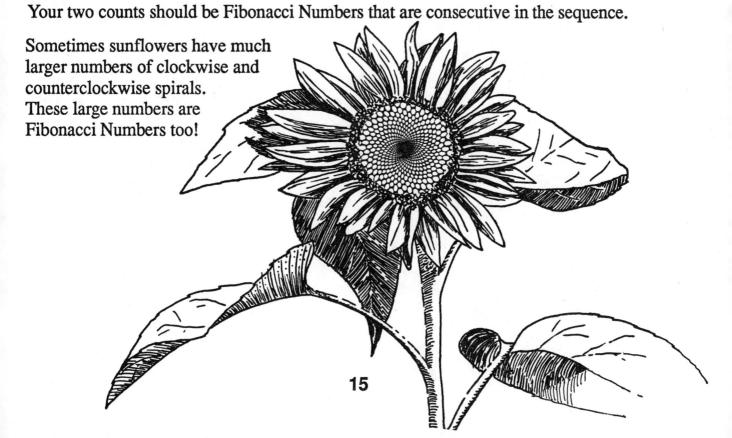

15

**COLORING SUNFLOWER SPIRALS, continued**

# SLANTS AND CURVES

The *clockwise* and *counterclockwise* spirals slant differently from each other. It's easier to see how if you color the spirals. Color the clockwise spirals red in this picture, but **color only every other one, like stripes, so you can see them better.**

Now count both colored and uncolored clockwise spirals. Number:_____

In the picture below, color the *counterclockwise* spirals blue. Remember, color every other one.

**WARNING:** You will end up with two blue ones next to each other at the end, but that's OK.
Count all counterclockwise spirals. Number:____

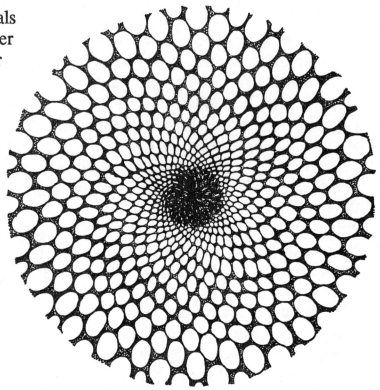

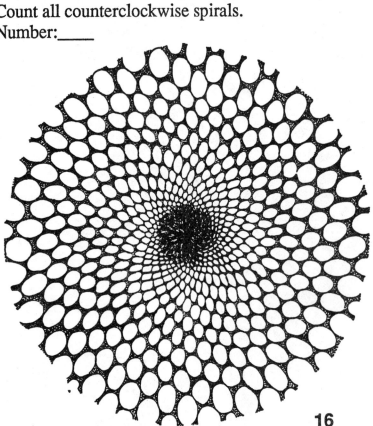

Now compare the reds and blues in **curve** and **slant.** That is, one color curves more than the other and also slants more at the top than it does on the base. This results in more of one color of curve than the other. Which will have to be more numerous, and why? Write your observations and explanations on a separate piece of paper.

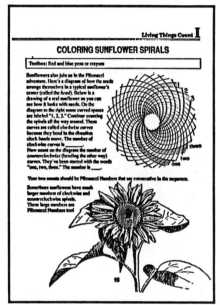

Student Page 15

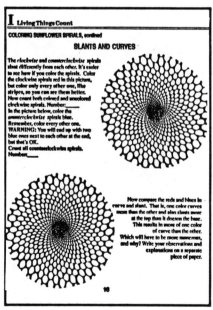

Student Page 16

# COLORING SUNFLOWER SPIRALS

## SUNFLOWER NUMBERS

In both the sunflower center and diagram, the number of clockwise-curving spirals is 34 and the number of counterclockwise-curving ones is 21. This is a fairly low set of numbers as sunflowers go. The ones your students try to count either in pictures or in real life could easily have 55 and 34 as their numbers or even 89 and 55. The highest known sunflower numbers are 233 and 144! All of these are, of course, Fibonacci Numbers, and they are consecutive in the sequence.

On page 16, students should observe that the less curved the spirals are, the more will fit around the circle.

## EXTENSIONS

• Have students compare and contrast the spiral appearances of spiral and helix arrangements in the pinecone, sunflower, and pineapple. There are subtle differences among each. Show the results in a chart or a table.

• Have them create fantasy flowers that have the Fibonacci Numbers operating in different ways on them. A good example is on the front page of the *Tour Guide* newspaper.

• Students can look up all the species of sunflower and daisy in a flower field guide. Some can make a display for others in the class, showing climates and soils that encourage these flowers.

• Students can buy sunflower seeds in the shells and study the shape of the shells as it relates to their Fibonacci arrangement.

• Students can plant a sunflower in a pot in the sun inside the classroom, and observe its growth. If it flowers, it will make another interesting study, as spirals can be observed in the center of the flower well before the seeds are developed.

# HOME PROJECTS:
# DAISIES, PINECONES AND PINEAPPLES

**1.** The centers of daisies and some other flowers look just like sunflowers but they're smaller. Some buds and seedpods on grasses, seeds, and flowers look kind of like pinecones; they have helical arrangements of bumps. This means the Fibonacci Numbers may be there too.

Go to a florist and count the clockwise and counterclockwise spirals in some daisies. (It's a good idea to take along a magnifying glass and a toothpick to point with.) Record your findings.

Also count the petals on the daisies and record the results. You may get very near some Fibonaccis. What are they?

Ask what species of daisy you are counting on and note it. Try to change to another species for petal-counting and see if the numbers change to being near another Fibonacci.

While you're there, search for other buds or flower centers that look *suspiciously Fibonacci*. Search your backyard or vacant lots for other Fibonacci plants.

On a separate piece of paper, write at least two paragraphs on your findings at the florist and vacant lots. If several students are doing this, consider putting all reports into a "Newspaper" for the class. Create a clever name for the paper and make copies for the library.

---

**2.** Find a pinecone and check its numbers. If you find more than one kind, all the better. Soak them for two hours if they are spread open, because this will close them up again and counting will be easier.

Using a separate piece of paper, describe your adventure and findings using at least two paragraphs.

## HOME PROJECTS, continued

**3.** Pinecones and pineapples have something in common besides starting with *pine-*. To see what it is, go to the grocery store, or have someone bring a pineapple home.

Notice that the bumps are shaped like this:

This shape is a hexagon.

Pick a hexagon on the pineapple. There are three directions hexagons can line up with your hexagon. (See the drawing.) Actually the *lines* are helices that curve their way up the pineapple— the way they did on the pinecone. So . . . count them like you did on the pinecone. That is, pick a *line* (helix) of hexagons, then count all the lines that are parallel to that line as you go around the pineapple.

Notice in the picture that there is even one line of hexagons where the hexagons are not touching at their edges (the dashed line). Every *other* hexagon is part of it.

Count how many lines of this kind there are; you should get a (guess-what-kind-of) number. If possible, check other pineapples to see if they give the same numbers.

**For advanced counters:**
See if the leaves are in spirals and try to count them in the same way. On a separate piece of paper, write a paragraph describing your results.

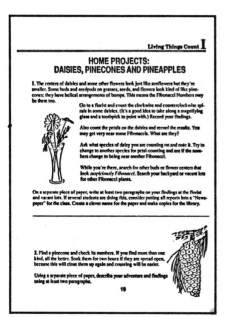

Student Page 19

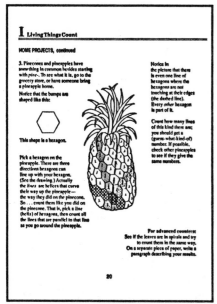

Student Page 20

# HOME PROJECTS: DAISIES, PINECONES AND PINEAPPLES

## DAISY PETALS

The numbers of petals on daisies are either Fibonacci Numbers or are very close to them. Most daisies have 21, 34, or 55 petals, depending on the species. Each species has its own preferred number. Encourage students to count daisy petals.

An interesting discussion: An old tradition is to pull daisy petals off one at a time and say, "She loves me, she loves me not . . ." until the last petal is gone. The last sentence said was considered true. Which species of daisy would you do this with to have a better chance of ending with "She loves me?" (An odd number will switch it back to "She loves me," so a 21 or 55 daisy is the best bet.)

## OTHER FLOWERS

Another source of flowers to count on is a garden shop that sells a large variety of seeds. The seed packets often have a good photograph of a flower. Other photos can be found in encyclopedias and resource books. And don't forget botanical gardens for year-round flowers, pinecones, and seed cones. The students can create reports containing drawings and verbal descriptions of their findings.

## PINECONE ACTIVITIES

Students can have Pinecone Treasure Hunts in their neighborhoods and bring their findings to school. That way everyone will have cones to count on.

For exhibit purposes, students could paint the scales of one helix white, the next yellow, and then white again all the way around. With a sharp felt-tip pen each spiral could be numbered near its base. That way, four cones of the same species can be painted to exhibit the four Fibonacci Numbers for that species. After the cones have been soaked to restore their tightness, and mostly dried out, you can spray them with clear lacquer to help prevent their opening up again.

## Teacher's Guide to Student Pages 19-20

### ABOUT HEXAGONS

Because hexagons cover the pineapple, and because an activity on beehives is coming up, students should feel comfortable with the definition, appearance, and behavior of a hexagon. You might want to introduce the hexagon before beginning the pineapple activity. One way is to have them play the game of HEX in the *Tour Guide* newspaper.

Another way is to paste or draw six circles on paper around a seventh, then connect their centers this way. This shows that six equilateral triangles compose a hexagon. It also shows why the ancient Egyptians and Greeks considered seven a number of *completion*—the seventh circle *completes* the other six to form a harmonious hexagon. (Six was considered the number of *harmony*.)

Incidentally, for thousands of years there were only seven bodies seen to be moving in the sky—Sun, Moon, Mercury, Venus, Mars, Jupiter, and Saturn. The solar system was complete. The ancient world view was shattered when the eighth, Uranus, was discovered by William Herschel in 1781. This was the dawning of the modern scientific age.

### DISCUSSION

Make sure students can verbalize, whether in class or groups, their conception of the journey thus far. This includes finding an infinite sequence of numbers implied by a natural object, then showing how several natural objects are connected by these Fibonacci Numbers.

Ask students why they think these particular objects all have Fibonacci Numbers in them. Their answers should include the observation that each object has elements arranged in spirals or helices.

# LEONARDO'S RABBITS

**Toolbox:** Red, blue, green pens; Rabbit Chart on page 24

Recall from the *Tour Guide* newspaper that in the 12th chapter of his book, Leonardo presented a problem about a growing population of rabbits:

> "A certain man put a pair of rabbits [that will breed during January] in a place surrounded by a wall. How many *pairs* of rabbits can be produced from that pair in a year if it is supposed that every month each pair begets a new pair which from the second month on becomes productive?"

This old-fashioned wording is a bit confusing. Let's work it out clearly so we get an answer that makes sense to us.

How about assuming that the first pair of rabbits has its litter of two by February 1? Because every litter has to wait two months before reproducing, this litter will not be ready to have its own babies until two months later (April 1). Once rabbits are old enough, they keep making new litters each month.

The best way to see this is to finish and color the rabbit chart on page 24 for January through June. Using your colored chart you can fill in this table. It's started for you up to April. After you fill it up to June, continue the number patterns up to January 1.

| MONTH | ADULTS | BABIES | YOUNGSTERS | TOTAL |
|---|---|---|---|---|
| January | 0 | 0 | 1 | 1 |
| February | 1 | 1 | 0 | 2 |
| March | 1 | 1 | 1 | 3 |
| April | 2 | 2 | 1 | 5 |
| May | | | | |
| June | | | | |
| July | | | | |
| August | | | | |
| September | | | | |
| October | | | | |
| November | | | | |
| December | | | | |
| January 1 | | | | |

You've seen that these orderly rabbits have used Fibonacci numbers to reproduce! How many *pairs* of rabbits are there by January 1 of the next year? _____. Now subtract one (the first rabbit pair) to get the answer to Leonardo's question. _____.

# THE RABBIT CHART

**1.** Color the rabbits before you start trying to understand this chart: Color the 1-rabbits **blue**. Color the 2-rabbits **red**. Color the 3-rabbits **green**.No need to color the rest of the rabbits. (If you want to you can, if you make each number a different color.)

**2.** Draw the chart as it continues to June. Remember, babies become youngsters, and youngsters become adults the next month. Adults, even the new ones, have a litter of two right away each month.

| | ADULTS | BABIES | YOUNGSTERS | |
|---|---|---|---|---|

**January** — #1 Rabbits are youngsters

**February** — #1 are adults and have #2 babies

**March** — #2 babies are youngsters #1 adults have #3 babies

**April** — #2 are adults and have #4 babies #1 adults have #5 babies #3 babies are youngsters

**May** — #4 babies are youngsters #5 babies are youngsters #3 are adults and have #6 babies #1 adults have #7 babies #2 adults have #8 babies

**June**

## Teacher's Guide to Student Pages 23-24

# LEONARDO'S RABBITS

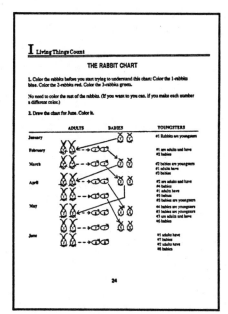

Student Page 23

Student Page 24

This Rabbit Problem of Leonardo Fibonacci is a well-known historical curiosity. Make sure students discuss the wording of the problem until they are sure what it is saying and asking.

The answers to the diagram are below.

To complete the diagram, students must be aware of what happens to **each** type of rabbit in a month. The babies become youngsters that are *too young*. The *youngsters* become adults *and* spawn a pair of babies. The adults stay adults and spawn a pair of babies.

The chart entry for May and June would be:

|       | Adults | Babies | Youngsters | Total |
|-------|--------|--------|------------|-------|
| May   | 3      | 3      | 2          | 8     |
| June  | 5      | 5      | 3          | 13    |

Those more ambitious students may wish to fill in another month or two on the diagram. They can then fill in the chart based on their diagram. It's sufficient, though, to let students simply finish the chart using their Fibonacci list.

Here's the rest of the chart:

| July   | 8   | 8   | 5   | 21  |
|--------|-----|-----|-----|-----|
| August | 13  | 13  | 8   | 34  |
| Sept.  | 21  | 21  | 13  | 55  |
| Oct.   | 34  | 34  | 21  | 89  |
| Nov.   | 55  | 55  | 34  | 144 |
| Dec.   | 89  | 89  | 55  | 233 |
| Jan. 1 | 144 | 144 | 89  | 377 |

So, there are 377 pairs of rabbits after one year, meaning that the first pair *produced* 376 pairs. This is the answer to Leonardo's question!

## Teacher's Guide to Student Pages 23-24

Keep in mind that these are very idealized rabbits, and we can't expect "everyday" rabbits to be so mathematical. The point of this exercise is for students to solve Leonardo's problem and experience how the numbers were introduced historically. If you wish, you can discuss the way mathematics gives only *ideal* answers, whereas real life has many more factors that may change the answers. The ideal answer is a guideline for what to expect real things to do.

Leonardo didn't really know these numbers had a connection to natural objects, and neither did anybody else for over 700 years. It's only been about 50 years since they've come to be known as one of the most important sets of numbers in the universe!

### EXTENSION

Have students research the reproduction patterns of *real* rabbits and compare them to Leonardo's idealized rabbits. Would the numbers come out about the same after a year?

# THE BIG MAP OF YOUR MYSTERY TOUR

Most important travel depends on a map. Your **Mystery Tour** is no exception. You need to know where you're going and see where you've been.

Your teacher will give you four sheets of paper with pieces of your Tour Map on them. Cut out each piece on the *inside* of the outside line (cutting *off* the outline) and fit the four pieces together like a puzzle. Then tape as follows:

> Use **small** pieces of transparent tape on the front to hold the map pieces together. Turn the map over and use larger pieces of tape along the seams to hold the map pieces tightly together.

## LOOKING AROUND ON THE MAP

● For this **Tour** we travel on a spiral. The **Tour** begins at the center of the spiral and moves around farther and farther from the center in a counterclockwise direction.

● Lines with arrows connect some places on the map to other places. This means that there is a connection between the ideas in both of these places. When an arrow points to a certain place, it means that the ideas in that place depend on the ideas of the place where the arrow begins. Notice that some arrows follow along the curves of the spiral.

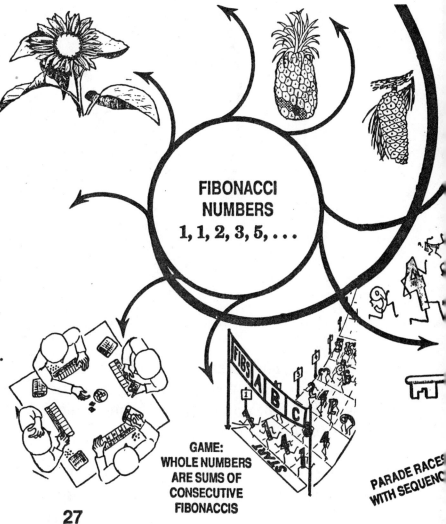

FIBONACCI NUMBERS 1, 1, 2, 3, 5, . . .

GAME: WHOLE NUMBERS ARE SUMS OF CONSECUTIVE FIBONACCIS

PARADE RACES WITH SEQUENC

## LOOKING AROUND ON THE MAP, continued

● At this point the map probably looks very complicated. Unexplored territory usually does. Fortunately, you will need to pay attention to only one piece of the map at a time. You have five units of activities and a few weeks of time to get familiar with this Territory.

● Look at the center of the spiral and you will see the part of the **Tour** you've taken so far. You know that a lot of other things happened that aren't on this map, like going to the florist shop or making a spiral mobile. But the way this map works is to give just a few pictures and symbols that trigger your mind to remember a whole bunch of things that connect to them.

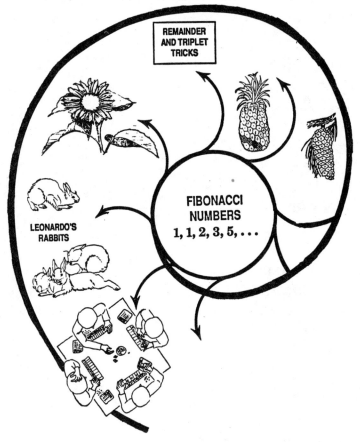

After you've finished each unit, you'll be asked to find the part of the map that shows where you've been. You can also see, at any time, a bit about what the next part of the Tour will be. The actual trip will be much more detailed, unusual, and interesting than just the few pictures on the map, of course.

**Now, fold your map and keep it near all your other work. Don't throw any work away because you will need to look at it again later.**

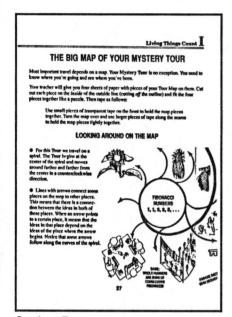

Student Page 27

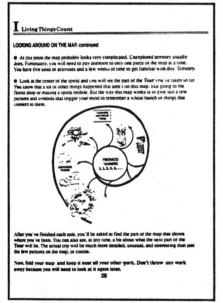

Student Page 28

# THE BIG MAP OF YOUR MYSTERY TOUR

The next page shows how the map looks when it's assembled. You will benefit more from the map by looking at a big one because it will seem far less complicated and easier to read. This one can serve as a quick reference. Mind mapping is an excellent activity for any subject. See Chapter 4 of Tony Buzan's book **Use Both Sides of Your Brain** or **Doodling Your Way to Better Recall** by McKenna. Both tell you all you need to know to bring this revolutionary method of study to your class.

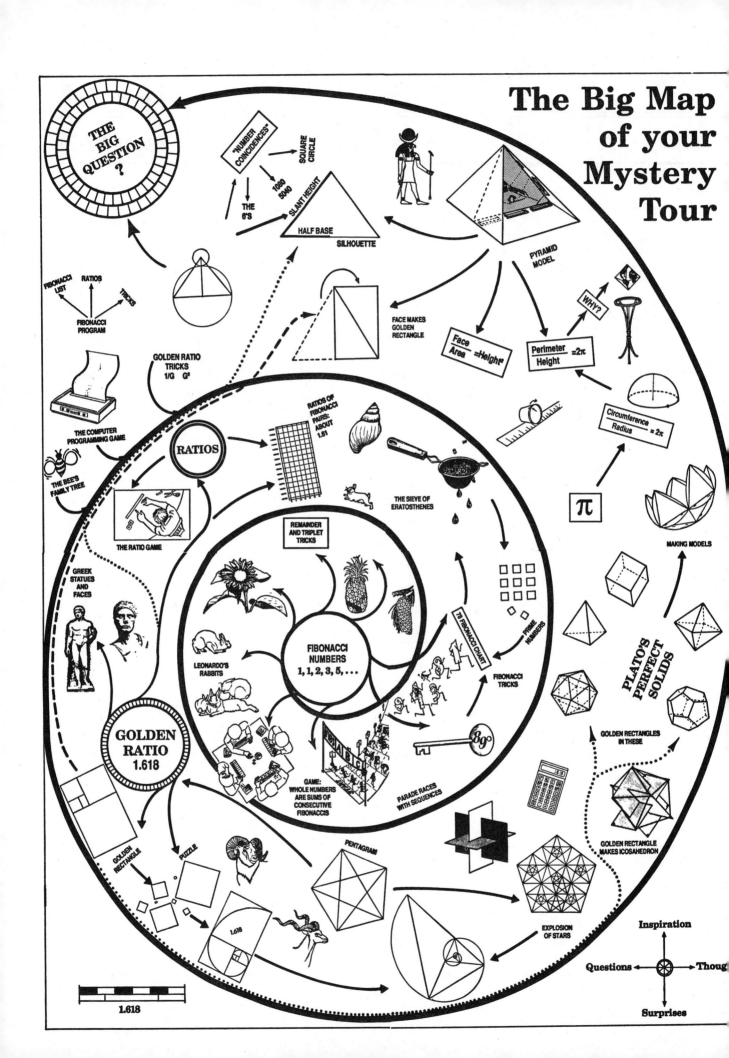

# The Big Map of your Mystery Tour

OPTIONAL ACTIVITY 1:

# THE NUMBER SECRET OF THE BEES

**Toolbox: The 78 Fibonacci List**

Bees are very mathematical. They know how to find directions well and how to make geometrical patterns (hexagon shapes) in their honeycombs. But the big surprise is that they make Fibonacci Numbers!

You won't fully understand or appreciate this activity until you first read the article in your *Tour Guide* newspaper about bee reproduction "Bees Form Labor Union and University." You may also want to play a game or two of HEX after reading the newspaper so that you can better appreciate the hexagons bees use. Then come back here.

**STOP**

● Now that you know how bees reproduce, you're going to draw a male bee's family tree. The first five generations are already done for you. To do the next generation, you should remember that every male bee has only *one* parent (a queen, marked F) and that every female bee has *two* parents (a queen and a drone, marked F and M).

● Study "A Male Bee's Family Tree" given to you on a separate page, and continue adding upper branches to it. **Be slow and neat.** Use a ruler! Draw lines straight upward. By the 9th generation, things will get pretty crowded!

● Fill in the number chart to the right of your tree as you go. This keeps statistics on the generations.

● When you're done, look over the number chart for patterns. Then answer the questions on page 34.

# A MALE BEE'S FAMILY TREE

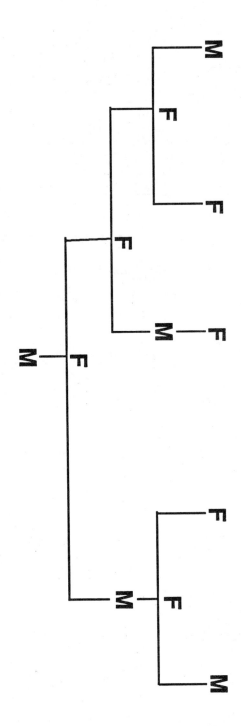

| Generation | Males | Females | Total Bees |
|---|---|---|---|
| 1 | 1 | 0 | 1 |
| 2 | 0 | 1 | 1 |
| 3 | 1 | 1 | 2 |
| 4 | 1 | 2 | 3 |
| 5 | | | |
| 6 | | | |
| 7 | | | |
| 8 | | | |
| 9 | | | |
| 10 | | | |
| 11 | | | |

THE NUMBER SECRET OF THE BEES, continued

# FIRST 78 FIBONACCI LIST

| Number | Fibonacci | Number | Fibonacci |
|---|---|---|---|
| 1 | 1 | 40 | 102334155 |
| 2 | 1 | 41 | 165580141 |
| 3 | 2 | 42 | 267914296 |
| 4 | 3 | 43 | 433494437 |
| 5 | 5 | 44 | 701408733 |
| 6 | 8 | 45 | 1134903170 |
| 7 | 13 | 46 | 1836311903 |
| 8 | 21 | 47 | 2971215073 |
| 9 | 34 | 48 | 4807526976 |
| 10 | 55 | 49 | 7778742049 |
| 11 | 89 | 50 | 12586269025 |
| 12 | 144 | 51 | 20365011074 |
| 13 | 233 | 52 | 32951280099 |
| 14 | 377 | 53 | 53316291173 |
| 15 | 610 | 54 | 86267571272 |
| 16 | 987 | 55 | 139583862445 |
| 17 | 1597 | 56 | 225851433717 |
| 18 | 2584 | 57 | 365435296162 |
| 19 | 4181 | 58 | 591286729879 |
| 20 | 6765 | 59 | 956722026041 |
| 21 | 10946 | 60 | 1548008755920 |
| 22 | 17711 | 61 | 2504730781961 |
| 23 | 28657 | 62 | 4052739537881 |
| 24 | 46368 | 63 | 6557470319842 |
| 25 | 75025 | 64 | 10610209857723 |
| 26 | 121393 | 65 | 17167680177565 |
| 27 | 196418 | 66 | 27777890035288 |
| 28 | 317811 | 67 | 44945570212853 |
| 29 | 514229 | 68 | 72723460248141 |
| 30 | 832040 | 69 | 117669030460994 |
| 31 | 1346269 | 70 | 190392490709135 |
| 32 | 2178309 | 71 | 308061521170129 |
| 33 | 3524578 | 72 | 498454011879264 |
| 34 | 5702887 | 73 | 806515533049393 |
| 35 | 9227465 | 74 | 1304969544928657 |
| 36 | 14930352 | 75 | 2111485077978050 |
| 37 | 24157817 | 76 | 3416454622906707 |
| 38 | 39088169 | 77 | 5527939700884757 |
| 39 | 63245986 | 78 | 8944394323791464 |

**THE NUMBER SECRET OF THE BEES, continued**

# QUESTIONS

Toolbox: **78 Fibonacci List**

**1.** Predict how many bees there will be in the 12th generation without making the chart.

**2.** Predict how many females will be in the 16th generation: _____

**3.** How many males will there be in the 23rd generation?_____

**4.** How far back does the family tree of a bee go?_____
_____

_____

**5.** Which goes further, the family tree of a bee or the Fibonacci sequence? _____

**6.** Which will there be more of in the 60th generation, males or females? (answer this without a lot of extra work.)_____
_____

How did you figure out this answer ?_____
_____
_____
_____

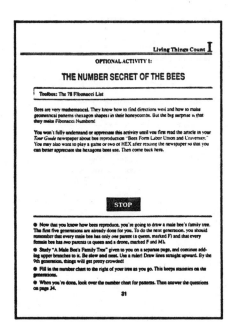

Student Page 31

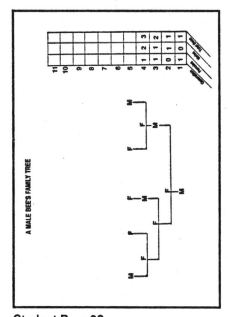

Student Page32

OPTIONAL ACTIVITY 1:

# THE NUMBER SECRET OF THE BEES

This first "Optional Activity" can be done now or anytime later, depending on your time and the interest of the students. If they liked the Nature themes in Unit I, they will like this bee activity.

Give the students a copy of the **78 Fibonacci List** to accompany this activity. This list will be necessary throughout Unit II and in the latter part of Unit III.

Students must be familiar with the parthenogenesis (reproduction by an unfertilized egg) system of bee reproduction before starting on this activity, or its full impact could be lost. Reading the article in the *Tour Guide* newspaper should do it, but you might want to ask the students for an oral explanation of the process, given either to you or to members of their study group.

The answers to questions in the *Tour Guide* newspaper are good discussion materials also. They are found in the Key at the back of this book.

It's good to point out that putting a lot of lateral distance on the diagram between a bee's male and female parents will ultimately create more room at the 9th generation. It may well happen that things get too messy by even the 8th generation, which is still plenty to show the Fibonacci pattern.

Some students might wish to start with a very large piece of butcher paper and, as a group project, make a few more generations. They should start by extending the first couple of generations very widely to leave room for generations to squish together in later stages. Wish them well!

## Teacher's Guide to Student Pages 31-34

**ANSWERS TO QUESTIONS ON PAGE 34**

**1.** Continue the Fibonacci pattern of the family tree to get 144 bees in the 12th generation.

**2.** Again continue along the Fibonacci pattern from the 9th generation to get 610 females. Another way is to notice, while using the 78 Fibonacci List, that in the 9th generation there are 21 females, 21 being the 8th Fibonacci. If the 9th generation produces the 8th Fibonacci, then the 16th generation will produce the 15th Fibonacci, 610.

**3.** In the 9th generation there are 13 males (7th Fibonacci), so in the 23rd generation there will be 10,946 males (21st Fibonacci).

**4.** The family tree of a bee goes back almost forever to the first bee couple. It's important to note that even though our male bee seems to gain more and more ancestors as we go back in generations, this is deceptive. There are many ancestors in the chart that are really the same bee. The females in any generation in the chart may all be the same queen bee, and the males could be all the same drone. Thus, this whole chart could eventually be traced to an original pair of bees.

**5.** The Fibonacci Sequence—it's infinite!

**6.** In the 60th generation there will still be fewer male bees than female bees because in each generation of the early chart this is so. The female bee count is always one Fibonacci ahead of the male count.

**EXTENSION ACTIVITIES**

• Play HEX in the *Tour Guide* newspaper (if students didn't do it during the pineapple activity). It's kind of a bee game and familiarizes students with hexagons.

Student Page 34

• Bring a honeycomb into class. If you don't know a beekeeper, you can buy a honey product that includes a piece of honeycomb. A good analytical question is "Why does the bee use hexagons?"

The answer is related to the way round balls would pack together if they were soft, like bubbles. They would create flat sides on each other and a slice through them would create hexagons. The bee anticipates this packing and makes them hexagonal in advance. Pretty smart!

• Visit beehives on a field trip. Interview the beekeeper.

• Research more about the life of bees and invent more mathematical questions like those in the *Tour Guide* newspaper article.

GREEK
STATUES
AND
FACES

FIBONACCI
NUMBERS
1, 1, 2, 3, 5, . . .

LEONARDO'S
RABBITS

GOLDEN
RATIO
1.618

GAME:
WHOLE NUMBERS
ARE SUMS OF
CONSECUTIVE
FIBONACCIS

GOLDEN
RECTANGLE

PUZZLE

PENTAGRAM

1.618

1.618

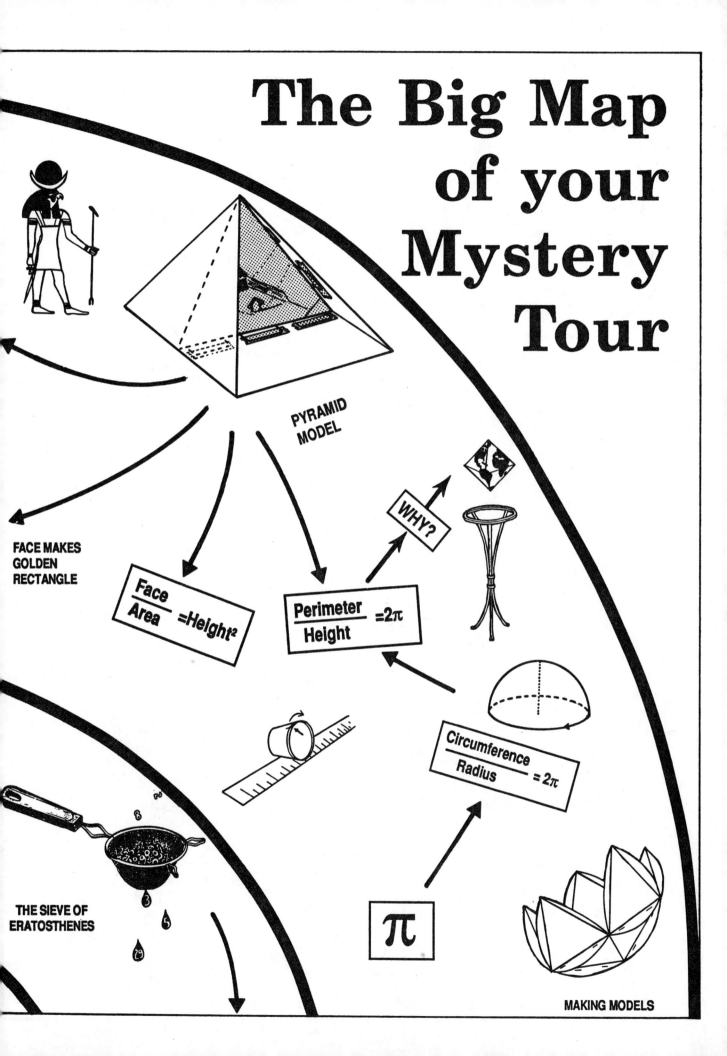

# The Big Map of your Mystery Tour

PYRAMID MODEL

FACE MAKES GOLDEN RECTANGLE

$$\frac{Face}{Area} = Height^2$$

$$\frac{Perimeter}{Height} = 2\pi$$

WHY?

$$\frac{Circumference}{Radius} = 2\pi$$

$\pi$

THE SIEVE OF ERATOSTHENES

MAKING MODELS

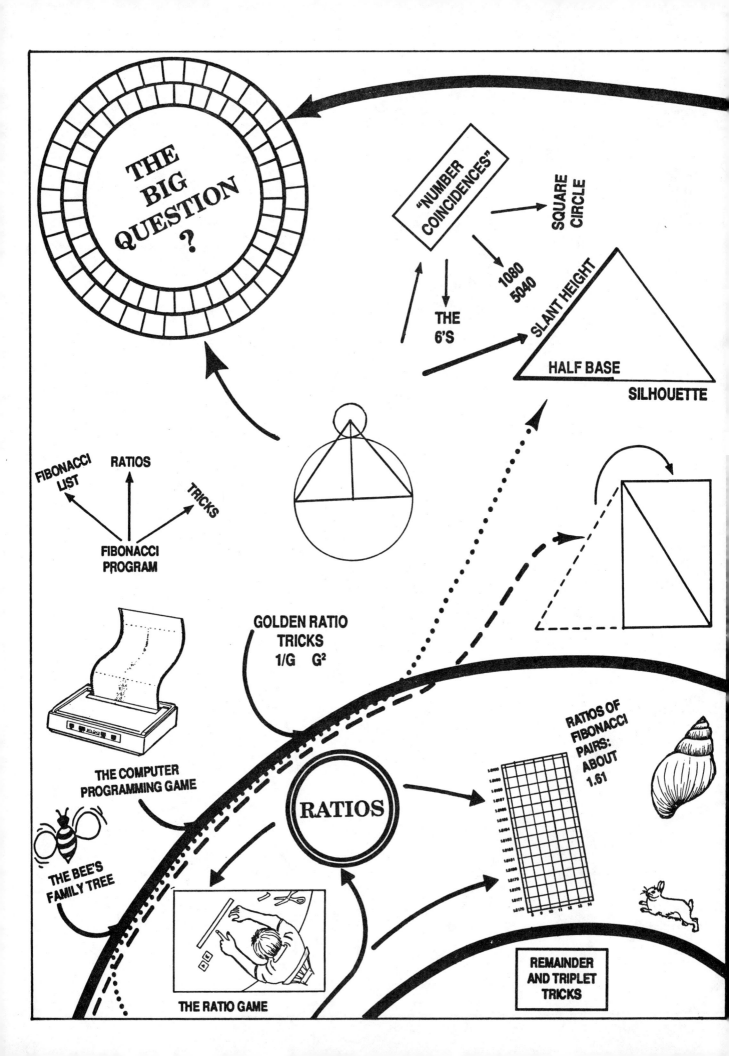

THE
BIG
QUESTION
?

"NUMBER COINCIDENCES"

SQUARE CIRCLE

1080
5040

THE 6'S

SLANT HEIGHT

HALF BASE

SILHOUETTE

FIBONACCI LIST

RATIOS

TRICKS

FIBONACCI PROGRAM

GOLDEN RATIO
TRICKS
1/G    G²

RATIOS OF FIBONACCI PAIRS:
ABOUT 1.61

THE COMPUTER PROGRAMMING GAME

THE BEE'S FAMILY TREE

RATIOS

THE RATIO GAME

REMAINDER AND TRIPLET TRICKS

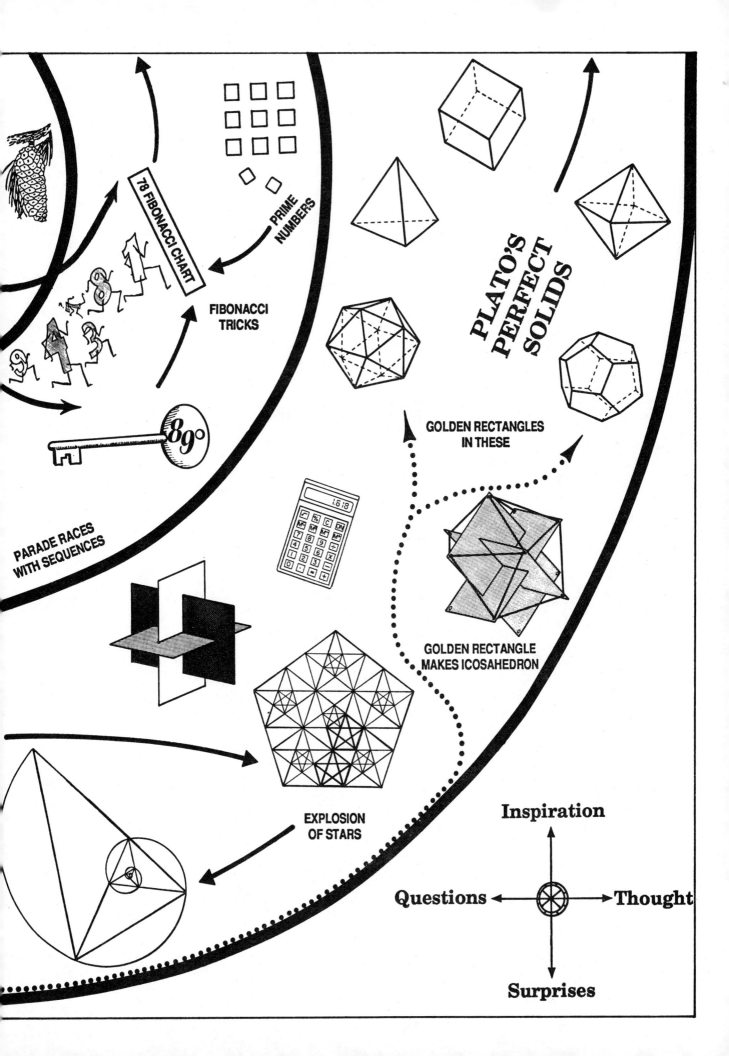

PRIME NUMBERS

78 FIBONACCI CHART

FIBONACCI TRICKS

89°

PARADE RACES WITH SEQUENCES

PLATO'S PERFECT SOLIDS

GOLDEN RECTANGLES IN THESE

1.618

GOLDEN RECTANGLE MAKES ICOSAHEDRON

EXPLOSION OF STARS

Inspiration

Questions ← → Thought

Surprises

# UNIT II: THE DANCE OF THE NUMBERS

## THE FIBONACCI PARADE

---

**Toolbox:** Calculator; **78 Fibonacci List**

---

You've met the sequence of Fibonaccis by seeing its smaller members peeking out of natural things. But a **sequence** really means an *endless* parade of numbers—numbers that all keep the same rule forever. The rule for the Fibonaccis says "To get the next one just add the two before it."

In this unit you'll see how tricky the endless Fibonacci sequence really is. One way to see how tricky the Fibonaccis are is to compare them with other sequences. You have probably never thought of a lot of them as sequences before.

For instance **2, 4, 6, 8, . . .** is a sequence. What is its rule?
(The rule has to say how you get the next member from the one before it.)

_____

_____

_____

_____

_____

## RACING SEQUENCES
(Your **78 Fibonacci List** will help you here.)

Now we're going to look at how fast the Fibonacci sequence grows. The Fibonaccis get big pretty fast, and so do some other sequences.

Let's have a race. In the race will be four well-known sequences. Fill them in up to their 15th member and watch how fast they grow in comparison to each other.

| Rank (Position) | Fibonacci | Sequence A | Sequence B | Sequence C |
|---|---|---|---|---|
| 1 | 1 | 1 | 4 | 1 |
| 2 | 1 | 2 | 8 | 4 |
| 3 | 2 | 4 | 12 | 9 |
| 4 | 3 | 8 | 16 | 16 |
| 5 | 5 | 16 | 20 | 25 |
| 6 | ___ | ___ | ___ | ___ |
| 7 | ___ | ___ | ___ | ___ |
| 8 | ___ | ___ | ___ | ___ |
| 9 | ___ | ___ | ___ | ___ |
| 10 | ___ | ___ | ___ | ___ |
| 11 | ___ | ___ | ___ | ___ |
| 12 | ___ | ___ | ___ | ___ |
| 13 | ___ | ___ | ___ | ___ |
| 14 | ___ | ___ | ___ | ___ |
| 15 | ___ | ___ | ___ | ___ |

## The Post-Race Wrap-Up

First, the racers:
  1. Give the rule for each sequence:
     **Sequence A:** _____
     **Sequence B:** _____
     **Sequence C:** _____
  2. Which two sequences start out faster but eventually get beaten by the Fibonaccis?
     _____

  3. At what rank (position) number do the Fibonaccis pass the first?_____
     The second?_____
  4. Which sequence starts out faster and never gets caught by the Fibonaccis?_____

So we see that our Fibonaccis are a medium-fast sequence!

## THE POST-RACE WRAP-UP, continued

Another thing that's interesting about the Fibonaccis is how their rank numbers play with the Fibonaccis themselves. For instance:

**5.** What two Fibonacci numbers are the same as their ranks in the sequence?

_____ , _____

**6.** What two numbers have *ranks* that are more than the *numbers* themselves?

_____ , _____

**7.** If you take a certain rank number and multiply it by itself (called **squaring** it), you get its Fibonacci. Which rank? _____ Which Fibonacci? _____

**8.** In what Fibonacci can you add its two digits to get its rank? _____

**9.** Here's a different kind of question: Compare the Fibonaccis in positions **5, 10, 15, 20,** and **25.** What do they have that no other numbers in between have?_____

_____

**10.** How are the Fibonaccis in positions **3, 6, 9, 12, 15, 18, 21,** and **24** alike?_____

_____

**11.** What do you think the Fibonaccis of rank **4, 8, 12, 16, 20,** and **24** have in common? Experiment until you find out._____

_____

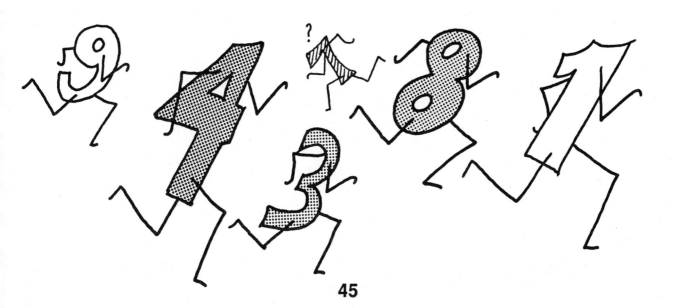

# UNIT II: THE DANCE OF THE NUMBERS

## THE FIBONACCI PARADE

This unit explores the Fibonacci sequence of numbers from several points of view. First we look at how fast the numbers of the sequence grow, and then we see how the **position** or **rank number** of the Fibonacci is related to the actual Fibonacci in that position.

We'll spend time on many amazing tricks the Fibonaccis can do. And there'll be a "Optional Activity" on the computer that can be done anytime. In fact, the whole of this unit need not be completed before going to Unit III. Some of its pattern work could be done as isolated activities later in the year.

Be sure each student has a copy of the **78 Fibonacci List** from the end of Unit I.

### RULE FOR 2, 4, 6, 8, . . .

In the sequence 2, 4, 6, 8, . . . the rule is "Add two to the previous number to get the next." This rule causes the sequence to go on forever.

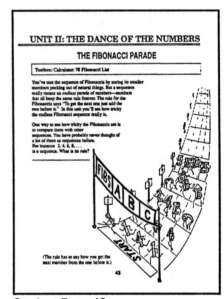

Student Page 43

## Teacher's Guide to Student Pages 43-45

Student Page 44

### RACING SEQUENCES

This is how the students' charts should look:

| Rank Number | Fibonacci | Sequence A | Sequence B | Sequence C |
|---|---|---|---|---|
| 1 | 1 | 1 | 4 | 1 |
| 2 | 1 | 2 | 8 | 4 |
| 3 | 2 | 4 | 12 | 9 |
| 4 | 3 | 8 | 16 | 16 |
| 5 | 5 | 16 | 20 | 25 |
| 6 | 8 | 32 | 24 | 36 |
| 7 | 13 | 64 | 28 | 49 |
| 8 | 21 | 128 | 32 | 64 |
| 9 | 34 | 256 | 36 | 81 |
| 10 | 55 | 512 | 40 | 100 |
| 11 | 89 | 1024 | 44 | 121 |
| 12 | 144 | 2048 | 48 | 144 |
| 13 | 233 | 4096 | 52 | 169 |
| 14 | 377 | 8192 | 56 | 196 |
| 15 | 610 | 16384 | 60 | 225 |

### ANSWERS TO QUESTIONS ON PAGE 43-45

1. Here's the rule for each sequence:

    Sequence A: To get the next, double (multiply x 2) the previous number.

    Sequence B: To get the next, add 4 to the previous number.

    Sequence C: To get the next, multiply the rank number *by itself*. (That is, **square** it.)

2. Sequences B and C start faster but get passed up.

3. The Fibonaccis pass B at rank 10 and C at rank 13.

4. The Fibonaccis never catch A, though they both start out at 1.

5. Both 1 and 5 are the same as their rank numbers in the Fibonacci sequence.

6. Rank numbers 2, 3, and 4 are more than their Fibonaccis, but after that the ranks are always less.

7. Rank number 12 times itself is 144, its Fibonacci.

## Teacher's Guide to Student Pages 43-45

**8.** In the Fibonacci 55, 5 + 5 = 10, and 10 is its rank number.

**9.** All these Fibonaccis end in 0 or 5 and are thus divisible by 5. None of the "in-betweens" is like this. In fact, this pattern is true throughout all the Fibonaccis.

**10.** All of these Fibonaccis are **even numbers!** The two in-betweens are always odd. This is true throughout the whole sequence, too.

**11.** All the rank numbers that are multiples of 4 have Fibonaccis that are divisible by 3.

**NOTE** for the Mathematically Minded Teacher: These last three questions have to do with a remarkable phenomenon in the Fibonaccis. That is, if one Fibonacci's rank number divides into another Fibonacci's rank number, the first Fibonacci will divide evenly into the second. Fibonacci 5 has rank 5 as well, which 5 divides into 10, 15, etc. This means 5 will divide into the Fibonaccis that have these ranks. Fibonacci 3 has rank 4. Any rank that is a multiple of 4 will be a Fibonacci divisible by 3. And so on. This is an excellent pattern for the more curious students to play with.

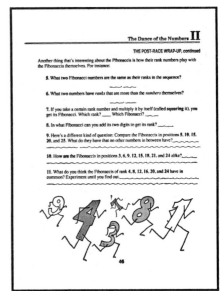

Student Page 45

## EXTENSIONS

• Ask students to invent other sequences and race them with the Fibonaccis. Can they invent one that will beat the fast Sequence A? (How about one with a rule of "triple the previous to get the next"?) Can they invent one that even the slow Sequence B can beat?

• Can they say what the size of, say, the 25th member of Sequences B and C would be without finding the ones in between? (Answer: In B, multiply 25 x 4. In C, multiply 25 x 25.)

**NOTE** for the More Advanced: The extension above can be done with Sequence A, but only with shrewdness. This is an excellent problem after students are more used to working with patterns. Ask students to experiment by picking two smaller members of Sequence A and multiplying them together. Have them repeat this. After a few times they will notice that their **answers** appear in Sequence A also. For instance, the 6th member times the 8th member gives the 13th member. When students notice that the multiplication always produces the member whose rank is **one less** than the sum of the ranks of the members they multiplied, they are there. The 25th can be found by multiplying the 12th by the 14th, for instance.

• Ask students to verify the Fibonacci patterns discussed above on larger numbers from the **78 Fibonacci List.**

# A FIBONACCI GAME
## (For Two or More)

**Toolbox:** Scissors; page with game pieces; paper; paper bag or cup; 10 pennies or tokens

**DESCRIPTION:** This game consists of a playing board with the first 11 Fibonacci Numbers listed on it, and a bag or cup containing numbers to be drawn on each play. The objective is to find the Fibonaccis that add up to the drawn numbers and to use as many of them as you can. You will learn something important about the Fibonaccis as you play.

**GAME PIECES:** You have been given a page containing your game pieces (gameboard, 20 numbered squares, and a scorecard). With your scissors cut them out on the **heavy black lines only.**

Place the gameboard in front of you with its numbers toward you. Place your scorecard near your writing hand. Place all 20 number squares in a cup in the center of the table. If there are more than two players, use only two players' numbers in the cup. Finally, place your 10 tokens or pennies on the table between you and your gameboard. (See the drawing below.)

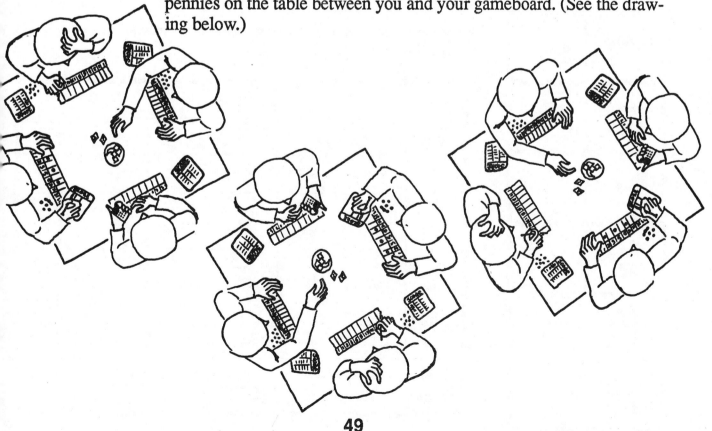

**A FIBONACCI GAME, continued**

## Fibonacci Gameboard

| 1 | |
| 1 | |
| 2 | |
| 3 | |
| 5 | |
| 8 | |
| 13 | |
| 21 | |
| 34 | |
| 55 | |
| 89 | |

## Number Squares (2 sets: 0-9)

| 0 | 1 | 2 | 3 | 4 |
| 5 | 6 | 7 | 8 | 9 |
| 0 | 1 | 2 | 3 | 4 |
| 5 | 6 | 7 | 8 | 9 |

CUT

| Play | Game I | Game II | Game III |
|---|---|---|---|
| 1 | | | |
| 2 | | | |
| 3 | | | |
| 4 | | | |
| 5 | | | |
| 6 | | | |
| 7 | | | |
| 8 | | | |
| 9 | | | |
| 10 | | | |
| Total | | | |
| Winner | | | |

# RULES

**1.** Players draw from the cup to see who starts. The player with the highest number begins—keep drawing if there's a tie. The next person to play will be to the left of the first player, and so on.

**2.** To make a play, the player draws two digits from the cup. These may be arranged in either order to make a number. The number made must not be a Fibonacci. The player must figure out which Fibonaccis add up to the drawn number. The more Fibonaccis the better. The player places pennies or tokens on his or her own gameboard next to the correct Fibonaccis.

**THIS RULE MUST BE KEPT: No two tokens on the gameboard may be in squares next to each other.**

**3.** If a player can't figure out a combination of Fibonaccis that makes his or her number, the other players can try for it on their gameboards one at a time, starting from the stuck player's left. The player who correctly makes the play enters the score in the parentheses by the play number on his or her scorecard.

**4. SCORING.** A player's score is the **number of tokens** used to make a play. It's written on the scorecard at the end of the player's turn. All tokens are then removed from the gameboard. The player with the highest total after 10 plays wins. (If there are three or more players, the game can be limited to six plays each.)

**ADVANCED GAME** (with a calculator): Make a playing board that goes up to the 16th Fibonacci Number (610). Put **three** sets of 0-9 number squares in the cup, draw **three** digits for each play, and otherwise play by the same rules. Use the calculator to try combinations. As you gain experience, try it without a calculator. Use the calculator only to check a play for accuracy.

## Teacher's Guide to Student Pages 49-51

# A FIBONACCI GAME

### PURPOSES OF THIS GAME

This game is great for plunging the students into practice of the vital skill of mental calculation. They use estimation also as they try to choose the Fibonaccis that add up to a drawn number.

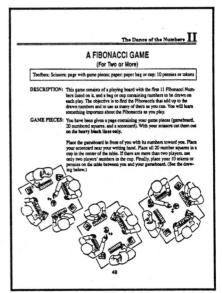

Because the opposing players can also score on a number (if the current player is unable to do so), all players get math practice on each play. Players can check a final total on a play with a calculator, and should do so unless your specific intention is to have them practice pencil-and-paper addition or higher-level mental math. No matter how the final addition is done, mental calculation and estimation are good goals that will be practiced with this game.

The game gives the players solid experimental evidence that indeed *any* non-Fibonacci number they draw can be expressed as a "special" total of Fibonacci numbers. And no two of the numbers are **consecutive** in the sequence. This should strike them as an amazing feat that not just any collection of numbers can do. A way to convince the skeptics is to try playing this game with any other sequence of numbers on the playing board. They won't be able to imitate this feat.

Student Page 49

### DISCUSSION OF THE PRINCIPLE

Discuss this idea with them after they play the game for a while: Mathematicians have proved that *every* whole number can be expressed as a sum of non-consecutive Fibonaccis. Your more eager beavers may wish to try to find much larger numbers and locate Fibonaccis to make them. The advanced game will meet their needs.

### THE ADVANCED GAME

This involves a change to a three-digit draw. The calculator should be used in this game, as addition by hand can really slow down the play and distract from the more important mental skills that are being developed. The search for Fibonaccis still involves mental math and estimation. The calculator's use should be restricted to the final tally-up on each play, to verify that the drawn number is indeed the sum of the chosen Fibonaccis.

**I hope you and your students enjoy this game!**

# PLAYING THE PATTERNS

**Toolbox: 78 Fibonacci List;** calculator

As you've seen so far, the Fibonacci Numbers are both playful and mathematically amazing. They seem to like creating patterns. You'll have a good chance here to watch these numbers do their stuff and boggle your mind. Your trusty calculator should be with you at all times to help you see and enjoy these patterns.

Find your copy of the **78 Fibonacci List.** Warm up your calculator.

## THE "SUBTRACT SQUARES" TRICK

**1.** Choose any two Fibonaccis that are just one apart in the string (like **3** and **8**): ____ , ____

**2.** Their rank numbers are: ____ ____

**3.** Add the two rank numbers: ____

**4.** Multiply each Fibo times **itself** (i.e., square them): ____ ____

**5.** Subtract the two answers in 4: ____

**6.** Is this a Fibonacci Number? ____

**7.** If so, what is its rank number? ____

**8.** Compare your answer in **7** with that in **3**: ____ equal ____ not equal

Do this with at least five more pairs of one-apart Fibonaccis from the list.

Now, describe what you found to be always true for one-apart Fibonaccis: ____

____

____

____

____

**53**

## THE "ADD SQUARES" TRICK

**1.** Pick any two **consecutive** Fibonaccis (like **8** and **13**).
_____ _____

**2.** Their rank numbers are:       _____ _____

**3.** Add the rank numbers:       _____

**4.** Square each Fibonacci:  _____ _____

**5.** Add the results from 4: _____

**6.** Is this a Fibonacci?    _____ yes _____ no

**7.** If so, give its rank number: _____

**8.** Compare answer in **7** with that in **3**:

_____ equal    _____ not equal

Do this five more times and then describe what is true about consecutive Fibonacci Numbers. (Choose your words carefully.) _____

_____

_____

_____

## THE "END DIGIT" TRICK

On a separate piece of paper, make two lists of digits. In the first, list each end (last) digit of Fibonaccis **2** through **25**. It begins **1, 2, 3, 5, 8, 3, . . .**

In the second list, write each end (last) digit of Fibonaccis **62** through **78**.

Compare the two lists. Does this similarity go further? _____ How far, do you suspect? _____

# AND THE *"FOUR-BONACCI"* TRICK

**Four** is *not* a Fibonacci, but it is a very popular number. The Fibonaccis treat **4** with respect and have a special dance they do with it.

To see it you simply need to make a list of *Four-Bonacci Remainders*. Do this by going to each Fibonacci, dividing it by **4**, and recording its remainder until you see a pattern.

Here are the numbers **1-18**. Next to each number, which is a position number for a Fibonacci, write the remainder you get when you divide the Fibonacci by **4**. This is best done by short division **without** a calculator. A few have been done for you.

1. ____          7. ____          13. ____

2. _1_           8. ____          14. ____

3. ____          9. ____          15. ____

4. ____          10. ____         16. _3_

5. _1_           11. ____         17. ____

6. ____          12. ____         18. ____

Now, **predict** what the remainders will be when you divide the 23rd, 54th, 75th, and 112th Fibonaccis by 4:

23rd: ____   54th: ____   75th: ____   112th: ____

State here what method you used to predict these: _____

_____

Using your **78 Fibonacci List**, check your predictions by actually dividing the 23rd, 54th, and 75th Fibonaccis by 4. Show your work on a separate piece of paper.

## Teacher's Guide to Student Pages 53-55

# PLAYING THE PATTERNS

### PATTERNS AND INDUCTIVE THINKING

There are many exercises coming up that involve **inductive** thinking. This type of higher thinking means that from a collection of data your students identify a general pattern and state that pattern as a rule. It's a type of thinking used in science all the time.

Usually mathematics books demand **deductive** thinking; that is, a rule is given to you and you have to make it work in several circumstances. With inductive thinking, on the other hand, the circumstances are given first with the rule implicitly working. The rule must then be constructed from observing these circumstances. Both kinds of thinking are necessary in our world, but inductive is seldom emphasized in the classroom.

Students may get tongue-tied trying to put into words something they observe. This formulation ability is an important aspect of language arts training and can be worked on in depth if you desire. Each group can try to come up with a good grammatical sentence or two that expresses what they observe. Then the whole class can perfect them with your guidance. As they experience well-formed rule statements, they'll be able to say the next ones better.

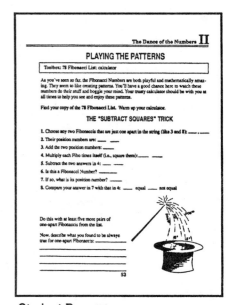

Student Page 53

### THE MAGIC TRICK EXTENSION

You can generally encourage students to turn most tricks or patterns into magic tricks of the "Pick a Fibonacci, Any Fibonacci" kind. They can use them on unsuspecting parents and friends. I'll show you a couple of these conversions as we go along. Then it's up to your students to keep the magic going.

### THE SUBTRACT SQUARES TRICK

Here's a high-level formulation of the first Subtract Squares Rule: "The difference of the squares of **two** *one-apart* Fibonaccis is a Fibonacci itself. The rank number of this Fibonacci is the sum of the ranks of the original two."

They may not get it this clean right away, but that's OK. They should be encouraged to shorten it and make it as grammatically correct as possible.

Student Page 54

## THE SUBTRACT SQUARES MAGIC TRICK

"Pick two numbers, one apart, from my **list of magic numbers.** On your calculator square each one. Now find the difference of those. Tell me the rank of the smaller one you chose, and I'll quickly tell you the answer you got on your calculator." (Student adds 2 to rank of smallest, gets both ranks, and adds them; the Fibonacci Number at that rank is the person's answer.)

## THE ADD SQUARES TRICK

This trick is generalized this way: "The sum of the squares of two consecutive Fibonaccis is a Fibonacci. Its rank number is the sum of the ranks of the original two Fibonaccis," or something like that. Its corresponding magic trick is almost identical to the one above.

## THE END DIGIT TRICK

The ending digits of the Fibonaccis 62 to 78 exactly copy the ending digits of Fibonaccis 2 through 18! Does this continue? I checked the pattern up to the 40th Fibonacci and found the ending digits match up to the 100th Fibonacci. Have students predict how far they think the pattern goes from there. My prediction is that the ending digits of Fibonaccis 2-60 duplicate those of Fibonaccis 62-120.

No great magic trick comes to my mind for this, but some students may think of one.

## THE *FOUR-BONACCI* TRICK

A regular pattern of six remainders repeats over and over again through the Fibonaccis as we divide each by 4. These are

$$...1\ 1\ 2\ 3\ 1\ 0\ ...$$

We can predict remainders later in the string this way. Take the 23rd Fibonacci remainder, for instance. Divide the rank number (23) by 6. The remainder is 5. This means that the 23rd Fibonacci remainder falls 5th in the cycle that goes from 19 to 24. It is therefore 1.

## Teacher's Guide to Student Pages 53-55

Using this method, the 4-remainder for the 54th Fibonacci (divide by 6, remainder 0) is 0, because 54 falls at the **end** of a 6-cycle. (54 is exactly a multiple of 6, and, like all the numbers at the end of 6-cycle, has a remainder of 0.) Because 75 has a 6-remainder of 3, the 75th Fibonacci has the third 4-remainder of the cycle (2). For the 112th, the 4-remainder comes out to be 3.

### THE *FOUR-BONACCI* MAGIC TRICK

Making it magic involves handing someone a list of Fibonaccis, saying "Pick one," and then having that person divide it by 4, remembering the remainder. The magician asks for the number of the Fibonacci on the list, and tells the person the remainder without even looking at the chosen Fibonacci! (The magician has the pattern ...1 1 2 3 1 0 ... memorized. She divides the rank by 6, gets the remainder mentally, and picks the 4-remainder from the pattern.)

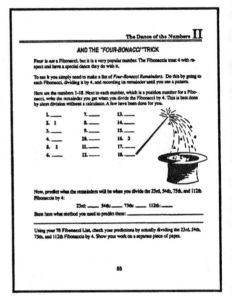

Student Page 55

# SOME FANCY QUICK TRICKS

**Toolbox:** Calculator; 78 Fibonacci List

## THE "SQUARED" TRICK

**To do this trick you need to know that $4^2$ (called "4 squared") means 4 times itself:**
$$4^2 = 4 \times 4 = 16$$

Keep your **78 Fibonacci List** in front of you. Fill in the first three blanks below. Notice the pattern. Then fill in the rest of the blanks without doing any calculating:

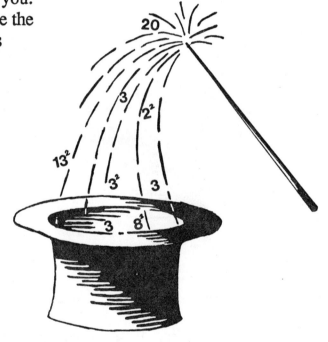

$$5^2 - 1^2 = \underline{\qquad} \times 3$$

$$8^2 - 1^2 = \underline{\qquad} \times 3$$

$$13^2 - 2^2 = \underline{\qquad} \times 3$$

$$\underline{\quad}^2 - \underline{\quad}^2 = \underline{\qquad} \times 3$$

$$\underline{\quad}^2 - \underline{\quad}^2 = \underline{\qquad} \times 3$$

$$\underline{\quad}^2 - \underline{\quad}^2 = \underline{\qquad} \times 3$$

$$\underline{\quad}^2 - \underline{\quad}^2 = \underline{\qquad} \times 3$$

**1.** Challenge: Write the line of this pattern that would start with "$377^2$":

_____

**2.** Choosing your words carefully, write a sentence or two describing how the pattern on each line is obtained from the list:

_____

_____

_____

_____

**SOME FANCY QUICK TRICKS, continued**

## THE "CUBED" TRICK

To do this trick you need to know that $2^3$ means that three copies of 2 are to be multiplied times each other: $2^3 = 2$ x $2$ x $2 = 8.$ It's pronounced "2 cubed."

Finish this pattern:

$2^3 + 3^3 - 1^3 = $ _____

$3^3 + 5^3 - 2^3 = $ _____

$5^3 + 8^3 - 3^3 = $ _____

$\_\_^3 + \_\_^3 - \_\_^3 = $ _____

$\_\_^3 + \_\_^3 - \_\_^3 = $ _____

$\_\_^3 + \_\_^3 - \_\_^3 = $ _____

**1.** The next four answers would be: _____ , _____ , _____ , _____

**2.** Challenge: Write the line of the pattern that starts with "$377^3$":

_____

**3.** Describe how the rank numbers in each line are related:

_____

_____

_____

_____

# THE "10-11" TRICK

Pick any 10 consecutive Fibonacci Numbers from the list. (Remember, *consecutive* means they start somewhere and count up with no skips.) Add them up.

Total: _____

Check, with your calculator, to see whether the total is divisible by 11. It should be!

Try it again with two more sets of 10 consecutive Fibonaccis.

Totals: _____ , _____

Is each divisible by 11?_____

A non-calculator shortcut for checking to see whether a number is divisible by 11 is to:

● Start at the right end of the number and add up **every other** digit as you move left. Then ...

● Add up all the digits that you skipped the first time.

● Subtract the smaller total from the larger. If this answer is divisible by 11 then the whole number is!

Try this trick on your three totals above. Fill in your work here:

| Number | _____ | _____ | _____ |
|---|---|---|---|
| **First digit total** | _____ | _____ | _____ |
| **Second digit total** | _____ | _____ | _____ |
| **Subtract totals** | _____ | _____ | _____ |
| **Divisible by 11?** | _____ | _____ | _____ |

State the general rule about the Fibonaccis you've learned in the "10-11" trick:_____
_____
_____

**SOME FANCY QUICK TRICKS, continued**

## THE "NUMBER TRIANGLE" TRICK

Finish this pattern by filling in four more lines. Then check all lines with your calculator to see if the patterns create true answers.

$$1^2 + 1^2 = 1 \times 2$$

$$1^2 + 1^2 + 2^2 = 2 \times 3$$

$$1^2 + 1^2 + 2^2 + 3^2 = 3 \times 5$$

$$1^2 + 1^2 + 2^2 + 3^2 + 5^2 = 5 \times 8$$

_____

_____

_____

_____

State the general pattern you see. Choose your words carefully and revise your statement twice on scrap paper before writing it here: _____

_____

_____

_____

_____

_____

_____

# THE "MYSTERIOUS 89" TRICK

The Fibonacci Number **89** is the key to all the other Fibonaccis. Here's how.

Find out what 1/89 equals as a decimal by punching on your calculator

$$\boxed{1} \quad \boxed{\div} \quad \boxed{8} \quad \boxed{9} \quad \boxed{=}$$

Notice that the first few digits look **very** familiar.
Here's how it would look if you had a bigger calculator screen:

### .01123595505617975 ...

The rest don't look very familiar, do they? However, this number has Fibonaccis *inside it*.
To show you, let's write some consecutive Fibonaccis, and you continue by filling in the blanks from your list:

```
.0 1 1 2 3 5 8
            1 3
              2 1
                3 4
                  5 5
                    8 9
                  1 4 4
                    2 3 3
                      3 7 7
                      6 _ _
                      _ _ _
                    _ _ _ _
                  _ _ _ _
                  _ _ _ _
```

To complete column totals on this side of the dotted line, you need to list more Fibonaccis.

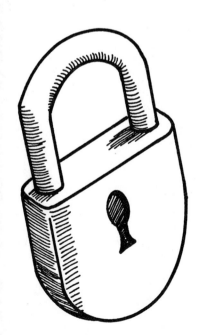

Now add up each column, starting to the left of the dotted line and moving left. The answer below the line gives you the same decimal digits of 1/89 as I gave you above! And it will do so for as long as you want to write Fibonaccis!

**SOME FANCY QUICK TRICKS, continued**

# Extension

You can get more digits of 1/89 by continuing to write more Fibonaccis diagonally. That is, each time start one more space to the right.

**Exception:** When there is an extra digit in the Fibonacci you are about to write, write it *without* jumping one place to the right. (For examples, look at 144 and 1597 on page 63.)

**FOR FEARLESS DIVIDERS:** You can check the digits of 1/89 by dividing by hand:

$$89\overline{)1.00000000000000000000000000000000000000\ldots}$$

## THE "FAST-ADD" TRICK

Starting with the first Fibonacci, begin adding up the whole string as you go. Write each sum you get along the way. See if you can begin to predict what the next answer will be. I'll start you off:

**1+1** is **2**
**2+2** is **4**
**4+3** is **7** (and so on).

**1.** Keep writing what you get when you add the next Fibonacci. Eventually you should see a pattern. When you do, describe it here:

_____

_____

_____

_____

**2.** Now predict what the sum of the first 83 Fibonaccis will be:

_____

_____

## THE "ODD-ADD" TRICK

Starting with the first Fibonacci, add up every other Fibonacci (that is, every Fibonacci with an odd position number). As you go, you will notice a pattern in your sums.

**1.** Describe the pattern: _____

_____

_____

_____

_____

**2.** Predict what the sum of odd Fibonaccis up through the 27th Fibonacci will be:

_____

_____

## Teacher's Guide to Student Pages 59-65

# SOME FANCY QUICK TRICKS

The Quick Tricks are more visual and rhythmic than the last set of tricks. They consist of patterns to recognize and continue. Here are the rules and answers.

### THE SQUARED TRICK

$5^2 - 1^2 = 8 \times 3$

$8^2 - 1^2 = 21 \times 3$

$13^2 - 2^2 = 55 \times 3$

$21^2 - 3^2 = 144 \times 3$

$34^2 - 5^2 = 377 \times 3$

$55^2 - 8^2 = 987 \times 3$

$89^2 - 13^2 = 2584 \times 3$

Calculation starts these off and recognition continues them. Make sure students try some of the last ones on the calculator to see that the patterns continue working.

**1.** $377^2 - 55^2 = 46368 \times 3$

**2.** To find the pattern for, say, the 22nd line, start with the 26th Fibonacci (4 more than the line number). The next Fibonacci used is the 22nd, same as the line number. On the right side of the equals, choose the 48th Fibonacci (always the sum of the two ranks of the Fibonaccis on the left) multiplied by 3.

### THE CUBED TRICK

$2^3 + 3^3 - 1^3 = 34$

$3^3 + 5^3 - 2^3 = 144$

$5^3 + 8^3 - 3^3 = 610$

$8^3 + 13^3 + 5^3 = 2834$

$13^3 + 21^3 + 8^3 = 10946$

$21^3 + 34^3 + 13^3 = 46368$

The key here is to notice that this relationship of cubes of increasing Fibonaccis generates every third Fibonacci.

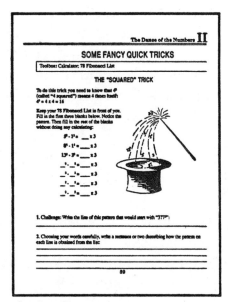

Student Page 59

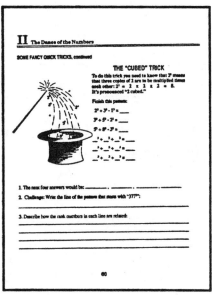

Student Page 60

## Teacher's Guide to Student Pages 59-65

**Student Page 61**

**Student Page 62**

**1.** The next four would be 196418, 832040, 3524578, 14930352.

**2.** $377^3 + 610^3 - 233^3 = 267,914,296$

**3.** In each line of the pattern, the rank of the first number is 1 less than the rank of the middle one, and 1 more than the rank of the last one. The rank of the answer Fibonacci is the sum of the ranks of the three Fibonaccis used.

### THE 10-11 TRICK

The pattern here is that any sum of 10 consecutive Fibonaccis is divisible by 11.

The 11s Divisibility Trick is more for the fun of it than a real time saver, though it can get pretty fast after a while. It's great for promoting quick mental arithmetic.

### THE NUMBER TRIANGLE TRICK

$$1^2 + 1^2 = 1 \times 2$$
$$1^2 + 1^2 + 2^2 = 2 \times 3$$
$$1^2 + 1^2 + 2^2 + 3^2 = 3 \times 5$$
$$1^2 + 1^2 + 2^2 + 3^2 + 5^2 = 5 \times 8$$
$$1^2 + 1^2 + 2^2 + 3^2 + 5^2 + 8^2 = 8 \times 13$$
$$1^2 + 1^2 + 2^2 + 3^2 + 5^2 + 8^2 + 13^2 = 13 \times 21$$
$$1^2 + 1^2 + 2^2 + 3^2 + 5^2 + 8^2 + 13^2 + 21^2 = 21 \times 34$$
$$1^2 + 1^2 + 2^2 + 3^2 + 5^2 + 8^2 + 13^2 + 21^2 + 34^2 = 34 \times 55$$

This pattern is saying that whatever sum of the squares of consecutive Fibonaccis you add, your answer can be also obtained by multiplying the last Fibonacci you used by the next one! See if students can say anything resembling this; then have them write it. If eventually you say it this way, see if they can repeat it.

## Teacher's Guide to Student Pages 59-65

### THE MYSTERIOUS 89 TRICK

When your students first find the reciprocal of Fibonacci Number 89 on the calculator, they may notice the progression of the first few Fibonaccis. Of course, if one went on dividing all day by long hand, an endless stream of digits would follow the ones seen on the calculator.

This same stream of digits can be created by adding up consecutive Fibonaccis. They have to be added just right, in the stairstep fashion shown:

```
                 3 7 7
                   6 1 0
                     9 8 7
Note here how an extra digit→ 1 5 9 7
changes the stairstep.         2 5 8 4
                                 4 1 8 1
```

You have to start with a complete column, that is, a column that won't change when more Fibonaccis are placed below. This means that only the column with 4 at the bottom can be added meaningfully. Then carry to the column before that and so on. You will get the long decimal shown on the student page.

This decimal can, of course, be obtained by a fearless long divider for practice.

### THE FAST-ADD TRICK: ADDING UP FIBONACCIS

**1.** Simply stated, adding up Fibonaccis consecutively from the beginning up to some Fibonacci always results in a total that is 1 less than the Fibonacci that is two more positions ahead.

**2.** The total up to the 83rd Fibonacci would be the 85th Fibonacci minus 1.

This has **magic trick** potential. "Start adding up the numbers on my list here. Go as far as you want. Just tell me which number rank you ended with." (The magician glances at the list and confidently says the total.)

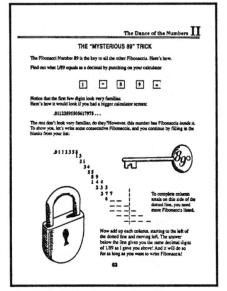

Student Page 63

Student Page 64

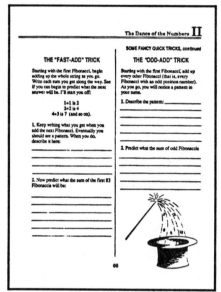

Student Page 65

## THE ODD-ADD TRICK: ADDING ALTERNATE FIBO-NACCIS

**1.** This trick is that if you add up every other Fibonacci, starting from the first, your total at any time is the next Fibonacci you're about to jump over!

**2.** The sum is the 28th Fibonacci, or 317,811.

This is the last of the short Fibonacci Tricks for now. Some go-getters in your class may want to look for more patterns on their own. Students often find one kind or another.

These references may be of help to you or them:

**Fascinating Fibonaccis** by T. H. Garland.

**The Divine Proportion** by Hogatt.

Larger libraries have all the back issues of the *Fibonacci Quarterly* in the periodical section. It is full of information on the Fibonaccis, but beware: it has some very high-level math in it, too. A few articles in each issue, especially the older issues, are readable by a serious student.

# USING THE SIEVE OF ERATOSTHENES ON OUR FIBONACCIS

**Toolbox:** Colored pens; **78 Fibonacci List**; a pile of cubes, coins, or squares; calculator

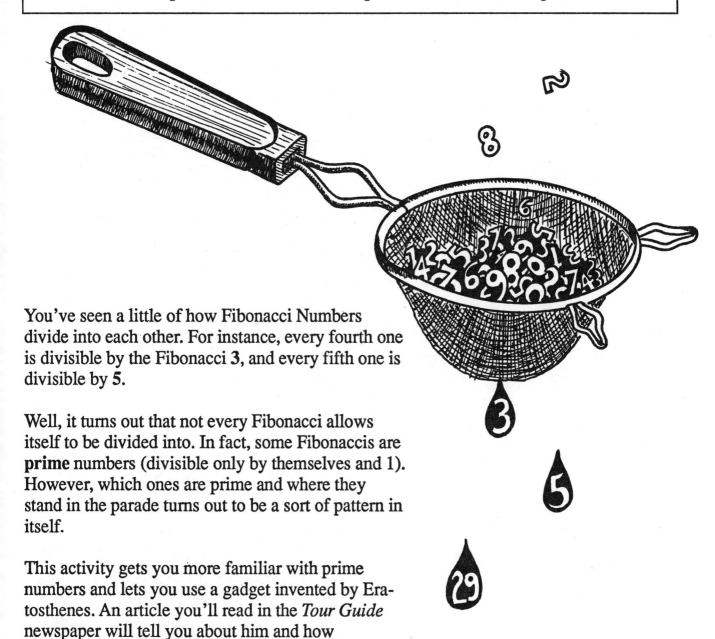

You've seen a little of how Fibonacci Numbers divide into each other. For instance, every fourth one is divisible by the Fibonacci **3**, and every fifth one is divisible by **5**.

Well, it turns out that not every Fibonacci allows itself to be divided into. In fact, some Fibonaccis are **prime** numbers (divisible only by themselves and 1). However, which ones are prime and where they stand in the parade turns out to be a sort of pattern in itself.

This activity gets you more familiar with prime numbers and lets you use a gadget invented by Eratosthenes. An article you'll read in the *Tour Guide* newspaper will tell you about him and how to pronounce his name. First, though, you need to explore *prime-ness*.

**THE SIEVE OF ERATOSTHENES, continued**

## PRIMES AND RECTANGLES

Take **41** cubes, coins, or squares. Try to arrange them into a solid rectangle with the appropriate number of rows and columns. Try it with **27**, **29**, and **24**, also. Describe your findings for each number:

**41:** _____

**27:** _____

**29:** _____

**24:** _____

A prime number can never be divided by any number (except itself and 1—how boring). Which numbers above must be prime numbers? _____ What's that got to do with being able to form a rectangle or not? _____

_____

_____

_____

_____

After you're clear about primes, read up on Eratosthenes in the article "Eratosthenes Measures the Earth" in your *Tour Guide* newspaper.

**STOP**

72

## THE SIEVE

Let's do his sieve (also called a strainer) so you can get used to it before we use it on the Fibonaccis. The rules for the Sieve of Eratosthenes are below. Do them on this square of numbers as you read the rules:

| 1 | 2 | 3 | 4 | 5 | 6 | 7 | 8 | 9 | 10 |
|----|----|----|----|----|----|----|----|----|-----|
| 11 | 12 | 13 | 14 | 15 | 16 | 17 | 18 | 19 | 20 |
| 21 | 22 | 23 | 24 | 25 | 26 | 27 | 28 | 29 | 30 |
| 31 | 32 | 33 | 34 | 35 | 36 | 37 | 38 | 39 | 40 |
| 41 | 42 | 43 | 44 | 45 | 46 | 47 | 48 | 49 | 50 |
| 51 | 52 | 53 | 54 | 55 | 56 | 57 | 58 | 59 | 60 |
| 61 | 62 | 63 | 64 | 65 | 66 | 67 | 68 | 69 | 70 |
| 71 | 72 | 73 | 74 | 75 | 76 | 77 | 78 | 79 | 80 |
| 81 | 82 | 83 | 84 | 85 | 86 | 87 | 88 | 89 | 90 |
| 91 | 92 | 93 | 94 | 95 | 96 | 97 | 98 | 99 | 100 |

● Cross off 1. (Use *black*.)
● Cross off **every even** number, **but not 2 itself**. (Use *pink*.)
● Cross off **every 3rd** number, starting at 3, **but not 3 itself**: 6, 9, 12, . . . (Use *red*, marking any numbers again that were already marked with pink.)
● Cross off **every 5th** number (multiple of 5) starting at 5, **but not 5 itself**. (Use *green*. Mark numbers again if they already have pink or red.)
● Cross off **every 7th** multiple, after 7, **but not 7 itself**. (Use *purple*, even on numbers already marked.)

All the numbers that are **not** crossed out are **PRIME NUMBERS**.

73

## THE SIEVE OF ERATOSTHENES, continued

**1.** How many primes are there between 1 and 100? _____

**2.** What pattern did you notice as you crossed off every 3rd number? _____
_____

**3.** What pattern did you notice as you crossed off every 5th number? _____
_____

**4.** What pattern did you notice as you crossed off every 7th number?_____
_____

**5.** If the sieve could continue up to 300, here are the prime numbers it would strain out:

| 101 | 137 | 173 | 223 | 263 |
|-----|-----|-----|-----|-----|
| 103 | 139 | 179 | 227 | 269 |
| 107 | 149 | 181 | 229 | 271 |
| 109 | 151 | 191 | 233 | 277 |
| 113 | 157 | 197 | 239 | 281 |
| 127 | 163 | 199 | 241 | 283 |
| 131 | 167 | 211 | 253 | 293 |

Now we've seen all the primes between 1 and 300.

Between 100 and 200 there are _____ primes. Between 200 and 300 there are_____
primes. Predict how many there would be between 300 and 400: _____.

There are many primes above 400, but my research shows that the three Fibonacci Numbers 1597, 28657, and 514,229 are the only Fibonaccis above 400 and under 64 million that are prime.

## PRIMES AND FIBONACCIS

It's time to find all the prime Fibonaccis you can and discover the secret of where they like to be in the Fibonacci List. Get your **78 Fibonacci List**. Use your sieve plus the number information I just gave you to do this:

- ● Circle all the **prime rank numbers** in the first column of the List.
- ● Then, circle all the **prime Fibonacci Numbers** you can find in the first column of the List.

**1.** There's not a perfect pattern here, but there's a partial one. It's a sort of **tendency.** Can you describe what is **often** true about the prime Fibonaccis and their position numbers?

_____

_____

**2.** What Fibonaccis seem to break the pattern? _____

**3.** Predict three Fibonaccis that **may** be prime: _____

### CONGRATULATIONS!

**This is your first work with a tendency.** As you've learned up to now, Fibonacci patterns always go on forever with no exception. Since ancient times the prime numbers have been known to be **very unpredictable,** and it's true when they show up in the Fibonaccis, too.

## Teacher's Guide to Student Pages 71-75

# USING THE SIEVE OF ERATOSTHENES ON OUR FIBONACCIS

This activity is about **prime numbers.** It's also about Eratosthenes in that students must read about him in the *Tour Guide* newspaper to do the activity. The article will also give them a tasty dose of earth science, geography, and history.

This activity is more sophisticated than the previous ones, as it includes a variety of interesting thoughts about primes and their predictability. The Sieve activity also displays number multiples in a colorful way. **If you are cutting activities because of time constraints, or your students have less curiosity about the Fibonaccis, this may be one to skip.**

### PRIMES AND RECTANGLES

Neither 41 nor 29 allows itself to be arranged as a rectangle of rows and columns. This means they are **prime numbers.** To see this, suppose that 41 **could** be arranged as, say, 6 rows and 7 columns. Then 6x7 would be the number of chips used and would equal the 41 (which of course they don't because 6 x 7 = 42). This would also mean that both 6 and 7 would divide into 41, which would mean 41 is **not** prime.

Note that 27 is odd but not prime because it can be arranged as a 3x9 rectangle. And 24 is interesting because it can make three different rectangles: 2x12, 3x8, and 4x6.

### THE SIEVE

This activity is more interesting if it's done on a large 100-grid and colored tokens are laid on the numbers. It's even better if the tokens are made of clear, colored acetate. This way the patterns referred to in the question become very evident and the numbers can be seen through the tokens.

Basically, I hope students will notice that the multiples of a number all repeat with a certain *rhythm* or pattern. Some students with sharp pattern recognition will notice that even numbers that share **two** tokens, or marks, of different colors repeat in a pattern. All of this can be a good exploration for a group.

Student Page 71

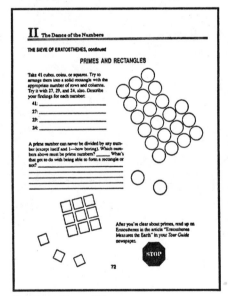

Student Page 72

## Teacher's Guide to Student Pages 71-75

Student Page 73

Here are the numbers that end up being struck and those that are left alone:

### A GOOD DISCUSSION

Ask why this works to filter out all the primes. Why aren't we instructed to cross out all multiples of 11? Or 13, and so forth? Let students discuss this for a while before you make any suggestions.

**Answer:** All multiples of 11 are magically crossed out because 11x2, 11x3, 11x4, 11x5, etc., were hit on other passes. The same with multiples of 13, and so on. If all multiples of everything are crossed out, it leaves the primes, which are not multiples of anything.

### A PRIME EXPLORATION

Students should be encouraged to check whether there is a pattern to the appearance of primes in the list. They will see some pattern that appears to work in a few instances but then it fades out. In fact, mathematicians have shown there is no overall pattern in the primes, which gives them the role of unpredictability in our number system. They have this role in the Fibonaccis too, as we'll see.

## Teacher's Guide to Student Pages 71-75

### ANSWERS TO QUESTIONS ON PAGE 74

**1.** There are 25 primes between 1 and 100.

**2.** Diagonals are created, slanting one down, one over to the left.

**3.** Straight lines are created in the 5 and 10 places.

**4.** Very slanted lines, one down and three to the left, go across the grid.

> **Note:** Encourage students to describe the patterns created by the numbers with **two** marks of certain colors.

**5.** 20; 15. Predictions for 300-400 will vary, but 10 is a good guess. The correct answer is 16.

### PRIMES AND FIBONACCIS

Part of the challenge of this activity is for students to interpret the number data about primes of various sizes and then use the data to mark Fibonacci primes throughout the first column. When the prime position numbers and the prime Fibonaccis of the first column are marked, a partial pattern begins to form.

We first note that there seems to be a correspondence, though not perfect, between position numbers that are prime and the prime Fibonaccis that tend to be in those positions. But some prime position numbers have non-prime Fibonaccis in them, namely positions 2, 19, 31, and 37. Not a very tight pattern!

But look at it more optimistically. *If* a Fibonacci is prime and over 3, it's *always* found in a prime position. Mathematicians have proved that this is true throughout the rest of the infinite Fibonacci sequence!

> **1.** It is quite often true that a prime position number will have a prime Fibonacci standing in it. The only exception that can be found from the data given the students is the number 4181: it is not given as prime even though its position number is the prime 19. There are other exceptions, including position 31 that has a non-prime in it.

> On the other hand, a Fibonacci that *is* prime (except for 3) will *always* choose to stand at a prime-ranked position.

Student Page 74

Student Page 75

**2-3.** The students should pick three prime rank numbers higher in the **78 Fibonacci List** and predict that the Fibonaccis in them are prime.

**NOTE:** It hasn't been determined, however, whether primes even continue to appear in the sequence forever or whether they run out at some point. Questions like this are part of the elusive nature of the primes that has always challenged mathematicians throughout the ages.

There's a statistical theme in these exercises, too. It first appears when students are asked to predict how many primes there will be between 300 and 400. Based on previous experience, with 25 the first hundred, 20 the second, and 15 the third, it would not be out of hand to say "10." But the elusive primes win again—there are 16! It's a good lesson that tendencies are not laws.

The next statistical theme arises when the students are asked to "Predict three Fibonaccis that may be prime." These would be any three Fibonaccis that are at prime position numbers in the second column. These prime positions are the highest probability places to look for prime Fibonaccis, but they don't guarantee anything.

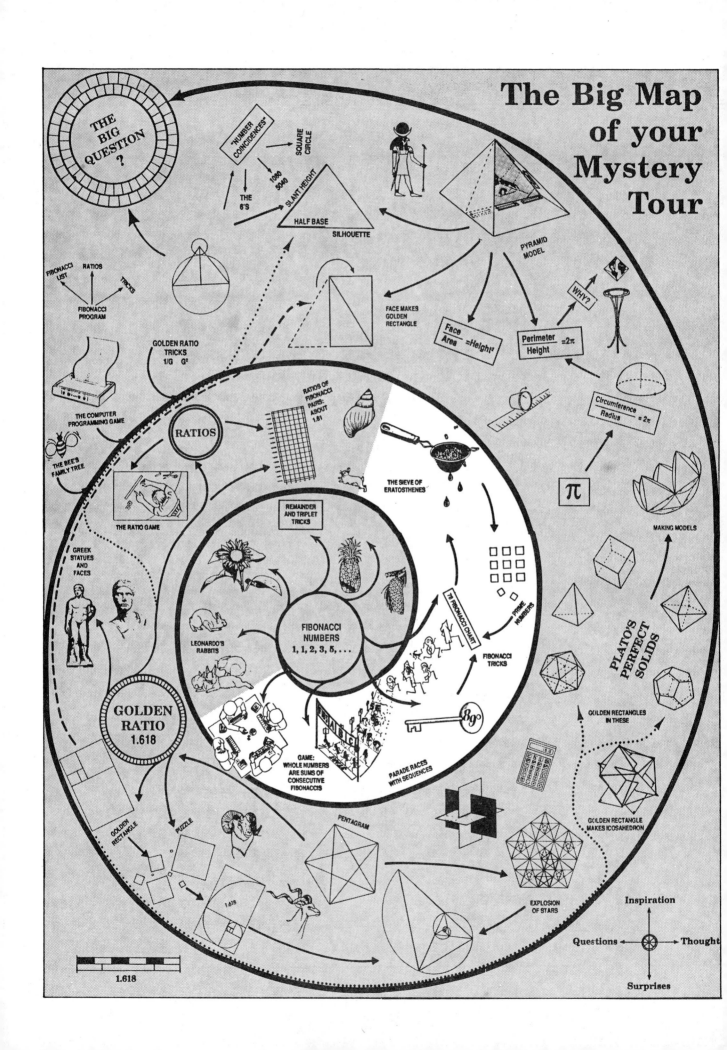

# The Big Map of your Mystery Tour

THE BIG QUESTION ?

"NUMBER COINCIDENCES"

SQUARE CIRCLE

THE 6'S

1080
5040

SLANT-HEIGHT

HALF BASE

SILHOUETTE

PYRAMID MODEL

FIBONACCI LIST

RATIOS

TRICKS

FIBONACCI PROGRAM

GOLDEN RATIO TRICKS 1/G   G²

FACE MAKES GOLDEN RECTANGLE

$$\frac{Face}{Area} = Height^2$$

$$\frac{Perimeter}{Height} = 2\pi$$

WHY?

$$\frac{Circumference}{Radius} = 2\pi$$

THE COMPUTER PROGRAMMING GAME

RATIOS

RATIOS OF FIBONACCI PAIRS, ABOUT 1.61

$\pi$

MAKING MODELS

THE BEE'S FAMILY TREE

THE SIEVE OF ERATOSTHENES

THE RATIO GAME

REMAINDER AND TRIPLET TRICKS

PRIME NUMBERS

PLATO'S PERFECT SOLIDS

GREEK STATUES AND FACES

78 FIBONACCI CHART

FIBONACCI TRICKS

FIBONACCI NUMBERS 1, 1, 2, 3, 5, . . .

LEONARDO'S RABBITS

GOLDEN RATIO 1.618

89°

GOLDEN RECTANGLES IN THESE

GAME: WHOLE NUMBERS ARE SUMS OF CONSECUTIVE FIBONACCIS

PARADE RACES WITH SEQUENCES

GOLDEN RECTANGLE MAKES ICOSAHEDRON

GOLDEN RECTANGLE

PUZZLE

PENTAGRAM

EXPLOSION OF STARS

1.618

1.618

Inspiration

Questions ← ⊕ → Thought

Surprises

# A LOOK AT THE TERRITORY: UNIT II

Here's the part of the Tour Map that shows the area you've just explored. The following activities will help you get to know it better.

- Look on your Tour Map to see where this chunk of territory lies.
- Discuss the map with someone else and explain why each arrow is placed the way it is.
- Study this map for 3 minutes; then put it away and redraw it from memory. (You don't have to be a great artist. Just make something to represent the picture.)
- Can you add the pictures from the Unit I part of the map? Try it! (If you can't, look them up on the Tour Map and add them.)
- Prove that this part of the journey is permanently stored in your mind. Here's how: without looking at any map, write two paragraphs or more about the journey you have taken in Units I and II. Briefly describe all main points, telling which ideas are connected and how. Use your mental map as your guide.

# LEARNING INVENTORY

---

**Toolbox: 78 Fibonacci List**

---

These questions are designed to see if you *got the point* of the activities you did in the first and second units. There are several types of questions, from memory to calculation to thought questions. There may be some answers you are fuzzy about. If so, after you have finished the inventory go back to reread, and perhaps rework, the pages these questions came from. Then write a short paragraph summarizing the important points of each topic you reviewed.

**1.** Draw a spiral and a helix:

spiral          helix

**2.** What Fibonacci Numbers are usually found on a pinecone?

_____

How do we get the whole sequence of Fibonaccis from these few?_____

_____

**3.** Write the first 10 Fibonacci Numbers and put a rank number below each:

___ ___ ___ ___ ___ ___ ___ ___ ___ ___

**4.** What other natural things have Fibonacci Numbers in them? (Name two)

_____    _____

**5.** Complete this statement: "Every regular counting number can be written as the _____ of some Fibonacci Numbers, and these Fibonaccis are also non- _____ ."

**6.** Underline one: Compared with other sequences, the Fibonacci sequence grows

**very fast**

**medium fast**

**slowly.**

**7.** If you square the 6th and 8th Fibonaccis, then subtract your answers, what Fibonacci will you get?

_____

**8.** If you square the 14th and 15th Fibonaccis, then add your answers, you will get

_____

**9.** The last digit of Fibonacci 19 should be the same as the last digit of what Fibonacci with rank in the 70s?

_____

**LEARNING INVENTORY, continued**

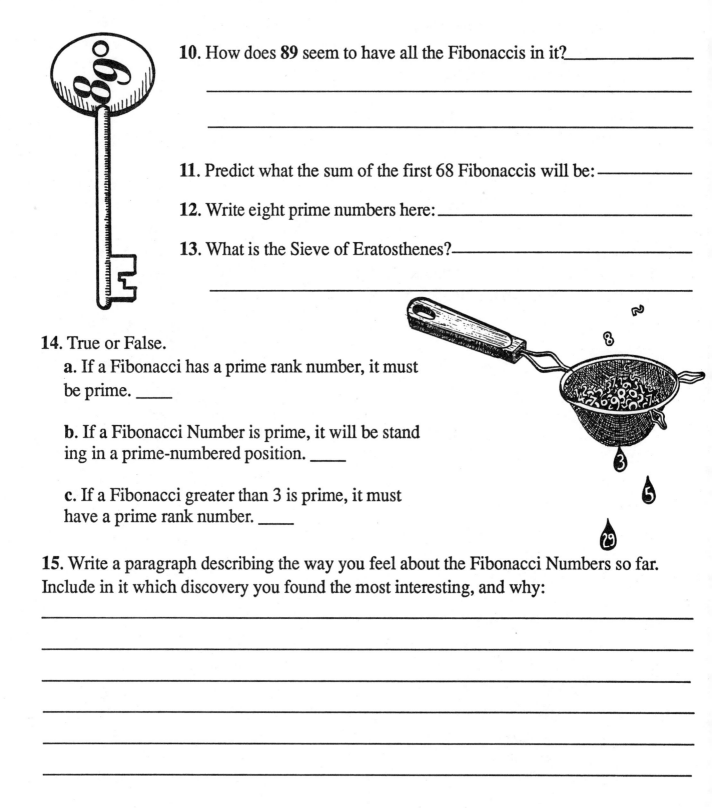

**10.** How does **89** seem to have all the Fibonaccis in it?_____

_____

_____

**11.** Predict what the sum of the first 68 Fibonaccis will be: ————

**12.** Write eight prime numbers here: _____

**13.** What is the Sieve of Eratosthenes?————————————

_____

**14.** True or False.
**a.** If a Fibonacci has a prime rank number, it must be prime. ____

**b.** If a Fibonacci Number is prime, it will be standing in a prime-numbered position. ____

**c.** If a Fibonacci greater than 3 is prime, it must have a prime rank number. ____

**15.** Write a paragraph describing the way you feel about the Fibonacci Numbers so far. Include in it which discovery you found the most interesting, and why:

_____

_____

_____

_____

_____

_____

## Teacher's Guide to Student Pages 82-84

# LEARNING INVENTORY

The purpose of this inventory is not to *zap* the students with stumpers, but to highlight areas that should be reviewed.

One method of review is to have students write a short paragraph on each section of material that was poorly remembered on this inventory. The answers to the questions can also be discussed in class or in small groups.

### ANSWERS TO QUESTIONS ON PAGE 82-84

**1.** Something like and

**2.**    3, 5, 8, 13, or 5, 8, 13, 21
Continue adding two to get the next Fibonacci.

**3.** Fibonacci     1  1  2  3  5  8  13 21 34 55
    Rank Number  1  2  3  4  5  6  7  8  9  10

4. Any two of these: Flowers, bees, pineapples, rabbits (only ideal rabbits, though)

**5.** sum, non-consecutive

**6.** medium fast (because some grow faster and some slower than the Fibonacci sequence)

**7.** The 14th Fibonacci; 6 + 8 = 14.

**8.** The 29th Fibonacci; 14 + 15 = 29.

**9.** Fibonacci 79. The last digit pattern of the Fibonaccis from rank 2 on repeats from rank 62 on. This means that if you add 60 to your Fibonacci rank, it will give you the rank of the Fibonacci with the same last digit.

**10.** The unending decimal for 1/89 can be constructed by adding the unending sequence of Fibonaccis in a particular way.

Student Page 82

Student Page 83

## Teacher's Guide to Student Pages 82-84

**11.** One less than the 70th Fibonacci, or, 190,392,490,709,134. "One-hundred-ninety trillion, three-hundred-ninety-two billion, . . ."

**12.** Answers will vary, but all must be the prime numbers discovered in the section on Eratosthenes' Sieve.

**13.** The Sieve of Eratosthenes is a *method* of eliminating all multiples and exposing the primes in the first 100 counting numbers.

**14.** a. F. There *can* be a Fibonacci with prime rank—like the 19th being 4181—but this number is not prime. There's only a tendency for these Fibonaccis to be the prime ones.
b. F. If the number is more than 3, this statement would be true.
c. T. This is the true rewrite of b.

**15.** Answers will vary. Some misunderstandings could be revealed by this answer.

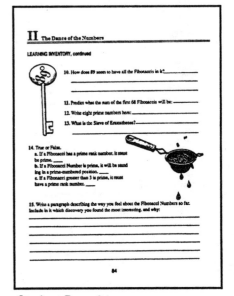

Student Page 84

Optional Activity 2:

# A FIBONACCI MACHINE AND COMPUTER PROGRAMS

**Toolbox:** Computer on which programming in BASIC Language is possible; scissors

If you've never programmed in BASIC Language, this section is for you.

**If you have programmed, and know what you're doing, you may decide to skip to the actual listing of the program at the end. This may be typed carefully into the computer and test run. There is a section afterwards on how to change the program. If you're fuzzy about how that program works, come back to this section for review.**

We're going to play with a machine and then program the machine into your computer. It'll spit out the **78 Fibonacci List** that you've been using. I hope you'll learn a lot about how computers think.

On the next page is a picture of a machine, kind of like a pinball machine, that fills boxes with number-marbles. It has a conveyor belt that moves the next box forward to be loaded each time the machine makes its moves. This machine is at the heart of the computer program you'll write, so you need to operate it.

**Starting Position**
● Cut out the 20 little circles of paper and pretend they're number-marbles. There's a "1" on one of them. Put it into **pan Y.**
● There's a "0" on another. Put it in the **B bowl.**
● Cut out the boxes with Fs in them. Cut slits along the thick line, so the boxes can hold a circle. Line the boxes up on the conveyor belt with F1 at the end of the spout coming from **pan Y.**

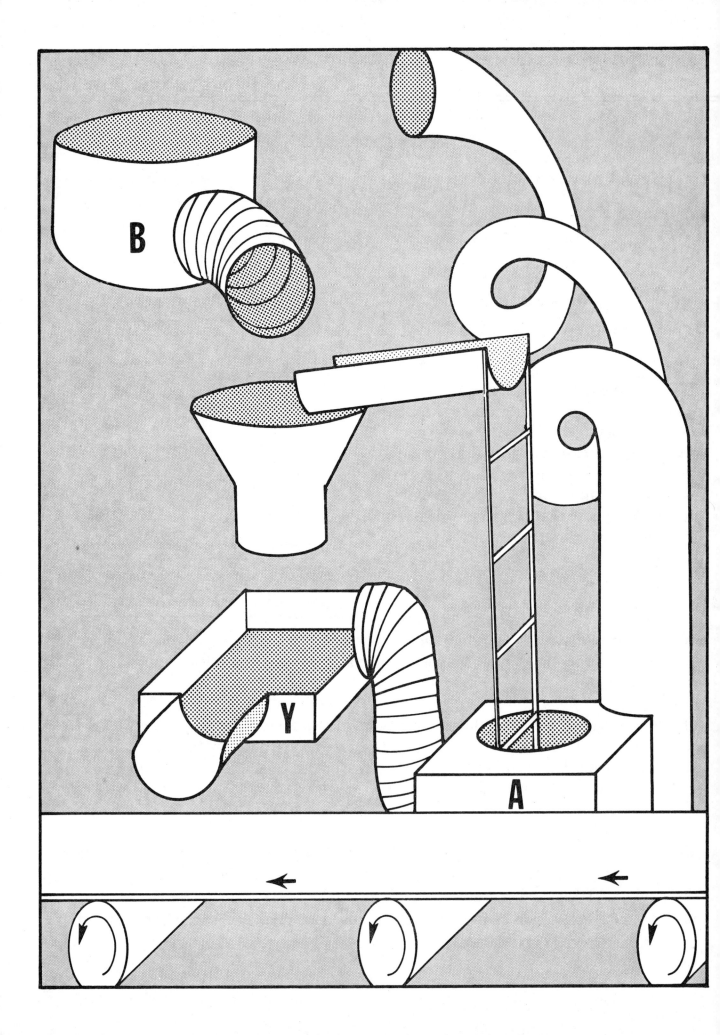

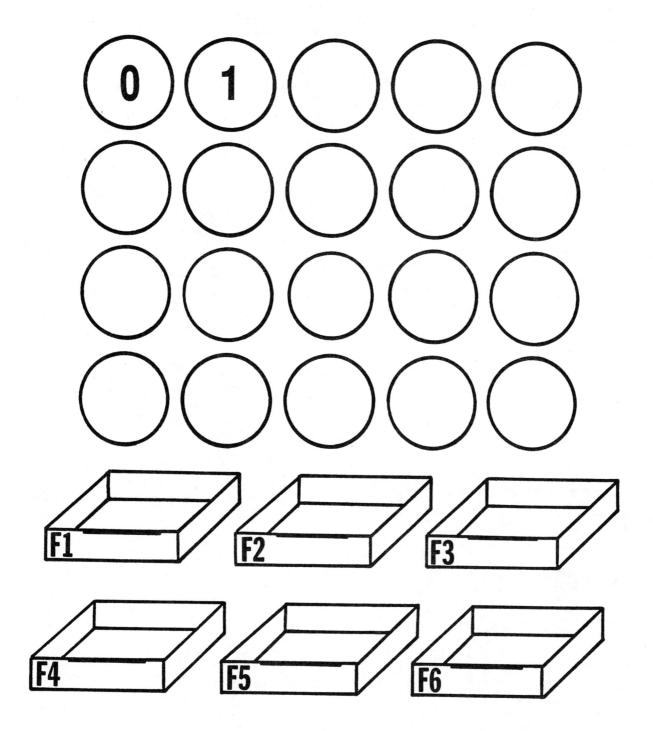

# FIBONACCI MACHINE

Here's what the machine does each time the conveyer belt has moved another box forward. Do every detail with your paper circles.

**1. Starting Position.** The **number-marble** in **pan Y** makes a **copy-marble** that has the same number.

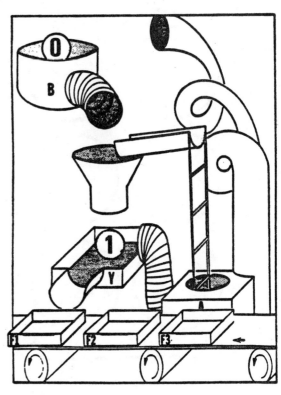

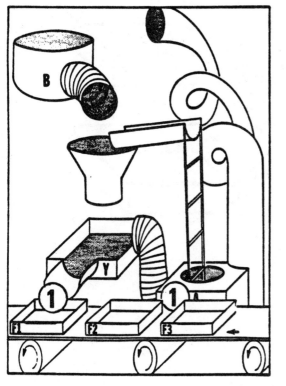

**2. One** of these rolls down the spout into the **F-box** waiting on the conveyor belt. The original number-marble drops through the tube into **box A**. It makes another copy-marble.

**FIBONACCI MACHINE, continued**

**3.** A marble from box A rolls up its ladder and down the trough just as the number-marble in **bowl B** drops to the funnel. They fall together through the funnel, adding as they fall to make one marble with their sum on it. The **sum-marble** drops into pan Y.

**4.** The other number-marble **copy** in box A *spirals* through the tube and *lands* in bowl B, bumping out whatever number is there so it disappears. Now the conveyor slips forward a notch, bringing the next F-box into place. Do this.

**5.** Then go to step 1 and do all moves again. Continue this at least six times, and watch what numbers end up in the F-boxes.

# WRITING THE PROGRAM

We'll write a program in BASIC language that will do exactly what your marble-machine did. It will

1. Calculate the first 78 Fibonacci Numbers.
2. Store that list so you can pull out any one you want later.
3. Print the list out in an orderly manner, showing the rank number of each Fibonacci.

Each step the computer has to do will be explained here. You'll recognize the steps you did with the marble game. All commands are numbered so that the computer can keep track of them. There are explanations with each command. Read through the whole program and explanations, then type the CAPITALIZED lines and numbers into your computer. Make sure it's set on BASIC language first!

### 5 PRINT "     A FIBONACCI LIST"

This is a command to print on the screen a set of blanks followed by the words "A FIBONACCI LIST."

### 10 PRINT

This command **prints** a blank line.

### 15 DIM F#(80)

This **Dimension** command tells the computer to make a conveyor belt of 80 empty boxes. These are to be named "F#"-boxes. (The little # mark tells the computer we want the F-boxes to hold up to 14-digit numbers instead of the usual 7 digits. Your computer may not have the ability to use this statement, saying "Syntax Error in 15." Change F#(80) to F(80) and remove the "#" from every command below which it appears. Your computer will then only print about 35 accurate Fibonaccis—the rest will look weird.)

### 20 PRINT"NUM";    "FIBO",,"NUM";"   FIBO"

This command says to print word headings with extra spaces between them. The punctuation and spaces are important as position cues for the computer screen. These words will label the tops of the columns of position numbers.

### 30 Y#=1

This command puts a 1 in the Y pan to start things off (as you did with the machine).

### 40 B#=0

This command puts a 0 in the B bowl for starters. (The computer automatically puts a 0 in any bowl you name anyway, but we're reminding ourselves how things start.)

### 50 FOR I=1 TO 78

This command says to start up a counter called "I" and do the commands that follow 78 times. Also, each time it does the commands it must change the counter by one notch. This will move our machine's conveyor belt one place after it has done a cycle.

### 60 F#(I)=Y#

In BASIC an "=" tells the computer to take a copy of the number in the box on the right side and put it in the container on the left side. So this command says to let the marble in pan Y roll into the F-box now in place and waiting on the conveyor belt. That box is now numbered by what's on the counter I.

### 70 A#=Y#

This command says to put a copy of what's in pan Y into box A (as you did with the machine).

### 80 Y#=A#+B#

This command adds what's in box A and in bowl B, then puts the sum through the funnel into pan Y, as in the machine.

### 90 B#=A#

This command makes the number in box A spiral through the tube into box B.

### 100 NEXT I

This command moves the conveyor belt forward one box, making counter I one number higher, and sends the computer to redo all the commands starting at the FOR in line 50. The computer won't get out of this **command loop** until it has moved the conveyor belt 78 times.

## WRITING THE PROGRAM, continued

```
110 FOR J=1 TO 39
```

After the commands above have been done 78 times, the computer looks here. This is a command to set up another counter called "J" that will count up as the commands below are done. The commands below will print the numbers from the F-boxes in two columns 39 lines long. The numbers on the counter J will rank the first column and those in box K (numbering from 40 to 78 because they're always 39 more than counter J) will be printed with the second column as rank numbers.

```
120 K=J+39
130 PRINT J;F*(J),K;F*(K)
140 NEXT J
150 END
```

This END command tells the computer to stop. It must appear only at the end of a program. You may now type in each of the steps above and run the program. Type RUN and press RETURN. I hope you made no errors and the computer gives you the list of the Fibonaccis on your screen.

If the computer dislikes one of your statements, it will tell you so. Check to see if you typed it correctly, and check your manual to see if *your* computer likes the same BASIC statements. Type the corrected statement over the old statement, then type RUN and press RETURN again.

If you want it to print the **78 Fibonacci List** on your printer, you add the command "3 PR #1" to the list for an Apple. For IBM compatibles, change PRINT to LPRINT everywhere in the commands above.

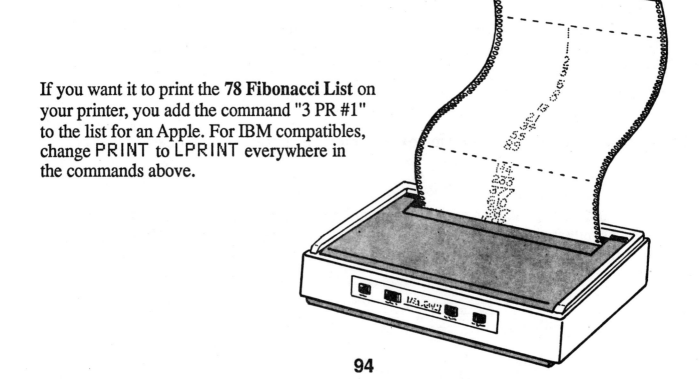

94

# EXTRA STUFF

If you want to program some more action and feel comfortable with what you have done so far, here are some suggestions:

**1.** Type
```
DELETE 120
```
then press RETURN

Do the same with 130. This will remove those two statements from the program. In line 110, type "20" over the "39," then push RETURN. (A "30" instead of a "20" in line 110 will give you a longer list.)

Now the Fibonaccis won't print, but we still have a counter J counting 20 steps of whatever we want to do. Let's print 20 **ratios** of consecutive Fibonacci **pairs**. Put this statement before 140:

```
120 PRINT F#(J+1)/F#(J)
```

Now RUN it and see what happens.

**2.** Use DELETE on statements 5, 20, 110, 120, 140 and150,

which removes the J counter too. Let's program a trick you've learned. Put these steps after 100:

```
110 INPUT "NAME TWO FIBOS THAT ARE ONE APART.
    TYPE THE SMALLER ONE (USE RETURN): ",A
120 INPUT "THE LARGER ONE: ",B
130 INPUT "GIVE THEIR RANKS, IN ORDER. FIRST: ",R
140 INPUT "SECOND: ",S
150 PRINT "HMMM, THEIR SUM IS ",R+S
160 C = B^2 - A^2
170 PRINT "I'M SQUARING YOUR SECOND FIBO GET-
    TING",B^2,"AND YOUR FIRST FIBO, GETTING"
    ,A^2,"THEN SUBTRACTING THE ANSWERS TO
    GET",C
```

**EXTRA STUFF, continued**

```
180 INPUT "PUSH C TO CONTINUE",C$
190 PRINT "BY GOLLY, THIS IS A FIBO OF RANK ",R+S
200 PRINT "CHECK IT! ITS RANK IS THE SUM OF THE TWO
    RANKS YOU GAVE ME!"
210 INPUT "IF YOU WANT TO DO ANOTHER, TYPE 1 (RETURN),
    OTHERWISE JUST PUSH RETURN",M
220 IF M=1 THEN GO TO 110
230 END
```

RUN it. State in your own words the pattern this is showing: _____

_____

_____

Predict the result of putting the two Fibonaccis 1597 and 4181 into the program: _____

_____

_____

_____

_____

## Teacher's Guide to Student Pages 87-96

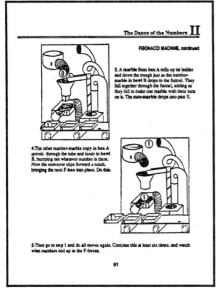

Student Page 90

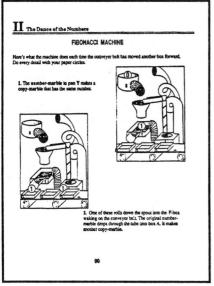

Student Page 91

OPTIONAL ACTIVITY 2:

# A FIBONACCI MACHINE AND COMPUTER PROGRAMS

This is a unique opportunity for your students to learn the *feel* of programming by doing the moves a computer does when it executes a program of BASIC Language commands.

The simulation is best done with pairs of students. As they do the moves of this cooperative activity, the Fibonacci Numbers should result. It is exactly these moves that the commands specify the computer to do.

The containers in the machine are analogous to actual cells in the computer that hold or combine numbers. A number can be moved from cell B to cell A by writing the command "A = B." This still leaves a copy of that number in B also.

There's one time in the activity when the pan Y is assumed to be empty after a number leaves it for the conveyor belt—but technically it's not empty. It retains another copy. Yet as soon as another number comes into the cell, the present member is annihilated anyway, so the analogy is close enough here.

The conveyor belt is set up by the FOR-NEXT statements. A counter moves waiting storage cells by one notch as it specifies another cycle of the activity. Each cycle of the activity builds the size of the numbers left behind in the game containers (computation cells) to be used in the next cycle. (You will learn this best yourself by doing the activity and reading the explanations of each step of the program.)

Even students who know some programming may benefit from the machine analogy. If they are quite at ease with this kind of program, they may want to simply try out the Fibonacci List program and the other features that can be added to it.

The more complex program is simply the "Subtract Squares" Trick. If 1597 (the 17th Fibonacci) and 4181 (the 19th Fibonacci) are fed into it, it should produce 14,930,352 (the 36th Fibonacci, 17 + 19 = 36) as an answer. I hoped when I wrote the more complex features that

## Teacher's Guide to Student Pages 87-96

students could spark off of them to program other Fibonacci tricks. We'll see.

A last note. Some computers are more limited in what type of **BASIC** commands they will accept. If your computer spits back one of my commands and says **syntax error** or something, check your manual for the way your computer likes the command to be written. This shouldn't be a problem on most computers.

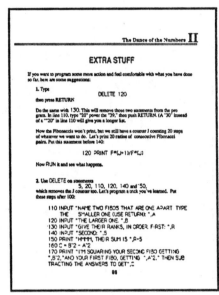

Student Page 95

Student Page 96

# Unit III: FINDING THE GOLD

## IMPORTANT INTRODUCTORY TEACHER INFORMATION

Time for a huddle along the trail . . .

Your students must be comfortable with three major concepts for success in the next three units. They don't have to be masters of every facet of these concepts. You don't, either. They should be able to do the following simple skills meaningfully with their calculators and rulers.

• They should know the meaning of the decimal part of a number, i.e., that it is a part of a whole and that the places represent tenths, hundredths, and thousandths of a whole.

• They should be able to convert any fraction to a decimal by dividing with the calculator.

• They should be able to measure something with a centimeter ruler down to the nearest millimeter and name the result as a decimal number of centimeters.

If your students are at grade six to grade twelve skill levels, they have been exposed to most of these ideas and should be about ready to go. Scan the Crash Course below to see if you want to emphasize anything. If your students are at grade six, they may need a little further coaching from the Crash Course.

If they are at grade five skill level, they have enough fraction savvy to develop skills 1 through 3 from the Crash Course with just a little practice. Grade fours—average or above average ability—can be coached from the Crash Course and need to practice more before proceeding. Below grade four depends on the courage and desire of both teacher and student, but it's possible.

Now here's the "Crash Course in Decimal Use." If you, the teacher, are rusty on this material, it's a good opportunity for you to brush up in a painless way. We are all better off in life with these skills at our fingertips!

**This, and the ideas in the first section of this unit, are the only major skill stops we'll have to make on the Tour. Allow two to four lessons on this if it's new for your kids. It'll save headaches later.**

## CRASH COURSE IN DECIMAL USE

### 1. Understanding the Meaning of the Decimal

**TEACHER:** "Climbers who want to go up Mt. Everest learn to hang from a tiny ledge by their fingertips. When any explorers plan to trek to exciting and rewarding territory, they often have to practice some new skills they're going to need. Our **Tour** will take us all the way to the moon, so you can guess we might want a few trusty tricks to take along!

## Teacher's Introduction to Unit III

### CRASH COURSE IN DECIMAL USE, continued

"You're going to get a chance to learn about decimals earlier than they usually come along in your textbooks. You won't be able to do everything with them, but you'll be quick with the few things we need. You'll be able to impress people who didn't think you'd be able to learn such things yet!

"A decimal is a way of naming how big a part of something is. Imagine your favorite football field, or any football field for that matter. See it clearly in your imagination. Imagine that it's marked off as 100 yards with 100 marks along the center, goal to goal. Each mark is 3 feet apart. There are lines across the field every 10 yards of marks. Try to see it clearly in your mind.

"A player at the 40-yard line is not quite halfway along the field—talking left to right. Using decimals we would say he is .40 of the way along the field. What decimal describes halfway along the field? .50 is correct. Stand a player at .80 along the field. If your desk or table is the field, where is he? Look around and see that all of you agree.

"The dot (decimal point) says 'Think **part** of something.' To see what part, we look at the numbers on the **right side** of the decimal point. They always mean part of something—not the whole thing. This part is usually made up of smaller parts, like our yards.

"They don't have to mean part of a football field. Estimate .80 of your pencil length (80 of 100 parts of your pencil) or .80 of the room height or .80 of your thumbnail." (Students practice naming and showing each other some different two-decimal-place parts of lengths of various things, using the football field image as a guide.)

"So .80 means '80 out of 100' and could be written as the fraction '80/100', which also means '80 out of 100.' What fraction is .46 of the field?" (At the 46th yard marker, almost halfway along the field.) " Yes, 46/100. And it's very close to halfway. Is .54? Yes." (Practice this fraction conversion and estimation process.)

"Now if we want to indicate the part of the field up to the 5 yard line, we still have to say .05 because the rule says to mean 'out of 100' you have to write two digits. It has something to do with the fact that 100 has two zeros. Now try this: Which means more field, .10 or .09?" (**Answer:** .10)

STUDENT: "The 1 looks smaller than the 9, but 10 out of 100 is larger than 9 out of 100."

TEACHER: "You've got it. That 0 before the 9 is crucial because there's another trick in this decimal parts-naming game. We can think of the football field as having just 10 big parts, each one being 10 yards of the field. Picture the 10 chunks of the field separated by the lines across the field placed every 10 yards.

"When there are only 10 parts to think about, we need only one digit to name how much of the 10 parts we mean. For instance, .5 can mean 'up to the fifth part,' i.e., halfway along the field."

## Teacher's Introduction to Unit III

### CRASH COURSE IN DECIMAL USE, continued

**STUDENT:** "But .50 meant that!"

**TEACHER:** "Yes, both mean halfway along! One means it when you are thinking of 10 big chunks, and the other means it when you are thinking of 100 little chunks. One means the 5th 10-yard line, and the other means the 50th 1-yard line.

"So we say that .5 =.50, since both mean the same amount of field. And this leads to the general rule that **ending zeros don't change the amount of field we mean**." (Students practice several examples of this rule.)

"There's a third way to think about the field. Imagine it marked with 1000 marks along its length. The marks would be about 3 1/2 inches apart. Now 1000 has three zeros, so it takes three digits to say how far along the field we are. And we could say it more accurately. For instance, .234 means we are at the 234th mark, 234 of the thousand marks. About where would that be on your desks?"

**STUDENT:** "Not far from the beginning. Sort of halfway between the beginning and the middle."

**TEACHER:** "OK, that's close. Now practice finding other three-digit locations on the field of your desks. Approximately, of course . . ." (Students practice.)

"So where would .500 be on the field? Halfway again, right. The 500 of 1000 marks puts us there. We could also say that the end zeros don't change the value, so .500 = .50= .5, right? And .250 is just .25 or the 25-yard line again.

"Now you know the decimal code for parts!"

### 2. Fractions to Decimals on the Calculator

**TEACHER:** "Your calculator can easily give you the decimal code for any part you can name as a fraction. Get your calculators out. Let's ask the calculator to first give us the code for 1/2 the football field. We certainly know that code! We interpret the fraction bar to mean the ÷ mark of your calculator.

"So push 1 ÷ 2 = .

"You will see 0.5 on the screen. The calculator has chosen to write a 0 before the point to mean there are no whole anythings—which is true when you have 1/2 of something. Following the point is 5 out of 10 parts. It doesn't like to write extra ending 0's, so it won't write .50 or .500.

"Try 5/8. That's right, 5 ÷ 8. You say .625? Good. How far along the field is this?"

## Teacher's Introduction to Unit III

### CRASH COURSE IN DECIMAL USE, continued

STUDENT: "Over halfway, but not 3/4 of the way."

TEACHER: "Correct. And 5 out of 8 parts is this way. It's a bit more than 4 out of 8, which would be half. So the decimal code gives us the same part information as the fraction code.

"Now I'll blow your minds. Try 5/7. You get gobbledy-gook, you say? Let's look closer at it. What we'll do here is just take the first three numbers, 714, after the point and throw away the rest. It's the closest number out of 1000 we can get that means the same as 5 out of 7.

"Try 8/9. Taking .888 is pretty close, but that fourth 8 was a lot to throw away. If the fourth number is 5 or more, we're going to change the last digit we keep to one higher. So .889 is better.

"Here's a last curve. Try 9/4. The 2.25 tells us that 9 of the things called fourths of a football field are really like two whole fields and another field up to the 25 yardline. From what you know about fourths, this should make sense."

### 3. Measuring Decimal Parts of Centimeters

TEACHER: "Now you're going to learn to put small measurements into decimal code. On the centimeter scale the centimeters are numbered up to 30, and each has small marks along it. These are millimeter marks. Six marks past the 7 means '7 cm and 6 mm.'

"Because there are 10 millimeter spaces in each centimeter, we use the one-digit decimal code (10ths) to describe *parts of centimeters* instead of saying *millimeters*. So, 7 cm and 6 mm is written 7.6 cm. The .6 says there are 6 out of 10 parts of a centimeter tacked onto the 7 cm. We choose this code because our calculator loves to munch decimals.

"Now you're initiated into the decimal code. Let's get on with our **Tour.**"

# UNIT III: FINDING THE GOLD

## INTRODUCING RATIOS

**Toolbox:** Metric ruler (with mm); scissors; paper; paper cup; calculator

You've come a long way with the Fibonaccis.
They seem to have jumped out of Nature and
they do some amazing mathematical stunts.
But, as the old saying goes,
"You ain't seen nothin' yet."

To show you where the Fibonaccis can go,
we have to leave them for a while to learn
about another amazing number, a relative of
theirs. And before you can do that, you need
to learn how to use ratios. You'll play a ratio
game for this, just to keep things light.

To get into the right frame of mind to play the game, read
the article in your *Tour Guide* newspaper called
"Scientists Vote Ratio Most Useful Tool."
Come back here after you've finished reading it.

**STOP**

# THE RATIO GAME

## MATERIALS

● To prepare for the game, cut out the 20 numbered tickets. These will be put in a cup to draw from.

● Also cut 10 strips from a regular piece of paper, making each about 2 cm wide. Give five to each player.

## PLAY:

**1.** To fight the duel, player A starts by

● cutting a length of paper from his strip,

● laying it on the table, and

● drawing two tickets and placing them on the table in order, then saying pointedly to player B, *Engarde!* (This means "on guard" in French; it's the way fencers like to start duels.) Players treat the two drawn digits as a two-digit decimal (with digits in the order drawn by player A) and think of this decimal as a ratio. For example: If a 3 then a 4 is drawn, it is thought of as .34.

**2.** To respond to this **outrageous** challenge, player B must do the following:
Cut a paper strip so that the ratio of its length to the length of the challenger's strip is .34.

Player B might think: ".34 of A's length means A's strip is the 100-yard football field and my strip has to reach to the 34th yardline. That's 1/3 of the way. I'll make my strip 1/3 as long as A's."

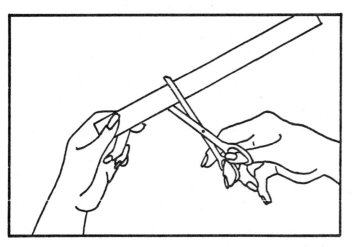

Player B cuts the strip and lays it on the table saying *Touché,* (pronounced "too-shay") meaning, in effect, "Take that!"

**3.** Players then measure the two strips to the nearest mm. Find the ratio with a calculator (divide the smaller measurement by the larger) to see how close that ratio is to the desired ratio (.34 in this case).

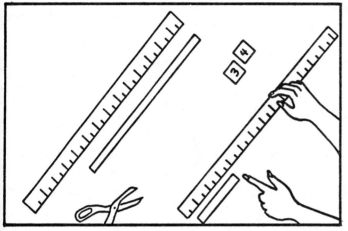

**For Example:** Suppose the calculated ratio is .2942698. Keep the first two digits (.29). Subtract this from .34 and get .05. As long as the calculated ratio gives a difference of no more than .05 from the desired ratio (.34), it is said to be *close enough*. Then .3832567 would be close enough, too, whereas .2724356 is too far away. (If you are comfortable with rounding decimals, use the answer **rounded off** to two places then compare it with the desired decimal.)

**4.** Each player whose *Touché* is close enough (within .05) gets 2 points. The first player to score 12 points wins, as long as both players have the same number of turns. In case of a tie, play continues until someone has the lead and becomes winner (who then gets to say *Voila!* which roughly translates "Behold the winner").

Here's a whole sample play:
- Pat cuts off a strip and draws a 2 and a 5, saying *Engarde!*
- Jon tries to cut a strip that is .25 (i.e., 1/4) as long as Pat's.
- Jon tosses it down saying *Touché!*
- They measure: Pat's is 6.6 cm and Jon's is 1.5 cm. They find the ratio 1.5/6.6 by dividing 1.5 by 6.6 = .2272727, and keep .22. (If you're good at rounding you would call it 23.) This .22 differs from .25 by .03 so it's *close enough*. Jon gets 2 points on the play.

### ADVANCED GAME

The same game is played with the only change being that the two digits drawn are played on a 1" high pattern shown at the right, making a ratio that is **greater** than 1.

$1.\square\square$

Jon must now try to cut a strip so that his strip is **longer** than Pat's. Jon ÷ Pat is the calculated ratio, which must still be within .05 of the drawn ratio.

# GAME PIECES

| | | | | |
|---|---|---|---|---|
| 0 | 1 | 2 | 3 | 4 |
| 5 | 6 | 7 | 8 | 9 |
| 0 | 1 | 2 | 3 | 4 |
| 5 | 6 | 7 | 8 | 9 |

## SCORE CARD

| Game I | | Game II | |
|---|---|---|---|
| Name | Name | Name | Name |
| | | | |
| | | | |
| | | | |
| | | | |
| | | | |
| | | | |
| | | | |
| | | | |

Total _____

# INTRODUCING RATIOS

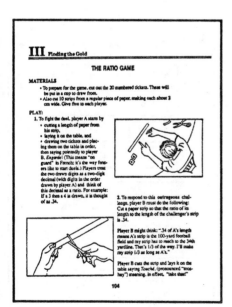

Student Page 103

Student Page 104

The concept of *ratio* is at the heart of many of the activities to come. Come to think of it, it's at the heart of thousands of number activities that will happen in your student's later life. Any time spent in better understanding ratio is math time well spent.

The article in the *Tour Guide* newspaper about ratios will help students master this subtle concept. And the **Ratio Game** will do much to make the concept lively and intuitive. Few youngsters have a real *sense* of what ratio is all about. You have to check at each stage to see how well your students *understand* the concept and its use.

### THE RATIO CONCEPT

To make sure you can do this, here's a condensed explanation of the ratio concept for you. (It's pretty painless!)

A **Ratio** is the comparison of two things by division. Two things can also be compared by subtraction. Here's an example of the difference:

If one teacher earns $300 a week and another earns $400, the difference in their pay (by subtraction) is $100.  This $100 may or may not mean a large difference, depending on how much they make.  If the $100 represented the difference of their **annual** salaries, we would say they make the same salary, for all practical purposes.  If it's the difference of their **daily** salaries, we would say that one was at the poverty level while one was in some special position. The $100 difference doesn't convey its **relative** size.

We could compare the weekly salaries by their *ratio* $300/$400, or 3/4, instead. This 3/4 is a *relative* comparison. It would give us the same impression of the difference of salaries whether we were told it applied to daily, weekly, monthly, or annual salaries. In the financial world people are usually interested in **relative** comparisons (with ratios). Subtraction is of interest when we want to know an **absolute** difference that is to be paid.

A funny thing is that the 3/4 is not expressed in dollars, even though the original ratio was a ratio of dollars. The units (dollars) on the top and bottom of the fraction *cancel* out and leave a pure *number*, a fraction with no units.

We could have taken the reverse ratio, $400/$300, or 4/3, or 1 1/3, instead, which gives just as much relative size information as 3/4. Because *proper* fractions are a little easier for our brains to chew on, it is more common to arrange it as 3/4, saying "The ratio of the lesser to the greater salary is 3/4." We could just as accurately say, though, that "The ratio of the greater to the lesser salary is 4/3."

Let's say we are told that the ratio of a person's salary to my salary ($400 per week) is 4/5. Another way to interpret this statement is that "The other person makes 4/5 of my salary." We could deduce that, as 1/5 of my salary is $80, 4/5 is 4 x $80, or $320, which must be the other person's salary. So if we know one salary and the ratio between, we can figure the other salary.

A ratio is usually first thought of as a fraction, but it's quite common to convert it to a decimal by dividing the top by the bottom. The 3/4 ratio becomes .75 when this is done. On the calculator, to get a ratio between two numbers, enter the first number. Push " ÷ ," then enter the second number. The decimal on the screen tells what part the first number is of the second number.

With all this in mind, you are equipped to make sure the students are playing the Ratio Game properly. Can they explain when asked "What is a ratio, and how is it used?"

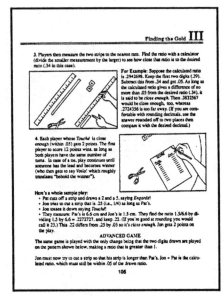

Student Page 105

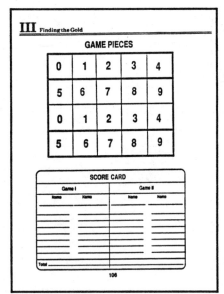

Student Page 106

# THE GREEKS AND THEIR GOLDEN RATIO

---

**Toolbox:** Metric ruler (mm); calculator

---

You now know what a ratio is and how to find it. The Greeks knew this, too, and they were in love with a particular ratio called "The Golden Ratio," whose value is 1.618 to three decimal places. Let's explore it as part of our Mystery Tour because it points the way to many fine things about the Fibonacci Numbers, history, and Nature.

**First we learn that Greek statues do cosmic math, and so do our own bodies.**

On the next page is a picture of a Greek statue. The Greeks liked to make their statues with Golden Ratios twinkling in them. To see how they did this, measure the lettered lengths on the statue as accurately as you can—to the **nearest mm**, written as a decimal number of centimeters. Write them in the spaces below.

A reminder about calculating in metric: If something is 7 mm marks past 3 cm, it's called 3.7 cm by your calculator.

After you've measured these lengths, calculate the ratios indicated. (Remember a/b means a ÷ b on your calculator.) Write just two decimal places for each answer:

| MEASURE | MEASURE | CALCULATE |
|---|---|---|
| **a.** Navel to Chin ———— | **b.** Length of Head ———— | **a/b** ———— |
| **m.** Navel to Ground ———— | **n.** Navel to Top-of-Head ———— | **m/n** ———— |
| **d.** Knee to Sternum ———— | **e.** Sternum to Top-of-Head ———— | **d/e** ———— |
| **a.** Navel to Chin ———— | **k.** Top-of-Leg to Navel ———— | **a/k** ———— |
| **g.** Top of Leg to Sternum ———— | **h.** Sternum to Chin ———— | **g/h** ———— |

I hope you've found that all these statue ratios are Golden Ratios of about 1.62. If they're not very close, recheck your work.

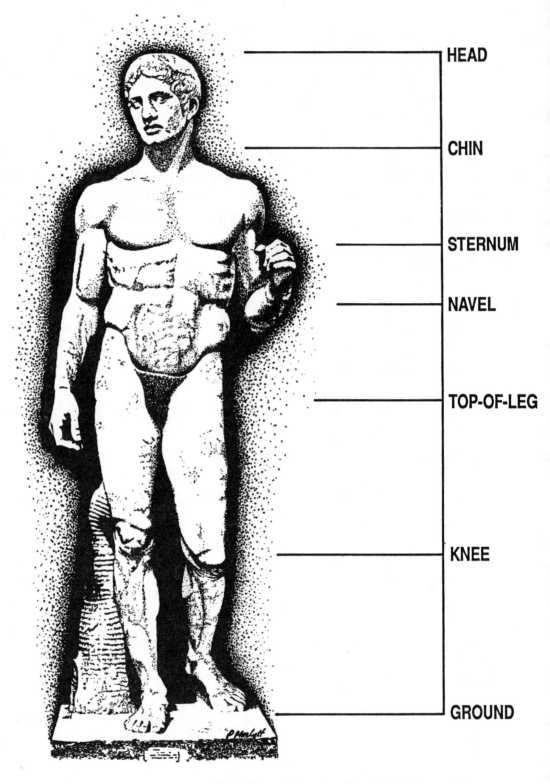

HEAD

CHIN

STERNUM

NAVEL

TOP-OF-LEG

KNEE

GROUND

"The Spear Thrower," by Polyleitos of Argos,
a 7' bronze statue sculpted in Greece in 440 BC.

## CLASS PROJECT

Measure body lengths and ratios on yourself and members of your class (to the nearest cm). To help you know where to measure, here are some definitions (see the Greek statue also):

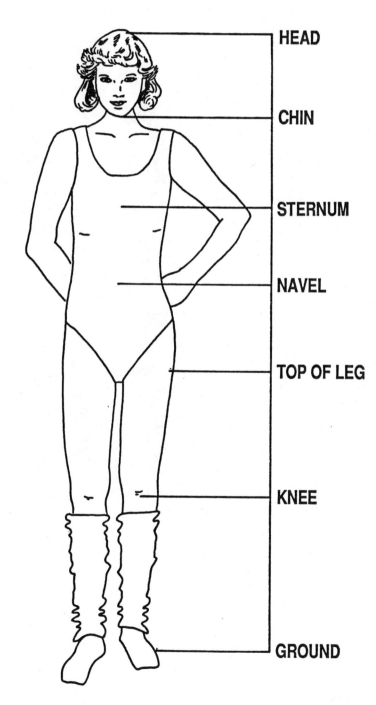

HEAD

CHIN

STERNUM

NAVEL

TOP OF LEG

KNEE

GROUND

**LENGTH OF HEAD:** Mark the height of the person on a wall and then mark the height of the chin from the ground. Subtract these to get the head length.

**CHIN:** With head level measure from just underneath the chin.

**STERNUM:** The indentation or "hole" in the bone at the center of the chest.

**TOP-OF-LEG:** Either measure from top of the inside seam of slacks or find a point 5 cm below the hip bone (the hard bump at the top of the outside of the leg) and measure from there.

**KNEE:** Measure from the "dent" below the knee cap.

# QUESTIONS ABOUT YOUR FINDINGS

**1.** Which of you has the most *Classic Greek* body? That is, who has the most ratios that are close to the Golden 1.618? (Between 1.60 and 1.64 qualifies.) _____

**2.** Find the average of all the a/b ratios of your classmates. (Add the ratios and divide by the number of classmates.) If this average is near 1.618, it will tell whether the class has a trend toward "Classic Greekness" in the torso.

Otherwise we say there's a trend away from "Greekness" (average far from Golden Ratio) for the a/b's of your classmates.

> **Technical Note:** If around 30 students were measured, this would be called a "large sample." From a large sample we can predict that the a/b's of all youths your age average close to this amount. Making predictions like this from large samples is what the science of statistics is all about. Your teacher may wish to tell you more about this.

**3.** On a separate sheet of paper do a scientific report. Show your work and report your conclusion for the average of this ratio, i.e., a/b, then do it for c/d, e/f, etc. *Then* write a conclusion about the **overall** "Greekness" of the faces and bodies of your classmates and of students your age based on the statistics you have gathered.

# HOME PROJECTS

● Measure the same ratios on your family members and decide who has the most "Classic Greek" face and body.
● Find pictures of animals (including fish) and see if you can measure Golden Ratios on their bodies.
● Find pictures of other statues or a real statue in a park, and measure as well as possible to see if they have the Golden Ratio.
● Check to see if a younger child you know has this ratio.
● Design a robot that has as many Golden Ratios as possible.
● Memorize the Golden Ratio to six decimal places so you can sound brilliant: 1.618034. If you like doing this, try nine places: 1.618033989.

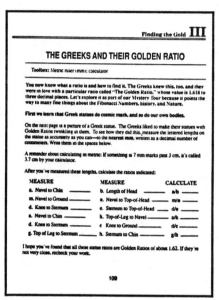

Student Page 109

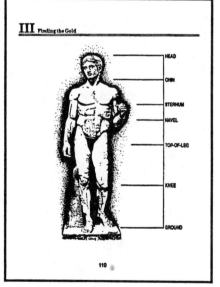

Student Page 110

# THE GREEKS AND THEIR GOLDEN RATIO

## STATUE RATIOS

Here are the measurements and ratios found on the statue:

| | | |
|---|---|---|
| a = 4.1 cm | b = 2.5 cm | a/b = 1.64 |
| m = 10.8 cm | n = 7.9 cm | m/n = 1.62 |
| d = 8.2 cm | e = 5.1 cm | d/e = 1.61 |
| a = 4.1 cm | k = 3.0 cm | a/k = 1.62 |
| g = 4.1 cm | h = 2.6 cm | g/h = 1.58 |

All of these are very close to the Golden Ratio of 1.62. There will be some discrepancies among these numbers depending on whether students rounded partial millimeters up or down.

This shows that the Greeks were very aware of this ratio. Later in this unit students will be assigned an article in the *Tour Guide* newspaper. It will discuss when and why the Greeks liked the Golden Ratio so much. You are welcome to read it now. It's called "The Golden Ratio Has Been In Style For Years."

Because Golden Ratios are in other human bodies besides Greek statues, we see—as in the case of spirals—how the Golden Ratio is one of the choice tools used by Nature in its design process.

## THE CLASS PROJECT

Have the students measure only the ratios on each other's bodies that they feel comfortable having measured. Girls should measure girls, boys should measure boys.

Note: The pre-adolescent and adolescent body does not fit these ratios as well as the adult body, so students should not feel "crushed" not to be "classical" yet. But still, some will be closer to this Greek ideal than others. Actually, not that many adult bodies are exactly Greek either!

## Teacher's Guide to Student Pages 109-112

### A STATISTICS LESSON

The class project is a great example of statistics in action and of how scientific reports get created. Two scientific methods are used:

First, a poll of statistics of each individual is taken. A group of individuals with a majority of statistics meeting a certain size criterion is searched for. This is a search for individuals of a certain *profile of characteristics*.

Second, a certain ratio (calculated body statistic) known throughout the group is averaged. Then other ratios of the group are similarly averaged. Finally, these averages are evaluated to check for a maximum number that fall within a certain criterion. If a large majority do, we have a *trend*.

This activity requires a lot of organization of information. Students should enter their own statistics in a table created by them or by you.

Another good aspect of statistical thinking is the notion of a *sample*. It is known that in a *random* sample of about 30, if we take a characteristic and average it among the 30, there is a very high chance that this characteristic would average about the same in the whole population from which the sample came. So, if the sample is large enough you can make a statement about the "Classical Greekness," on the average, of all "typical students of that age."

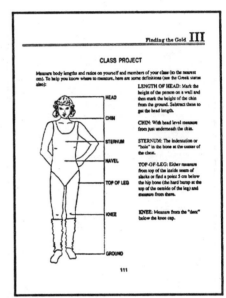

Student Page 111

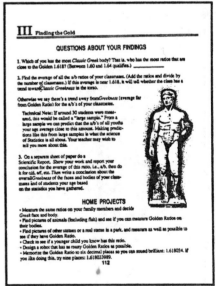

Student Page 112

# GOLDEN FACES

> **Toolbox:** Calculator; metric ruler (mm)

You now know that Nature seems to have designed the human body using a lot of Golden Ratios. Or, at least, human bodies considered most perfect by the Greeks had many Golden Ratios. It turns out that the *perfect* human face has a whole flock of Golden Ratios as well.

You'll be measuring the ratios on faces by using the instructions on this page as you measure. Before you start, notice that letters are given on the face on the next page to name either a location on the face or a measurement on the face.

● Using your cm ruler, find each measurement below to the nearest millimeter (__.__ cm). Remember, you are measuring the distance between the two locations mentioned. You can use the lines for your measurements

a = Top-of-Head to Chin = ____.____ cm

b = Top-of-Head to Pupil =____.____ cm

c = Pupil to Nosetip = ____.____ cm

d = Pupil to Lips = ____.____ cm

e = Width of Nose = ____.____ cm

f = Outside Distance between Eyes = ____.____ cm

g = Width of Head = ____.____ cm

h = Hairline to Pupil = ____.____ cm

i = Nosetip to Chin = ____.____ cm

j = Lips to Chin = ____.____ cm

k = Length of Lips = ____.____ cm

l = Nosetip to Lips = ____.____ cm

## GOLDEN FACES, continued

● Now, find these ratios to three decimal places, using your calculator:

**WIDTH OF HEAD**

EYE  LIPS  EYE

NOSE

$$\frac{a}{g} = \frac{\text{cm}}{\text{cm}} = \underline{\hspace{2cm}}$$

$$\frac{b}{d} = \frac{\text{cm}}{\text{cm}} = \underline{\hspace{2cm}}$$

$$\frac{i}{j} = \frac{\text{cm}}{\text{cm}} = \underline{\hspace{2cm}}$$

$$\frac{i}{c} = \frac{\text{cm}}{\text{cm}} = \underline{\hspace{2cm}}$$

$$\frac{e}{l} = \frac{\text{cm}}{\text{cm}} = \underline{\hspace{2cm}}$$

$$\frac{f}{h} = \frac{\text{cm}}{\text{cm}} = \underline{\hspace{2cm}}$$

$$\frac{k}{e} = \frac{\text{cm}}{\text{cm}} = \underline{\hspace{2cm}}$$

TOP OF HEAD

HAIRLINE

PUPILS

NOSE TIP

LIPS MEET

CHIN

Your answers to the above ratios should be near the Golden Ratio, 1.618. If you're very far off on any one of them, recheck both your measurements and your calculations.

## CLASS PROJECT

● Have a friend measure lengths on your face while filling in the information requested below.

**Measurer:** It's best to hold the ruler as far away from your eyes as possible when measuring these distances on the other's face. Otherwise you will get measurements that are distorted and inaccurate.

Then calculate each of the ratios listed above for your face. Would you say your face is "classically Greek" (since classical Greek statues show all of these Golden Ratios)?

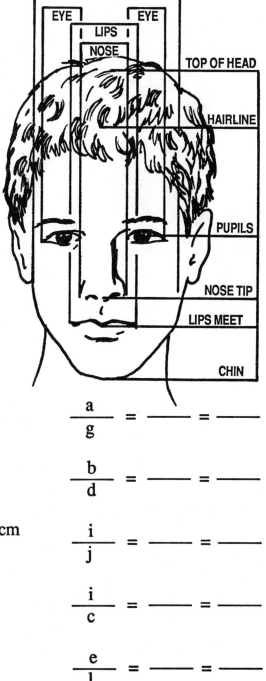

a = Top-of-Head to Chin = _____._____ cm

b = Top-of-Head to Pupil = _____._____ cm

c = Pupil to Nosetip = _____._____ cm

d = Pupil to Lips = _____._____ cm

e = Width of Nose = _____._____ cm

f = Outside Distance between Eyes = _____._____ cm

g = Width of Head = _____._____ cm

h = Hairline to Pupil = _____._____ cm

i = Nosetip to Chin = _____._____ cm

j = Lips to Chin = _____._____ cm

k = Length of Lips = _____._____ cm

l = Nosetip to Lips = _____._____ cm

$$\frac{a}{g} = \underline{\qquad} = \underline{\qquad}$$

$$\frac{b}{d} = \underline{\qquad} = \underline{\qquad}$$

$$\frac{i}{j} = \underline{\qquad} = \underline{\qquad}$$

$$\frac{i}{c} = \underline{\qquad} = \underline{\qquad}$$

$$\frac{e}{l} = \underline{\qquad} = \underline{\qquad}$$

$$\frac{f}{h} = \underline{\qquad} = \underline{\qquad}$$

$$\frac{k}{e} = \underline{\qquad} = \underline{\qquad}$$

## GOLDEN FACES, continued

● Average the ratios for faces in the whole class to see how "Greek" the faces are in your room.

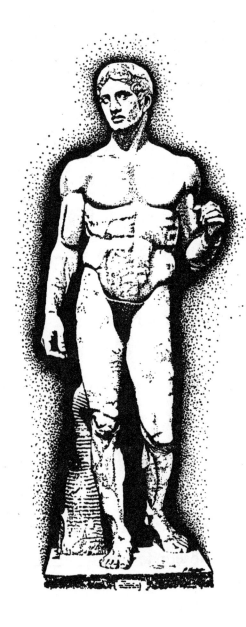

● On a separate piece of paper, write a paragraph answering the following question after thinking about it a few minutes or discussing it with others who have done the same work:

"Why do you think the Greeks wanted to use the Golden Ratio to design the bodies and faces of statues of their gods and heroes?"

(Remember, not **every** body and face has a lot of Golden Ratios.)

## Teacher's Guide to Student Pages 115-118

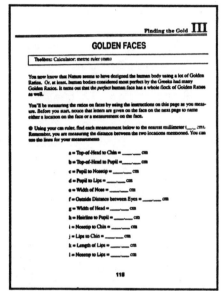

Student Page 115

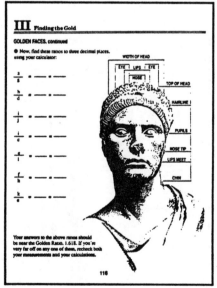

Student Page 116

# GOLDEN FACES

## ANSWERS TO THE QUESTIONS ON PAGE 115-116

Here are the measurements:

| | |
|---|---|
| a = 9.3 cm | g = 5.7 cm |
| b = 4.6 cm | h = 2.7 cm |
| c = 1.8 cm | i = 2.9 cm |
| d = 2.8 cm | j = 1.8 cm |
| e = 1.6 cm | k = 2.6 cm |
| f = 4.4 cm | l = 1.0 cm |

Here are the ratios:

$$\frac{a}{g} = 1.63 \qquad \frac{e}{l} = 1.6$$

$$\frac{b}{d} = 1.64 \qquad \frac{f}{h} = 1.63$$

$$\frac{i}{j} = 1.61 \qquad \frac{k}{e} = 1.63$$

$$\frac{i}{c} = 1.61$$

The class projects for this section resemble those done on the Greek body in the last activity. The discussion of statistics presented there is just as applicable here. In fact, this activity can be used to reinforce points made then.

## EXTENSION ACTIVITIES

• Draw a strange face, but make sure it has lots of Golden Ratios in it.

• Redraw the Greek face so that it has none of the Golden Ratios in it.

• Make up a new ratio and give it an interesting name. You can even make up some history and lore about it in a write-up. Draw a face that has lots of this ratio. Compare and contrast it with the Golden Ratio face.

• Find photographs of faces in magazines and books. Check them for the Golden Ratios you measured on the Greek face. Find faces of other nationalities and see if they have more or fewer Golden Ratios than the ideal Greek ones.

• Make up a better word than "classic Greek" to mean a face with lots of Golden Ratios in it. A *non-* in front of this word will mean it doesn't have many. Have a vote among all those invented words and adopt this *best* term as the *official* one.

### GOOD REFERENCES

**The Geometry of Art and Life** by Matila Ghyka is a good reference with good illustrations for more detail on these concepts. Parts of it are technical.

**The Power of Limits** by Georgi Doczi is a beautifully illustrated book showing the Golden Ratio in Nature and architecture. It's available through most bookstores.

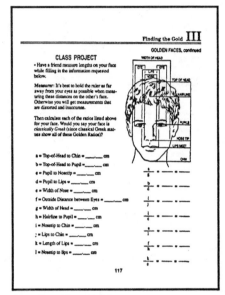

Student Page 117

Student Page 118

# THE GOLDEN RECTANGLE

**Toolbox:** Ruler; calculator; compass; protractor

We won't leave the Fibonacci Numbers behind forever, but we need to see how this Golden Ratio 1.618034 . . . "gets around." We'll discover that besides appearing in the *ideal* human body, it pops up in Nature and in the knowledge of some very ancient peoples. Then we'll find out that this number is a very close relative of the Fibonaccis. So, let's continue on our **Tour.**

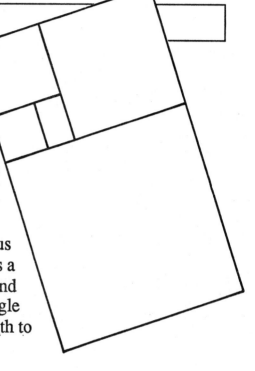

One attraction the Greeks saw in this number was the curious behavior of a figure called the Golden Rectangle, which has a whole family tree of Golden Rectangle *children* inside it, and which can make a beautiful curved shape. A Golden Rectangle is easy enough to define: it's a rectangle whose ratio of length to width is the Golden Ratio.

On the next page I'd like you to draw your own Golden Rectangle. From it you will produce a very surprising natural shape. Here are the instructions for doing it. **Draw accurately and slowly.**

**1.** Draw lines **DL, GI, GD,** and **IL.** This should give you a perfect rectangle. Measure sides **GD** and **GI** to the nearest millimeter:

GD:__.__cm          GI:___.__cm

Check to see that you have a Golden Rectangle by finding, with your calculator:

$$\frac{GD}{GI} = \frac{length}{width} = \underline{\hspace{3cm}}$$

Is the ratio close to 1.618? _____ If so, you have a Golden Rectangle!

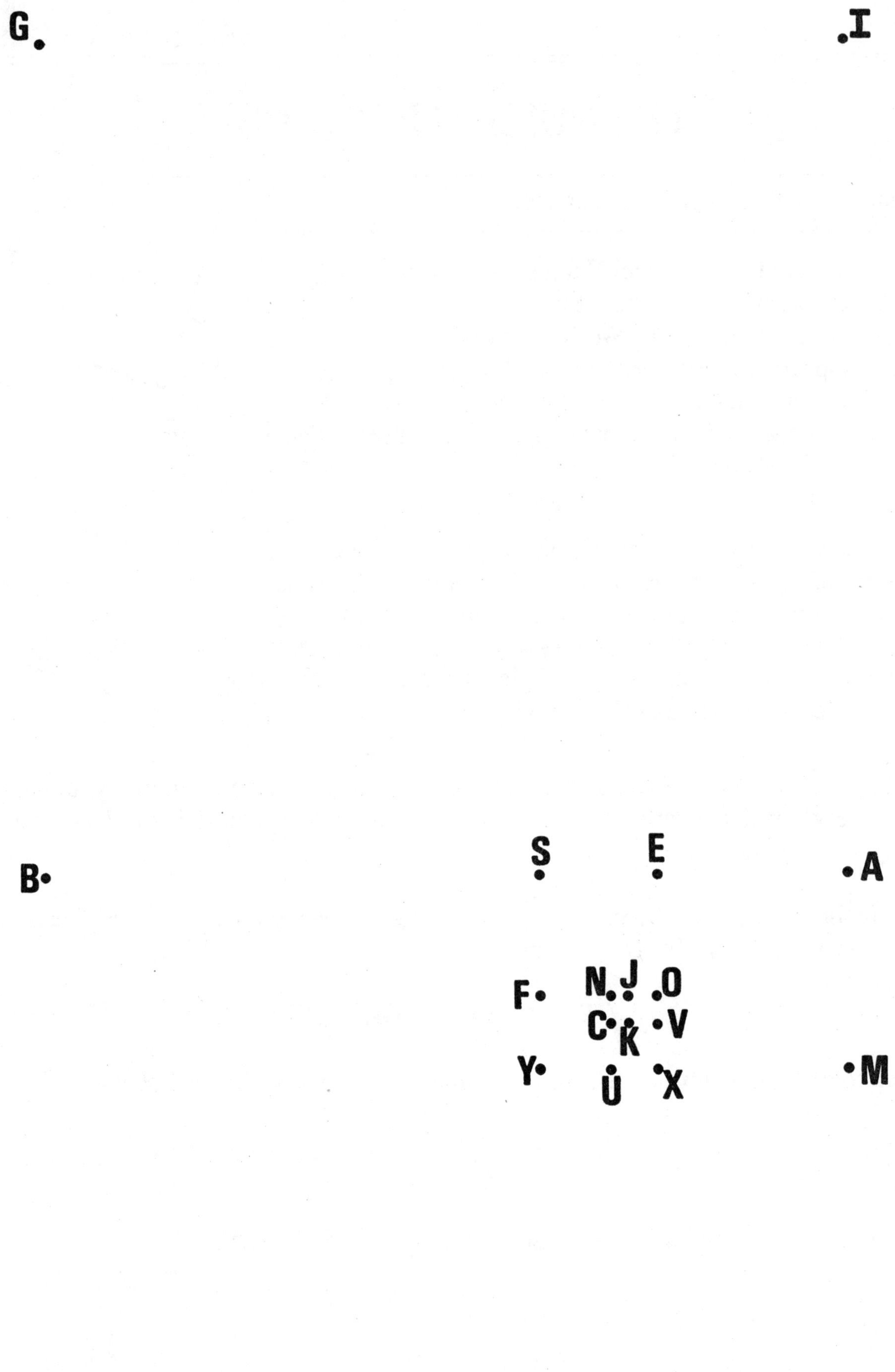

G.

.I

S.                E.                •A

B•

F•   N•J   •O
     C•V
      •K
Y•   U•  X   •M

D•

P•                •L

## THE GOLDEN RECTANGLE, continued

**2.** Draw **AB**. Measure the sides of **GIAB**. What kind of familiar figure is **GIAB**?

Now, for something surprising: Find the ratio of length to width in rectangle **BALD**. Length **BA** = _____.\_\_\_\_cm.  Width **BD** = _____.\_\_\_\_ cm. Ratio length/width = \_\_\_\_\_.

> **That's right, BALD is a Golden Rectangle made by removing a square from a bigger Golden Rectangle!**

**3.** Because **BALD** is a Golden Rectangle, we do the same dance again—remove a square from it.  That is, draw **SP**. You should be able to see the square **BSPD**. The leftover rectangle **ALPS** should again be a Golden Rectangle. Check it:

$$\underline{\hspace{2cm}} / \underline{\hspace{2cm}} = \underline{\hspace{2cm}}$$

This should be very close to the Golden Ratio.

**4.** Do the same thing again! Because **ALPS** is golden, draw **YM**. Check to see that **SAMY** is golden (but keep in mind that the slight inaccuracy when measuring small numbers of centimeters and millimeters can cause the ratio to be off some):

$$\underline{\hspace{2cm}} / \underline{\hspace{1.5cm}} = \underline{\hspace{1.5cm}}$$

How's it look? I hope it's near 1.6.

**5.** Since **SAMY** is golden, make a square in it by drawing **EX**. Check rectangle **SEXY** for the Golden Ratio.  What did you get?

$$\underline{\hspace{2cm}}$$

**6.** Even if it's getting off a bit from 1.6, continue by drawing **FO**, making the square **SEOF** and Golden Rectangle **FOXY**. Measure and find **FOXY**'s ratio:

$$\underline{\hspace{1.5cm}}.$$

**7.** Draw **NU**, **CV**, and **JK** to get the next-sized Golden Rectangles.

**THE GOLDEN RECTANGLE, continued**

# SPIRAL TIME

It's time to get your compass. You're going to draw **arcs** in your rectangle. (Arcs are pieces of circles.) To draw an arc, you need to know four things:

**1.** How long your compass should **reach** from point to pencil. (Open it big enough to reach between the two letters you'll be given.)
**2.** On which letter to place its **point** (the sharp point).
**3.** At which letter to **start** touching the pencil to paper (while holding the point at **its** place).
**4.** At which letter to **stop** touching the pencil to paper.

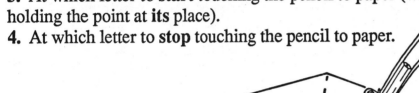

Here are some arcs I
would like you to draw in
that Golden Rectangle drawing
you made. (See the drawing on
this page for how the first arc will look.)

| REACH | POINT | START | STOP |
|-------|-------|-------|------|
| IA | A | B | I |
| SB | S | B | P |
| PY | Y | P | M |
| XM | X | M | E |
| OE | O | E | F |
| NF | N | F | U |

Each of the curves you make will join the last one. Each curve is inside a square that is smaller than the last one used.

Continue drawing curves *freehand* in the smaller squares, following the same pattern.

**THE GOLDEN RECTANGLE, continued**

# CONGRATULATIONS!

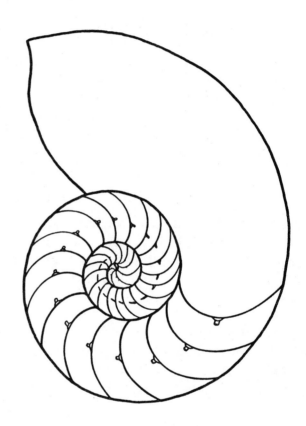

You've just drawn a special **spiral** that is the shape Nature uses to make shells, horns, tusks, and DNA. Some of these curves are wound tighter than yours and some are looser, but all are close relatives of the curve you got from the Golden Rectangle.

125

## Teacher's Guide to Student Pages 121-125

# THE GOLDEN RECTANGLE

It's very important to continue reminding students where the journey has come from and where it's going. This sheet does this a bit with its first paragraph. Students may race over this without recalling that their main experience with the Golden Ratio thus far has been that it shows up all over in the ("ideal Greek") human body and face. It might also appear in their own or a friend's or family member's face. Thus far no connection with the Fibonacci Numbers is evident. Later in this unit students will see that the Golden Ratio 1.618 . . . and the Fibonacci Numbers are intimately related.

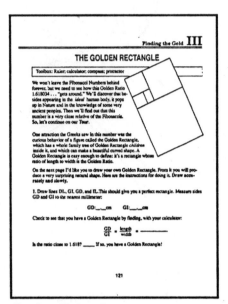

Student Page 121

### THE GOLDEN RECTANGLE MAKES A SPIRAL

This activity brings up the Golden Rectangle, a rectangle whose ratio of length to width is 1.618 . . . It is considered to be a very aesthetic shape and, as the activity reveals, it is intimately associated with Nature's workings. This rectangle has also been used in architecture and art throughout the ages.

There are 7 steps to this exercise. Each has very precise instructions, a kind of connect-the-dots. As students work you may want to see if they are grasping the overall pattern of moves they are making (while things get smaller and smaller). Here's the pattern:

a. In a Golden Rectangle make a square.

b. The leftover is a Golden Rectangle, so do "a" again.

Make sure students are comfortable checking each rectangle at each stage to see if it's a Golden Rectangle. They do this by measuring length and width in millimeters and then dividing the larger by the smaller number. Each time the answer should be around 1.6 (allowing for small errors in measurement).

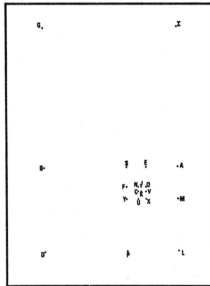

Student Page 122

### EXTENSION ACTIVITIES

• You may wish to find pictures of shells and mountain-goat horns in the library, or have students find them, to verify that the shape obtained from the activity is the general shape of these things.

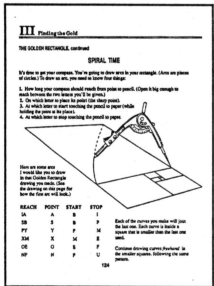

Student Page 123

Student Page 124

As mentioned on the sheet, some shells have tighter spirals than others, but all have the same "property of growth" as the Golden Rectangle spiral. This property is that as the spiral makes more turns and grows larger, the whole spiral exactly duplicates the proportions it had as a younger spiral. (The younger spiral forms the tinier inside part of the adult spiral.) That is, a photographic enlargement of the central part of one of these spirals would look identical in curvature to that of a "grown" shell. It's important to realize that most growing things do *not* retain *exactly* the same shape as an adult that they had as a *child*. Human beings are a good example of this difference.

From books of animal pictures make a list of all the species you find that have spiral or helical horns, tusks, teeth, and so forth. Some things that curve only a little , like a rhino horn, a wolf fang, a beaver tooth, and a fingernail, would grow in the spiral curve if it continued, so include these curved objects in your list.

• Get a book of shells and notice all the different ways Nature plays with the helix and spiral shapes. Compare and contrast the spirals of five very different shells.

• Make a bulletin board exhibit of spirals in Nature. Use clipped pictures or tracings that are colored. Make the exhibit in spiral form. Or, you may choose a mobile or a collage to express the spiral theme.

• Get your ruler and calculator handy. Check several common rectangular objects, both big (door, playground, wall of school) and small (light switch, license plate, page). See if they are Golden Rectangles. Document your findings, both positive and negative.

• Make a **"Handy-Dandy Quick Golden Rectangle Checker"** that would make most of the work in the extension above a piece of cake. From a piece of tagboard, cut out a rectangle 8.9 cm by 5.5 cm. (Make your measurements carefully and your lines straight.) **You want to save the hole, not the rectangle!** Use the hole as a viewer. By holding it closer or farther from your face you can get the hole to "frame" most rectangles you want to check.

## Teacher's Guide to Student Pages 121-125

Use the viewer to check a whole flock of rectangles, including buildings and windows, to find Golden Rectangles. Have a contest to see who can find the most Golden Rectangles in magazines, the school, or the neighborhood.

• Do a report on the United Nations building, its architect, when it was built, how it was built, its floor plans, and so forth. Why? Because its side was designed to be a Golden Rectangle! (See "The Golden Ratio Has Been in Style for Years" in the *Tour Guide* newspaper.)

• Sometimes things that are not rectangle-shaped are still related to the Golden Rectangle. They **just** fit inside a Golden Rectangle. One example is the Parthenon, discussed in the article in the *Tour Guide* newspaper. Certain classic vases, a chicken egg, and the human face are other examples. Use the Golden Rectangle viewer decribed above to go on another search for Golden Objects.

• One striking example of a universal **natural** object fitting inside a Golden Rectangle is this: the DNA double helix makes one twist every 34 Angstroms and the twisted DNA is 21 Angstroms across. The ratio of length to width is 1.62, a Golden Rectangle! This means that every twist of a DNA molecule can just fit into a Golden Rectangle, and the whole DNA helix is a chain of Golden Rectangles! (For more information about this, see the teacher notes for the first pinecone activity.)

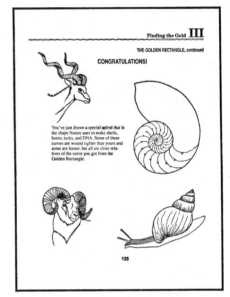

Student Page 125

# A GOLDEN RECTANGLE PUZZLE

**Toolbox:** Scissors; glue; construction paper

The pieces on the next page will make one large Golden Rectangle— if you put them together properly. In your last Golden Rectangle activity you drew a figure just like this one will make. Recall that you were constantly making squares inside the Golden Rectangle. In fact, this activity will show you that a *large* Golden Rectangle can be made from many squares and one *small* Golden Rectangle.

## INSTRUCTIONS

Carefully cut out all the square pieces on the next page along with the one tiny rectangle. On a piece of colored construction paper, assemble them to make one large rectangle (**no glue yet**).

## CONGRATULATIONS, YOU DID THE PUZZLE!

But now, before you glue, you should have the puzzle make a spiral, too. Notice that each square (except the first) has a second possible position—just moved over, with the littler stuff on its *other* side. Starting with the second largest, look quickly at the center of each square in order of size.

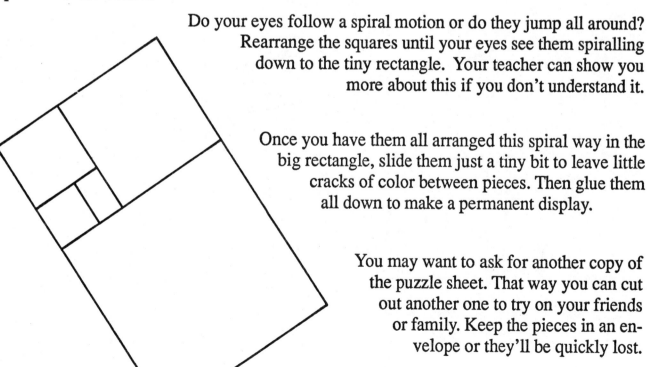

Do your eyes follow a spiral motion or do they jump all around? Rearrange the squares until your eyes see them spiralling down to the tiny rectangle. Your teacher can show you more about this if you don't understand it.

Once you have them all arranged this spiral way in the big rectangle, slide them just a tiny bit to leave little cracks of color between pieces. Then glue them all down to make a permanent display.

You may want to ask for another copy of the puzzle sheet. That way you can cut out another one to try on your friends or family. Keep the pieces in an envelope or they'll be quickly lost.

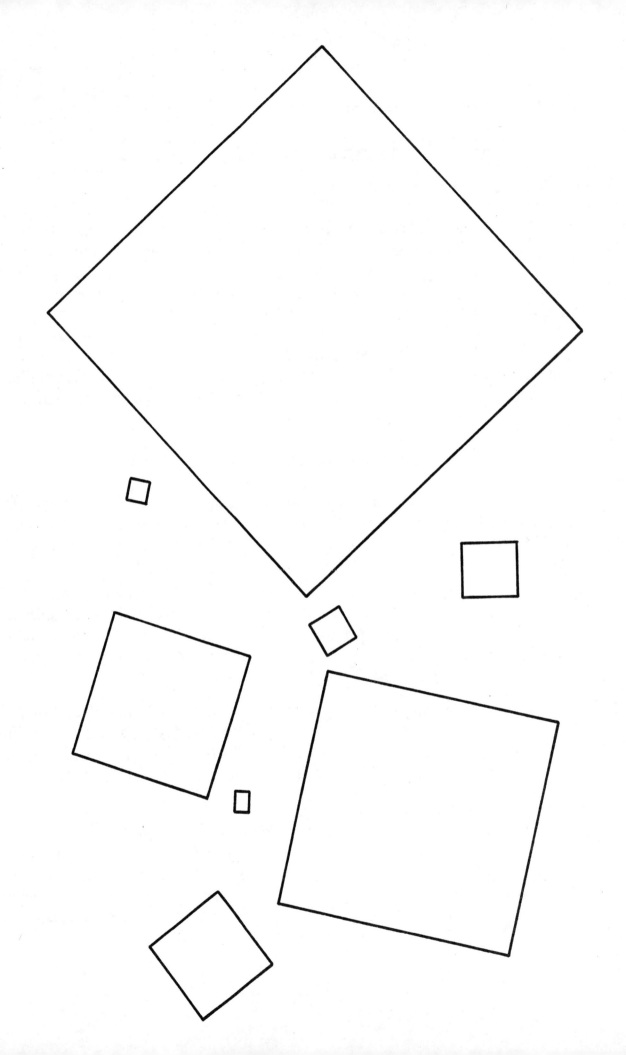

## Teacher's Guide to Student Pages 129-130

# A GOLDEN RECTANGLE PUZZLE

The learning objective for this activity is to reinforce the spatial relationships of the Golden Rectangle activity done earlier.

Encourage students to cut out the puzzle pieces slowly and carefully. You may want to photocopy page 130 in another color of paper to add to the visual effect of the finished product assembled on construction paper. Before you allow students to paste the pieces down, check that the pieces are arranged in the correct spiral form (see discussion below). Also verify that there are thin cracks left between pieces so that the color below can highlight each junction.

The correct arrangement for the puzzle is the same as the rectangle on page 124. (Its mirror image is also correct.) An *incorrect* arrangement could *still make a rectangle*. How? A student may not have the progressively decreasing squares arranged in a spiral. Scan the figure so that your eye tracks from the center of the largest square to the center of the next largest, and so on down to the smallest. Notice that your eye follows a spiral motion as it goes. Help students adjust their squares to this spiral progression if necessary.

Finally, it would be a good idea to run off an extra copy for your students and provide them with envelopes so they can try it on friends and/or family.

# THE FIBONACCI NUMBERS STRIKE AGAIN!

> **Toolbox:** Metric ruler (mm); calculator; colored pens

You may not have noticed when you made your Golden Rectangle that you were given Fibonacci Numbers in disguise!

First, the largest rectangle was 23.3 cm by 14.4 cm. How many mm are each of these?_____, _____ Notice that you have written two Fibonacci Numbers (check your list to confirm). Notice also that their ratio is _____. (Calculate it.)

We said that a Golden Rectangle has a ratio of length to width of 1.618, and you can see once again that the large rectangle is Golden. But the amazing part is that two (consecutive) Fibonaccis have produced the Golden Ratio!

The next largest rectangle you created was 14.4 cm by 8.9 cm, which is 144 mm by 89 mm.

Find their ratio: _____.

Notice again that both of these numbers are consecutive Fibonacci Numbers!

The **next** largest rectangle you made was 8.9 cm by 5.5 cm. This is the same as _____mm by _____mm, and these create the ratio _____.

**Surprised?**

You should be because two consecutive Fibonaccis have again produced the Golden Ratio.

This leads us to the idea of looking at **all** the ratios of consecutive Fibonacci Numbers to see how many turn out to make the Golden Ratio.

1.618

Here goes. Here are the first 16 Fibonaccis. Next to each pair write the ratio you calculate to **five decimal places** (if the calculator gives you that many, of course). Always divide the bigger by the smaller in each pair.

| FIBONACCI | RATIO | RATIO NUMBER |
|-----------|-------|--------------|
| 1 | | #1 |
| 1 | 2 | #2 |
| 2 | | #3 |
| 3 | | #4 |
| 5 | 1.6 | #5 |
| 8 | | #6 |
| 13 | | #7 |
| 21 | | #8 |
| 34 | 1.61765 | #9 |
| 55 | | #10 |
| 89 | | #11 |
| 144 | | #12 |
| 233 | | #13 |
| 377 | | #14 |
| 610 | | #15 |
| 987 | | |

How do these ratios compare with the Golden Ratio of **1.618034**? _____

Look at each one and see whether it is more or less than the Golden Ratio. (There is a pattern.) What pattern do you see? _____

# GRAPH OF THE FIBONACCI RATIOS

Now, graph 14 of the ratios you just calculated. Make a dot for each ratio **decimal** on the vertical line that corresponds to the **number** of the ratio. Take your time figuring out where to put dots, and check with other students to make sure you are doing it right. When you've finished, connect the dots.

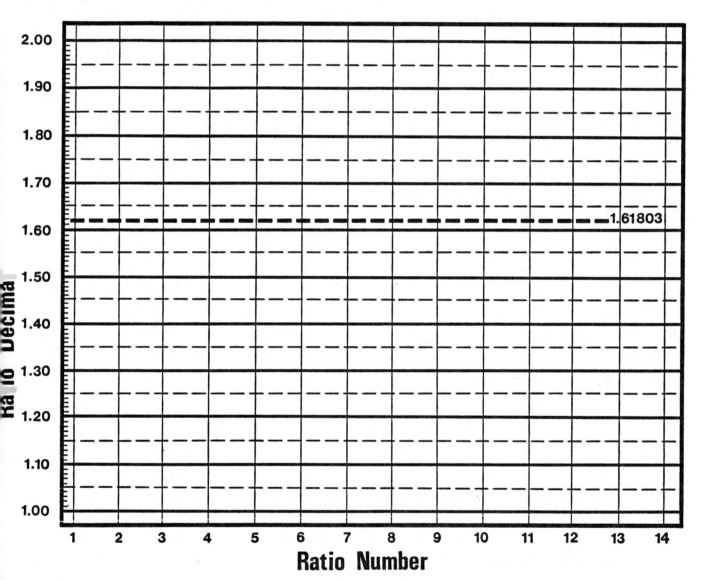

How do the ratios of the Fibonacci Numbers seem to relate to the Golden Ratio?

_____

_____

_____

_____

# "CLOSE-UP" GRAPH OF THE FIBONACCI RATIOS

**Toolbox:** Colored pens; metric ruler (mm)

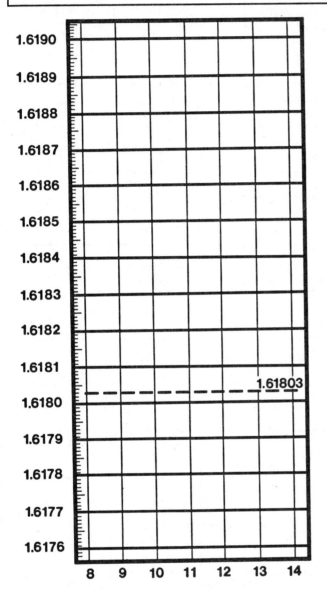

Here's another graph. It's sort of an enlargement or close-up of your first graph. It shows only the tiny movements of your ratios that occur after ratio number #7, so we graph only ratios #8 through #14.

Enter your ratios on the graph only after *carefully* reading the scale and paying attention to each decimal place. The scale has 10 marks between each four-decimal-place number to represent the **fifth** decimal place of the number you're trying to graph.

As an example, practice putting ratio #11 on the graph: 1.61798 is more than 1.6179 even though the two look exactly alike up to the fourth decimal place; the first is 8 more than the second in the fifth decimal place. (The **fifth** decimal place of 1.6179 is an invisible **0.**)

So, on the vertical line marked **11** on the graph place a dot at the level of the 8th tiny mark above 1.6179, where the arrow is pointing. Notice that this ratio is just a little bit below the level of the Golden Ratio on your graph.

After you've graphed the ratios and joined the dots with lines (use your ruler), accurately describe how the ratios of Fibonacci Numbers change as you go farther and farther along in the sequence. _____

_____

_____

**Thanks to these graphs we've seen that the Golden Ratio has been hiding out in the Fibonacci Numbers all along!**

# THE FIBONACCI NUMBERS STRIKE AGAIN!

What this activity leads to is that **the ratio of any two consecutive Fibonacci Numbers approximates the Golden Ratio. The approximation grows more accurate as larger Fibonaccis are chosen.**

If your students are newcomers to decimal notation in this activity, they will have trouble graphing and comparing longer decimals. Even those who know decimals might brush up here. They need to be able to tell when one long string of decimal digits is larger than another. The "Crash Course in Comparing Decimals" will be of great help in teaching this skill.

If they're pretty shaky on decimals it may be too much to have them do the "Close-Up Graph" on page 136. A good goal is to get through the first graph and discuss what it means. The relationship of the Fibonaccis to the Golden Ratio is the important concept of this whole activity.

## A CRASH COURSE IN COMPARING DECIMALS

**TEACHER:** "You know how to tell whether one three-digit decimal is bigger than another. Just see which number looks bigger, meaning which has more of those thousand parts of the football field. But let me point out that 1.7 is bigger than 1.624 or 1.67. Why?"

**STUDENT:** "The other two look bigger because they mean 624 parts and 67 parts. The .7 means only 7 parts."

**TEACHER:** "Remember that 1.7 is the same as 1.700. Now which seems biggest?"

**STUDENT:** "You're right, 1.7 is!"

**TEACHER:** "I'm going to give you a simple rule for comparing *any* two decimals, no matter how many digits they have after the point. Here it is." (Writes on board.)

**If the numbers before the point are different, the larger wins. Otherwise, start at the point and compare the decimals digit-for-digit from left to right. The first time you come to a place where the two numbers have different digits, the one with the larger digit is the larger number.**

"So, by this rule, 1.7 would win over 1.624 because they differ in the first place after the decimal point. The 7 there is larger than the 6, so 1.7 wins."

"Now, how about 1.61806 versus 1.618026?"

**STUDENT:** "As I scan along, I see that in the fifth place the first has a 6 and the other has a 2. So the first is bigger."

## Teacher's Guide to Student Pages 133-136

**TEACHER:** "That's it! Now let's practice some more and then we'll use this skill on some Fibonacci ratios."

### ANSWERS TO QUESTIONS ON PAGE 133

23.3 cm = 233 mm; 14.4 cm = 144 mm. Both are Fibonacci Numbers. Their ratio is 233/144 = 1.61803, the Golden Ratio.

Similarly, 144/89 = 1.61798, rounded to 1.618, the Golden Ratio.

And again, 89/55 = 1.61818.

### THE FIBONACCI RATIOS REACH 1.61803

The answers to the ratios of successive Fibonaccis are on the next page. Students should record them rounded off to five decimal places (unless it comes out to a simple decimal), to aid comparison. The last three are shown to six decimal places to show how the up-and-down effect continues past the first five places. It also shows how the 1.61803 . . . value, the known five-place value for the Golden Ratio, is finally "pinned down" by the 15th ratio.

| Ratio Number | Ratio | Ratio Number | Ratio |
|---|---|---|---|
| 1 | 1 | 8 | 1.61904 |
| 2 | 2 | 9 | 1.61765 |
| 3 | 1.5 | 10 | 1.61818 |
| 4 | 1.66667 | 11 | 1.61798 |
| 5 | 1.6 | 12 | 1.61806 |
| 6 | 1.625 | 13 | 1.618026 |
| 7 | 1.61538 | 14 | 1.618037 |
|  |  | 15 | 1.618033 |

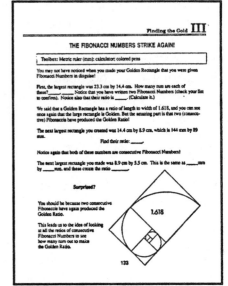

Student Page 133

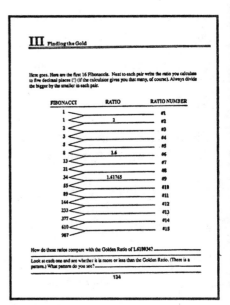

Student Page 134

## Teacher's Guide to Student Pages 133-136

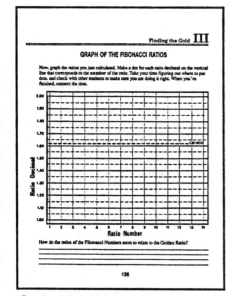

Student Page 135

Student Page 136

Peruse these numbers while comparing them to 1.618034 . . . You will find that they are alternately above and then below that number. Also, they approach 1.618034 . . . whether they are above or below it. The full effect of this will be illustrated by the finished graphs on this page and the next page.

### FIBONACCI RATIOS ON A NUMBER LINE

Before graphing these results, students may need some instruction on how to locate a decimal on a number line. For instance, for graph interval from 1.6 to 1.7:

**1.61** is at the first mark above **1.60, 1.62** is at the second, and so forth.

**1.61798** is 8 parts of the 10-part distance between the **1.6179** and **1.6180** marks.

It's impossible to enter a further decimal place on the first graph. The second graph is a *magnification* and allows for further decimal places. (See left for that graph.)

### GRAPHING THE FIBONACCI RATIOS

To graph the ratios of successive pairs of Fibonaccis, points must be centered on the graph at the appropriate height for each ratio number. Students should carefully estimate by first locating the value along the left scale. They should then use a ruler to extend this value over to its position on the appropriate line above its ratio number. There they make a dot.

Afterwards, students should draw straight line segments connecting the points (see finished graph). The point of this graphing exercise is for the student to visualize how the values of successive ratios of the Fibonaccis rapidly jump up and down but eventually approach the Golden Ratio value as we use larger and larger Fibonaccis. It's as though the Golden Ratio were *hidden* in the Fibonaccis and slowly gets *unveiled* to more and more decimal places as we divide higher and higher Fibonacci pairs.

## Teacher's Guide to Student Pages 133-136

### THE CLOSE-UP GRAPH

It looks on the graph as if the Golden Ratio is reached by about the time the 10th ratio is plotted. That's just because the scale of the graph is too *gross* to pick up the fine variations in the ratio numbers after that. So I made a second graphing page for ratios 8-14 only. It's on a much finer scale.

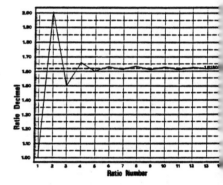

There the student must simply locate each ratio's fifth decimal place on the scale and transfer the value to the line above the ratio number. In this way we see that successive ratios are jumping up and down as wildly as ever (see finished graph). But again they diminish in their jumping as the Fibonaccis get larger. Some students may speculate that even another, more magnified graph of **six** decimal places would show more jumping and tapering off. They're right!

### DISCUSSION OF A SIMPLE CALCULUS IDEA

Some discussion of this phenomenon may reveal that, indeed, the unending decimal value of 1.618034 . . .will never be *exactly* duplicated by dividing two Fibonacci Numbers. If we choose two Fibonaccis that are large enough, we could divide them and achieve a value of the Golden Ratio accurate to as many decimal places as we desired.

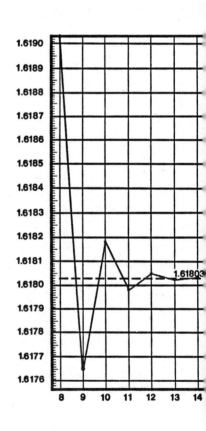

Some students may enjoy knowing that this kind of closer-and-closer approach to a number is studied in **calculus**. There the Golden Ratio is called a **limit**, which is reached only if we could continue dividing Fibonacci numbers forever. This could be discussed in the context of human behavior, also, because many people believe that in their youth they deviated more from the "correct" Golden values, but as they get into their larger age numbers they are *focusing in* on the "correct" values with growing accuracy. They still hit above and below it, though. Students could discuss their opinions of this belief.

### THE FINISHED GRAPHS

Here is how the finished graphs should look. See comments on the previous teacher page about interpreting and discussing these graphs.

# THE FIBONACCIS, THE GOLDEN RATIO, AND SOME CALCULATOR TIPS

These calculator exercises will explain and use what you learned from graphing the Fibonacci Ratios.

**1.** Divide the Fibonacci 233 by the Fibonacci 144. _____ (Should be the Golden Ratio.)

**Don't remove your answer from the screen.**

**2.** Multiply your answer by 144. _____
Of course, you get 233 back.

**This obvious exercise suggests something important: If you multiply a (reasonably large) Fibonacci by the Golden Ratio, you'll get the next Fibonacci (or very close to it).**

**3.** Multiply the Golden Ratio by 3 (a small Fibonacci).

Do you get the next Fibonacci? _____

Do you land close to one? _____

Why won't this work on a small Fibonacci as well? (Consult your list and graph of Fibonacci ratios before you answer.) _____
_____
_____

## THE FIBONACCIS, continued

**4.** Now we'll use what we found in **1** through **3** above. Here's a way to generate a whole bunch of Fibonacci Numbers using your calculator.  Put 1.618034 (Golden Ratio) on the screen. Push the

$$\boxed{\text{M+}} \text{ or } \boxed{\text{M}} \text{ key,}$$

which puts a copy of this number into a memory cell of the calculator.  Test that it's stored in there by pushing the

$$\boxed{\text{C}} \quad \text{(clear screen) button,}$$

then call the number back from memory by pushing the

$$\boxed{\text{MR}} \quad \text{or} \quad \boxed{\text{M}^{\text{RC}}} \text{ (memory recall) button.}$$

**5.** Now, push

$$\boxed{3} \ \boxed{4} \ \boxed{\text{X}} \text{ , then } \boxed{\text{MR}} \text{, then } \boxed{\text{X}} \text{ .}$$

This will give you something very close to the next Fibonacci. **Don't clear anything.**

$$\text{Push } \boxed{\text{M}^{\text{R}}} \text{ then } \boxed{\text{X}} \text{ again}$$

to get (near) the next Fibonacci. Punch these two keys a few more times, checking the screen to see that you are near Fibonaccis each time (check your Fibonacci list).

How close to 987 (the 16th Fibonacci) do you get? _____ (Give the difference to five decimal places.) How many times did you multiply 34 by the Golden Ratio to get near 987? (Check it again.) _____

**6.** This time just push

$$\boxed{\text{M}^{\text{R}}} \text{ and } \boxed{\text{X}} \text{ a total of seven times}$$

$$\text{and } \textbf{then} \text{ push } \boxed{3} \ \boxed{4} \text{ and } \boxed{=} \text{ .}$$

What do you get? _____ Surprised? Why should this **not** be surprising? (Use a separate piece of paper.)

## Teacher's Guide to Student Pages 141-142

# THE FIBONACCIS, THE GOLDEN RATIO, AND SOME CALCULATOR TIPS

Student Page 141

Student Page 142

These sequenced exercises help students realize another meaning of the fact that the ratio of two large consecutive Fibonaccis is essentially the Golden Ratio. What this means is that I can take any Fibonacci greater than 34, multiply it by the Golden Ratio, and get the next Fibonacci (if I round off the tiny decimal part of my answer).

The calculator can be used to store the Golden Ratio and then multiply it by 34, then by that answer, then by that answer again, and so on. The result will be that a sequence of answers very closely resembling the Fibonacci Sequence will appear number by number.

### ANSWERS TO QUESTIONS ON PAGES 141-142

1. 1.61806

3. No. No. Won't work because the ratios of consecutive Fibonaccis like 2,3 or 3,5 are not really near the Golden Ratio. Thus multiplying 3 by the Golden Ratio won't give anything very close to 5.

5. 987.17107—very close to 987;  7 times

6. The same: 987.17107. It doesn't matter whether we multiply 34 x 1.618034 x 1.618034 x 1.618034 x etc. or multiply 1.618034 x 1.618034 x 1.618034 x etc. and *then* multiply by 34, because multiplication is **commutative**, allowing it to be done in any order.

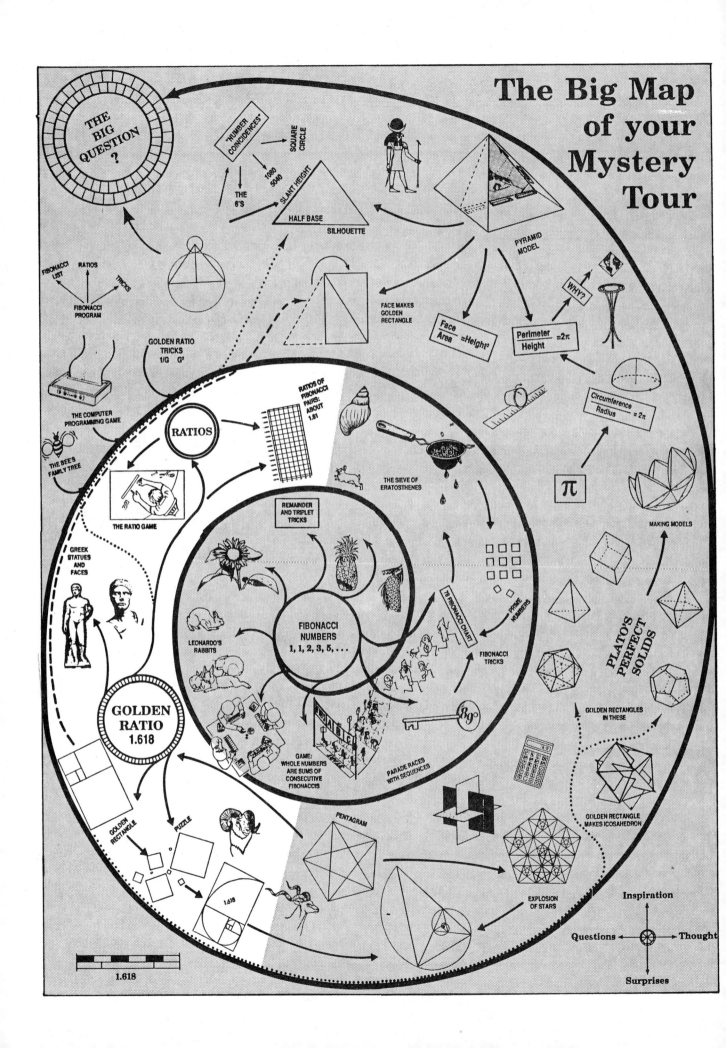

# The Big Map of your Mystery Tour

THE BIG QUESTION ?

"NUMBER COINCIDENCES"

SQUARE CIRCLE

THE 6'S

1080
5040

SLANT HEIGHT

HALF BASE

SILHOUETTE

PYRAMID MODEL

FIBONACCI LIST

RATIOS

TRICKS

FIBONACCI PROGRAM

GOLDEN RATIO TRICKS 1/G    G²

THE COMPUTER PROGRAMMING GAME

FACE MAKES GOLDEN RECTANGLE

WHY?

$\dfrac{\text{Face Area}}{} = \text{Height}^2$

$\dfrac{\text{Perimeter}}{\text{Height}} = 2\pi$

$\dfrac{\text{Circumference}}{\text{Radius}} = 2\pi$

RATIOS

RATIOS OF FIBONACCI PAIRS: ABOUT 1.61

THE SIEVE OF ERATOSTHENES

THE BEE'S FAMILY TREE

THE RATIO GAME

REMAINDER AND TRIPLET TRICKS

PRIME NUMBERS

π

MAKING MODELS

GREEK STATUES AND FACES

LEONARDO'S RABBITS

FIBONACCI NUMBERS 1, 1, 2, 3, 5, ...

'1 TO FIBONACCI CHART'

FIBONACCI TRICKS

PLATO'S PERFECT SOLIDS

GOLDEN RATIO 1.618

GOLDEN RECTANGLES IN THESE

GAME: WHOLE NUMBERS ARE SUMS OF CONSECUTIVE FIBONACCIS

PARADE RACES WITH SEQUENCES

GOLDEN RECTANGLE

PUZZLE

PENTAGRAM

GOLDEN RECTANGLE MAKES ICOSAHEDRON

1.618

EXPLOSION OF STARS

Inspiration

Questions ←⊕→ Thought

Surprises

1.618

# A LOOK AT THE TERRITORY: Unit III

You've come a long way! Here's the piece of the map you've covered. Check where it sits in the Tour Map. Now let's do the map activities again.

● Discuss the map with someone else. Use your Tour Map, too, so that you can explain why every arrow is pointing the way it is. If you're unsure about something, go back in your work and remind yourself what that section was about.

● Study this map piece for four minutes and then redraw it from memory. If you miss some parts, restudy the sections and then redraw your map.

● Can you add the parts of Unit II from memory? Try it. Then check your Big Map and correct what you missed.

● Can you fill in the Unit I pictures from memory? Try it. Check the Tour Map and correct your try.

● Now translate the map into words. Write one page about your recent Unit III journey, pointing out the sights and connections you discovered. Go into more detail on what you especially liked. Write questions that pop up in your mind. Suggest answers for them and use them during a class discussion.

# LEARNING INVENTORY

**Toolbox:** Ruler (mm); calculator; colored pens

These questions are designed to let you know which areas of Unit III you understand and which you should review. Your teacher will tell you whether you should

- look back at your worksheets as you do this inventory, or

- try the inventory first and then look back to research your incorrect answers. Your teacher may also ask you to write about the corrected answers from memory, or to answer further questions about them.

**1.** From the Ratio Game...

- Try to "cut" strip "A" (by drawing a line across it) so that it is .41 of the length of strip "B."

- Make your mm measurement of the cut length of strip "A" and of strip "B," marking these numbers on the strips.

- Calculate, with your calculator, the ratio of the measurement of strip "A" to the measurement of strip "B."
        Ratio: _____

- Is your ratio more or less than .05 away from .41? _____

**2.** If the ratio of a long strip to a short strip is 1.5 and the short strip is 6 cm, what is the length of the long strip? _____

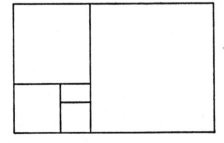

**3.** What is the Golden Ratio? What does it have to do with Greek statues? (Answer clearly in a couple of sentences on a separate piece of paper.)

**LEARNING INVENTORY, continued**

**4.** If you wanted to check to see if someone's body had a Golden Ratio, what would you measure? ____________________

____________________

If you were checking for a Golden Ratio on someone's face, what would you measure?

____________________

____________________

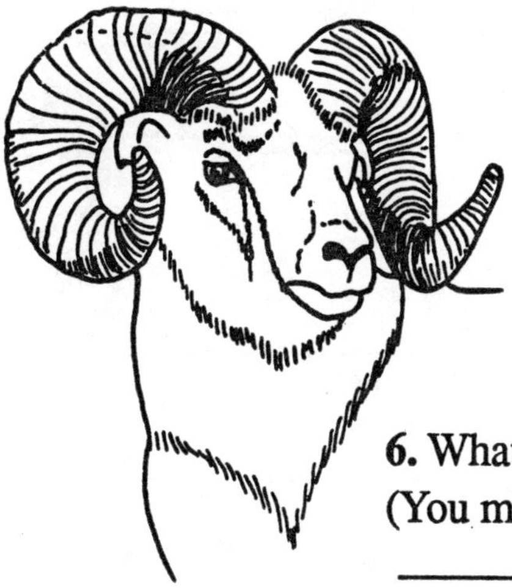

**5.** What is a Golden Rectangle? ____________________

____________________

____________________

What does it have to do with Nature? ____________________

____________________

**6.** What happens if you cut away a square from a Golden Rectangle? (You may draw a diagram and label it or answer in a sentence.)

____________________

____________________

**7.** How do the Fibonacci Numbers produce the Golden Ratio? ____________________

____________________

**8.** How can you make more Fibonaccis from one Fibonacci using the Golden Ratio?

____________________

____________________

____________________

____________________

____________________

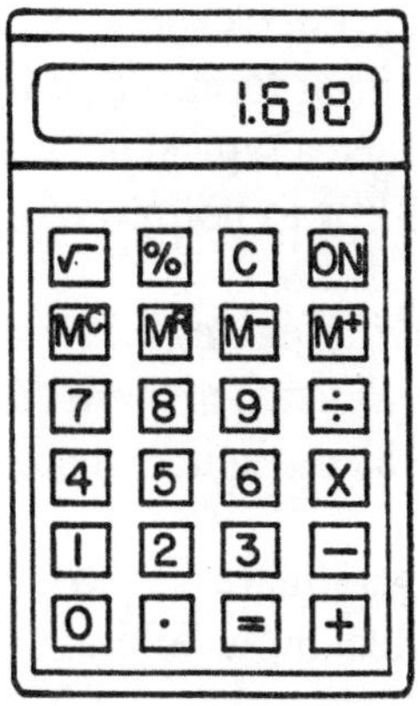

## Teacher's Guide to Student Pages 146-147

## LEARNING INVENTORY

This Learning Inventory has questions that involve the ability to summarize or apply ideas. Even if students have to go back through their papers to find the answers, there will be some synthesis and review going on.

If they miss some of the answers or simply can't figure them out, it's important to provide them with an opportunity to summarize their knowledge in either a written summary or an oral discussion. The whole inventory could be done as a small group endeavor with the introductory warning that any member of the group can be called on to explain any answer.

### ANSWERS TO QUESTIONS ON PAGES 146-147

**1.** Strip "B" should show a measurement of 80 mm, while the cut part of strip "A" should be somewhere in the neighborhood of 33 mm. If the cut measures **very** much lower or higher than 33 mm, the student probably still has some inability to estimate what part of a whole a decimal is. Point out to the student that the two-digit decimal simply creates a scale of 1 to 100 on strip "B," and that he/she must figure out where 41 would be on that scale; then mark that length on strip "A."

**2.** 9, because 1.5 x 6 = 9. If the ratio of two numbers is 1.5, then the larger is 1.5 times the shorter.

**3.** 1.618 . . . This number shows up as the ratio of several key body measurements on Greek statues.

**4.** Answers will vary among the several measurements that were done on the Greek statue earlier. A typical answer might be "measure from floor to navel and from navel to top of head." Similarly with the face a typical answer might be "measure from eyes to lips and from lips to bottom of chin."

**5.** A Golden Rectangle is a rectangle with a length-to-width ratio of 1.618 . . . Several of them can be assembled to make a spiral that is the same as the spiral in seashells and horns.

**6.** Cutting a square from a Golden Rectangle leaves another smaller Golden Rectangle behind.

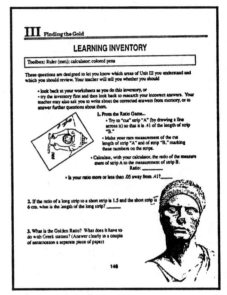

Student Page 146

Student Page 147

## Teacher's Guide to Student Pages 146-147

**7.** If successive ratios of consecutive Fibonacci Numbers are calculated, these ratios will be seen to be extremely close to the Golden Ratio number, growing closer as we choose larger and larger Fibonacci pairs.

**8.** If any relatively large Fibonacci Number is multiplied by the Golden Ratio, the next larger Fibonacci will result, and this in turn can be multiplied by the Golden Ratio to get the next larger Fibonacci.

# UNIT IV: MATHEMATICAL ARTFORMS

## SUPERNOVA: THE EXPLOSION OF STARS

**Toolbox:** Ruler; pencil; colored pens; calculator

You're in for a lot of careful drawing with your ruler. You'll be making some interesting geometric designs in this unit. You'll also put together some complex paper solids. And all the while you'll be learning more about the Golden Ratio!

This first activity will produce for you three things—a terrific design you can improvise on, a whole bunch of Golden Ratios, and a key to Nature's designs. Get your ruler ready. . . .

A.

B.

C.

D.

E.

F.

G.

H.

I.

J.

K.

L.

M.

N.

O.

P.

# THE PENTAGRAM

Start with the five dots on the accompanying sheet, **A**, **B**, **C**, **D**, and **E** (ignore all other dots) and follow these instructions to end up with a whole family tree of shapes:

● Connect *each* dot of the five to *each of the other four* dots. Pick dot **A**, for instance, and from it draw **straight** line segments connecting it to **B, C, D** and **E. Do the same** with dots **B, C, D,** and **E** until all dots are joined with every other dot. (You will notice that you have one less line to draw each time you change letters.)

● You've created a large pentagon (five-sided figure) with a star inside it. We'll call them **Great Pentagon** and **Great Star** in the instructions below.

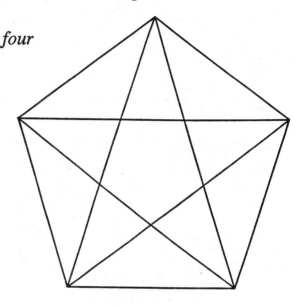

**GREAT PENTAGON**
**GREAT STAR**

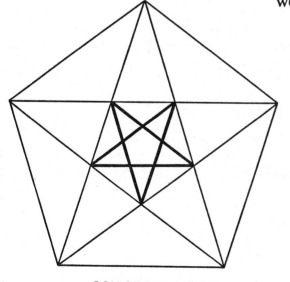

**SON OF PENTAGON**
**SON OF STAR**

● Inside Great Star is a smaller **pentagon, FGHIJ**, which we'll call **Son of Pentagon.** Join its five points with segments. (Remember how you did it with Great Pentagon?) Call this newborn star **Son of Star.**

● This design already looks interesting, but you "ain't seen nothin' yet." Before we explode the drawing to make more stars, let's measure the ones we have—there are some secrets these star measurements will tell.

## SUPERNOVA: THE EXPLOSION OF STARS, continued

With your ruler, measure (to the nearest mm) the long segment AC. _____.____ cm.

Now measure the next longest segment, a side of Great Pentagon, AB. _____.____cm.

The ratio of the longer to the shorter measurement is _____.____ .

I hope this answer is a familiar number to you by now!

But there's more. Measure these segments on your drawing (nearest millimeter). You've already found the first two:

AB _____.____cm         JF _____.____ cm         FH _____.____ cm

AC _____.____cm         FK _____.____ cm         IH _____.____ cm

BF _____.____cm         KO _____.____ cm

Then find these ratios (two decimal places):
You found the first one before.

AC/AB=____        JF/FK= ____

AB/BF= ____        FK/KO= ____

BF/JF= ____        FH/IH= ____

**1.** Make an observation here about what you've seen in your answers:———————

————————————————————————————————————

**2.** Predict five more ratios in your drawing that will be Golden Ratios:

_____ _____ _____ _____ _____

Put the measurements for each segment of your predicted ratios above and below these lines:

_____ _____ _____ _____ _____

(These should be the same as measurements you've already done.)

Calculate the five ratios: _____ _____ _____ _____ _____

### SUPERNOVA: THE EXPLOSION OF STARS, continued

**3.** Knowing that segments are in the Golden Ratio to each other allows you to find one segment's length from another. For example, multiply length **ID** (_____.____.cm) by **1.618.**

This should give you about the length of **ED** (____.__cm).

Multiply this answer by **1.618** and get about the length of **EC** (____.__cm).

If these didn't come out exactly, what could have caused it?

---

The star you have been exploring has been known from ancient times as a **pentagram**. It was believed to be a magical symbol in early Greece. It was the official sign of the Pythagorean Brotherhood on the beautiful Greek island of Samos. There are two articles about the history of the pentagram and the Pythagoreans in your *Tour Guide* newspaper. You will be asked to read them after finishing this design.

Now, add to your design so that it makes a supernova explosion of stars.

● Go to work on Son of Star. Find segment JG and extend it (with your ruler) to P and Q, so that PQ is one long segment. Now we can say, "One of Son of Star's arms reaches to the sides of Great Pentagon."

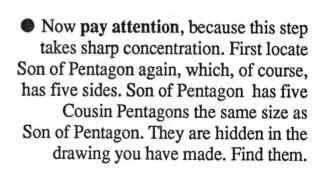

● Son of Star has four other segments (*arms*). Each of these also has to reach out to touch the sides of Great Pentagon. Use your ruler and pencil to make them reach.

● Now **pay attention**, because this step takes sharp concentration. First locate Son of Pentagon again, which, of course, has five sides. Son of Pentagon has five Cousin Pentagons the same size as Son of Pentagon. They are hidden in the drawing you have made. Find them.

**HINT:** Each Cousin Pentagon shares a side with Son of Pentagon.

**COUSIN PENTAGON**          **155**

## SUPERNOVA: THE EXPLOSION OF STARS, continued

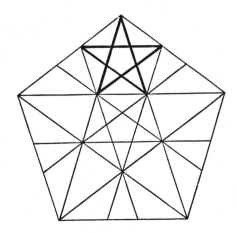 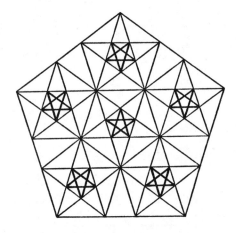

● With your ruler and a sharp colored pen, outline each **Cousin** so you can see it. Inside each Cousin (using a colored pen with a different color), create a star that looks just like **Son of Star**. These are **Son of Star's Cousins.**

● Inside Son of Star and his Cousins are **Grandsons of Pentagon** (tiny pentagons). Make a **Grandson of Star** inside each one of these.

### THIS IS ONE PLACE TO STOP THIS DESIGN AND COLOR IT.

Otherwise, if your eyes aren't falling out or your picture doesn't have smeared lines and a hole erased through it, you are invited to find even more pentagons and stars *before* you color. Whether you're going to color now or later, I'll give a few tips about coloring your design:
   ● Use fairly sharp pens.
   ● Choose colors that "get along with each other."
   ● Shapes that are alike repeat in a circular path around the inside of the pentagon. Color these "like" shapes the same color.
   ● Leaving some parts of shapes (like star centers) uncolored can look sharp. But it's up to you.

**Continuing the design (for courageous designers):**

● Explore your design searching for pentagons that are a *bit smaller* than Son of Pentagon. These are touching the points of center Grandson of Star and lying on the arms of each other Grandson of Star. (See Figure above right.)

### SUPERNOVA: THE EXPLOSION OF STARS, continued

● When you find these pentagons, use a different-colored pen to draw (with ruler) a star inside each in the usual way. (The star will usually already have three of its lines in place.)

● You might want to draw more smaller stars inside the center pentagons of stars you see floating around.

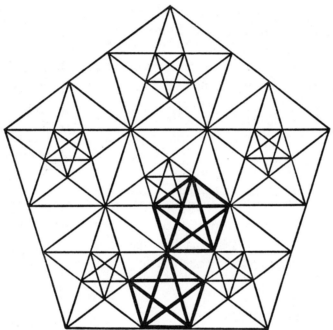

You're done, at least as far as I dare take you. If you are really hot, you can search for more pentagons all over the place in your diagram and put stars in them. Keep changing pen colors to keep track. It takes practice to keep them neat. Then color it in an interesting way! The next activity will show you how your design has a secret seashell in it.

### Done Coloring?

Read two articles in your *Tour Guide* newspaper. They are entitled "Secrets of Pythagoras's Community Exposed" and "The Powerful Pentagram." They'll help you get to know how people used to think of geometry and numbers—a very different way from how we think of them today.

# UNIT IV: MATHEMATICAL ARTFORMS

## SUPERNOVA: THE EXPLOSION OF STARS

### AN OVERVIEW OF THE ACTIVITY

Some students will enjoy the more mathematically abstract lessons of this **Tour**. Some will relish the more visual exercises. Some will like the hands-on, physical experiences. Others will like the people-oriented, historical aspects. Still others will remember the mysterious things. All of these are ways to appreciate mathematics.

This unit has all of the above. Be ready for some of the more *intellectual* students to turn *klutz* during the constructions. A periodic helping hand will steady them.

The pentagram design is excellent practice in precision, spatial perception, and the ability to follow a lengthy series of directions. The payoff is a very aesthetically pleasing image, especially if it is taken far. Before starting, you can avoid mistakes by making sure your students are comfortable holding the ruler steady and drawing lines that exactly touch two points.

### MEASUREMENTS AND GOLDEN RATIOS IN THE PENTAGRAM

AC = 15.8 cm

AB = 9.8 cm

AC/AB = 1.6, which is the Golden Ratio! This means every pentagon automatically creates Golden Ratios. Pythagoras was in awe of this, as the articles "Secrets of Pythagoras's Community Exposed" and "The Powerful Pentagram" in the *Tour Guide* newspaper will attest.

Here are the other measurements in the design:

| | |
|---|---|
| BF = 6.1 cm | KO = 1.4 cm |
| JF = 3.8 cm | FH = 6.1 cm |
| FK = 2.4 cm | IH = 3.8 cm |

Student Page 154

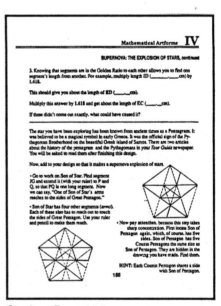

Student Page 155

## Teacher's Guide to Student Pages 151-157

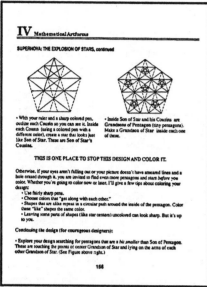

Student Page 156

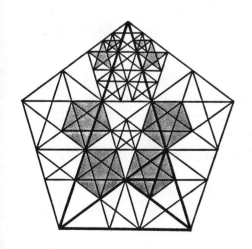

Calculate:

AB/BF = 1.64      FK/KO = 1.71
BF/JF = 1.61      FH/IH = 1.61
JF/FK = 1.58

### ANSWERS TO QUESTIONS ON PAGES 154-155

**1.** These values, all near the Golden Ratio, show that the pentagram is an explosion of Golden Ratios! They would come out exactly to 1.618 . . . if measurements were extremely precise.

**2.** There are many more segments that make the Golden Ratio. Basically, any segment in the pentagram is in the Golden Ratio to any next-shorter segment that can be found in the diagram.

**3.** Make sure students know that if

$$\frac{FD}{ID} = 1.618, \text{ for instance, then FD} = 1.618 \times ID.$$

The study of ratios in the last chapter brings this out. Note that there will be times when exact lengths of segments will not be given by this multiplication because of imprecision in measuring the segment to be multiplied. Have students experiment with this on their calculators.

If the design progresses much further, what it looks like is shown here. Only some of many possible pentagons have been used to make this sample. Every pentagon found can have a star in it.

Show students this design and tell them to find pentagons that arrange to make stars they want in their design. The possibilities are endless, as they, and you, will find out.

Encourage students to color it carefully no matter what stage it was taken to. Hang designs up in the room. They create a lot of pride in accomplishment.

## EXTENSION ACTIVITIES

• Some students really take off on this and have a good sense of precision. Have them start with five equally spaced points on a 3x3-ft. piece of paper and take it all the way to small **grandson** stars. They should color it along the way to keep the stars sorted out.

Place the five starting points by taping a completed pentagram in the middle of the paper on the floor. Mark its center. Place the end of a yard or meter stick at the center, and have the ruler just graze past one of the five pentagram points. Make a dot at 18 inch or 45 cm. Do the same at each of the other four points of the pentagram. Now you have the points of a large pentagram.

• Redraw the pentagram design and try a whole new coloring scheme, which may bring out another pentagon scheme.

• On the bulletin board, a central pentagram can have five others joined to its edges to form a super-design.

• Many mobiles, ornaments, and the like are possible with these colored pentagrams. Other crafts—needlepoint, quilting, and so forth—can also make good use of these as a design element.

• A stimulating reference for more elaborate designs of this kind is **Patterns in Space** by Colonel R. S. Beard. A visual feast for students interested in constructions.

• A book called **Creative Constructions** is also available from Creative Publications. It shows how to make many simple constructions with ruler and compass.

• The film **Donald Duck in Mathemagicland** is a 1950s classic. District media centers and public libraries often have it. Many of your students may already have seen it. Show it again, because now they have the understanding to really follow the details. It has a lot on the pentagram, the Pythagoreans, the Golden Rectangle, and so forth. Replay some of the geometrical scenes more than once until the students fully understand the sequences shown. Some students may wish to try to draw some of the sequences—for instance, the way a Pentagram translates to a plant.

• Have students research **supernovas** and report on their astronomical importance. Is the supernova's real definition symbolized well by our star design?

# FROM THE STAR EXPLOSION TO A SEASHELL

**Toolbox:** Protractor; ruler (mm); calculator

The star explosion you drew is the secret code of a seashell. You saw that the Golden Rectangle contained a seashell also. The thing in our explosion that gives us the same seashell is a **Golden Triangle.**

A Golden Triangle, **ACD,** is outlined in Figure 1, below. Its lines appear in the star explosion you drew. (There are some other smaller triangles also outlined. We'll discuss these later.) Triangle **ACD** looks very balanced because it's **isosceles,** which means that it has two equal sides.

It also has two equal angles. Remember that angles are formed when two line segments come together at a point (**vertex**). If two angles are equal, one could be laid on top of the other to make an exact fit. Put your two fingers on the two equal angles.

Put a finger on each equal side.

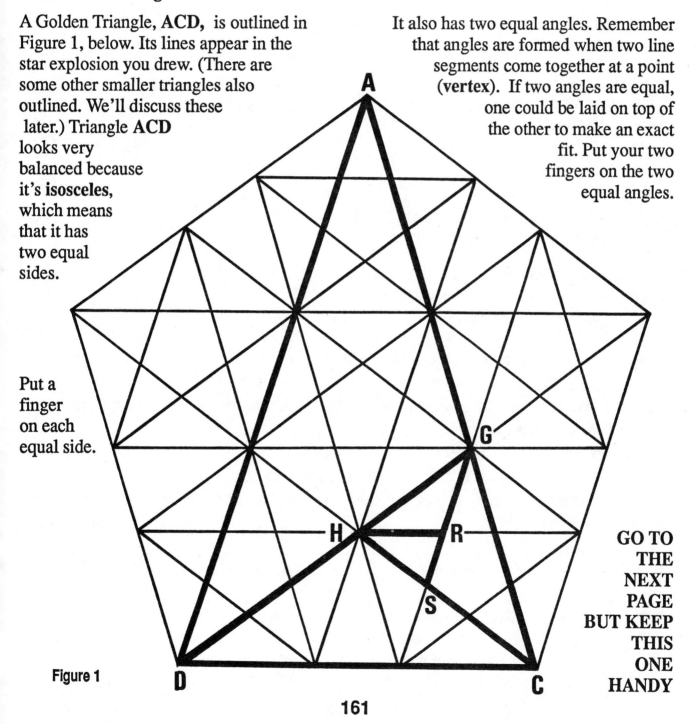

**Figure 1**

GO TO THE NEXT PAGE BUT KEEP THIS ONE HANDY

## FROM THE STAR EXPLOSION, continued

The Golden Triangle found in your pentagram star explosion is special for some other reasons besides being isosceles. To find out, you will need to measure the angles of your triangle on the previous page. This requires a protractor. (**If you're a "pro" with a protractor, skip the instructions below.**)

**If you've never used a protractor, here's a set of instructions to measure an angle:**

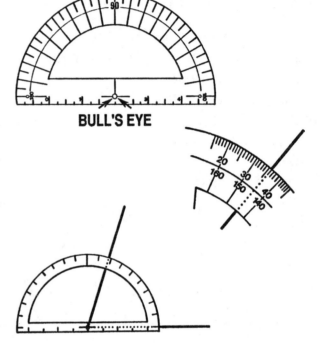

**BULL'S EYE**

● Put the protractor "bull's eye" exactly on the point of the angle.

● Rotate the protractor so that a zero (**0**) mark on the scale lands on one line segment.

● Make sure the other line segment crosses over the number scale of the protractor.

● Read the number on the same protractor scale that had the **0** mark you used. Each mark means **1°** of spread between segments.

**1.** Measure the three angles of the Golden Triangle of Figure 1. Their measurements are _____, _____, _____. Remember, *all triangles* have three angles that add up to **180°** exactly. Make sure your three measurements do this. If not, remeasure and adjust the numbers. (Make sure two are equal!)

**2.** Each bottom angle is exactly *twice* as big as the top angle. Do your measurements show this? _____ This is a special feature of the Golden Triangle.

**3.** Now measure the three angles of the smaller triangle **GCD**. (Your measurements should add to 180°, remember?) _____, _____, _____ Can you tell that this triangle is also a Golden Triangle? How? _____

**4.** Is **GCH** also a Golden Triangle? _____ Measure the angles and see: _____, _____, _____

**5.** Does it seem that **GSH** and **HRS** are Golden Triangles? _____

**6.** Try to draw a line segment that will make the next-sized Golden Triangle in the figure. Then draw the next one after that and the next one after that. How many Golden Triangles can there be inside one Golden Triangle? _____

**FROM THE STAR EXPLOSION, continued**

Here's how the Golden Triangle looks with its little Golden Triangles inside (Figure 2). Compare it with your sketch. You may notice that you drew yours inside different angles of some Golden Triangles. These triangles were drawn so that they **rotate** counterclockwise as they get smaller. See Figure 3, which shows how they'd look if they were drawn separately outside their triangles. Find each triangle shown in Figure 3 inside the triangle in Figure 2.

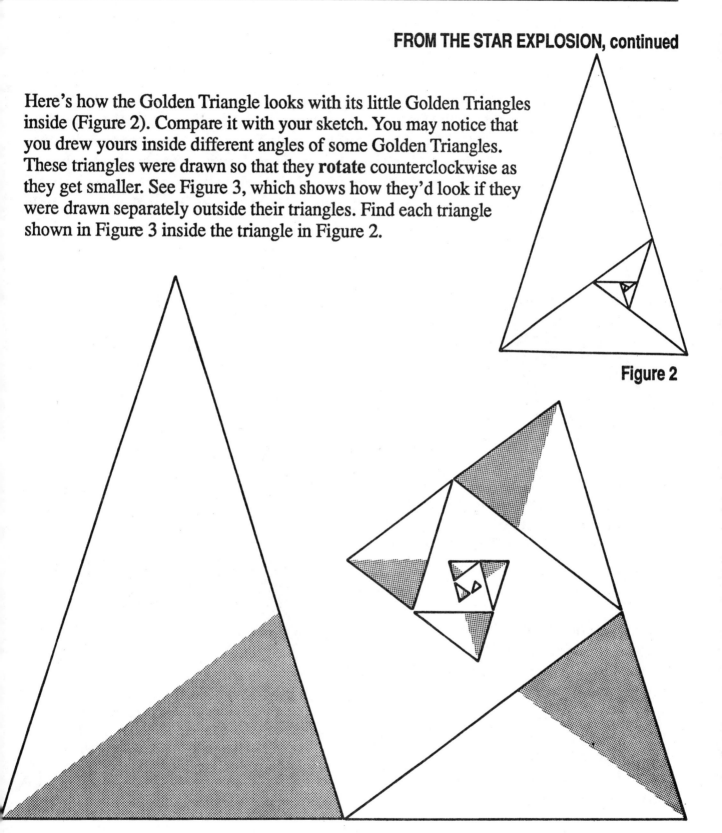

Figure 2

Figure 3

## FROM THE STAR EXPLOSION, continued

Now notice in Figure 2 how each triangle has another isosceles triangle inside it that **isn't** a Golden Triangle. Call it the **Big Sister** of the little Child Golden Triangle, where both Sister and Child are found in their Parent Golden Triangle. The Sister's vertex (top angle) touches the side of the Parent triangle in a place that's not the middle of the side. Figure 4 shows how it looks in one Golden Triangle.

**Figure 4**

On the next page you will find a Golden Triangle taken from Figure 1. Start with the biggest Golden Triangle. Open your compass so that it's just the length of one side of the isosceles triangle. (See Figure 5.) Place the compass point at **G**, pencil at **A**, and draw a curve (arc) down to **D**.

Next with your compass point at **H**, draw a curve from **D** to **C**. And with the point at **S** make a curve from **C** to **G**. Continue drawing such curves for each triangle.

When you're finished, you'll have a spiral that looks like the (familiar) seashell shape.

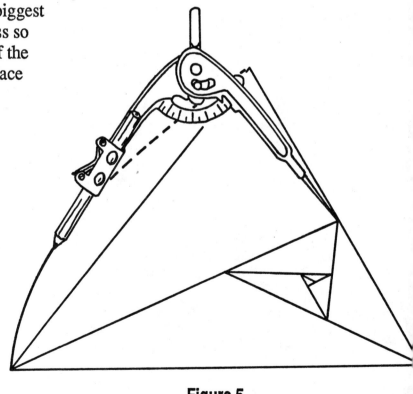

**Figure 5**

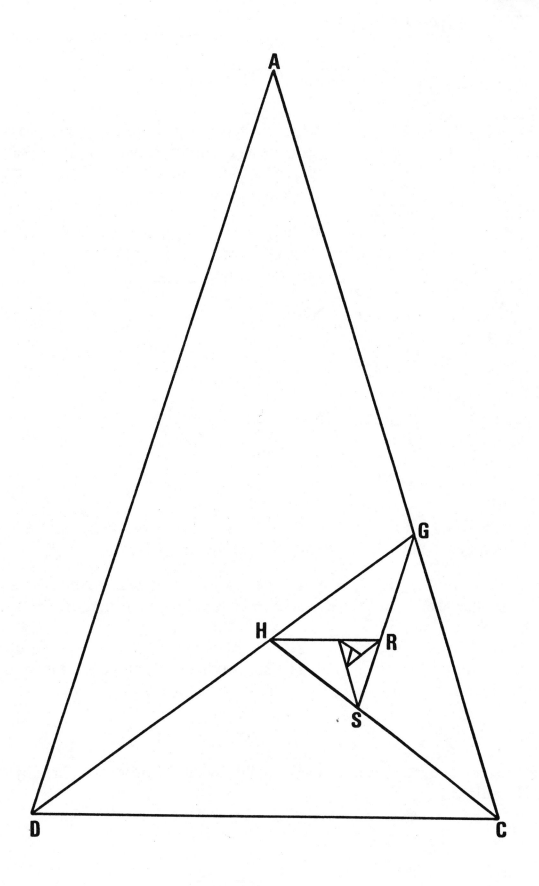

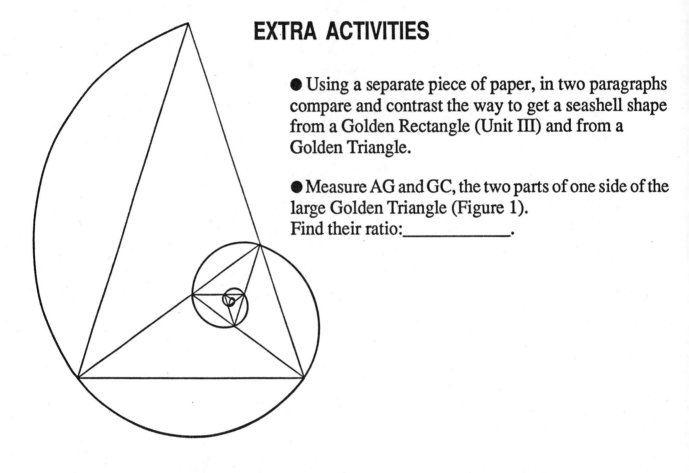

## EXTRA ACTIVITIES

● Using a separate piece of paper, in two paragraphs compare and contrast the way to get a seashell shape from a Golden Rectangle (Unit III) and from a Golden Triangle.

● Measure AG and GC, the two parts of one side of the large Golden Triangle (Figure 1).
Find their ratio:_____.

How near to 1.618 is it? It should be right on! (In fact it's one of the Golden Ratios you calculated in your supernova design.)

● Challenge: You need to know how to find the area of a triangle to do this one. By measuring the base and height of the largest Big Sister triangle of Figure 1 to the nearest mm, calculate its area (A =1/2bh).

Do the same for the Child Golden Triangle. (Both of these triangles add up to the area of the Parent Golden Triangle.)

Now find the ratio of the **areas** of the two triangles by dividing the larger area by the smaller. The ratio is _____.

Does it look familiar?

## Teacher's Guide to Student Pages 161-166

# FROM THE STAR EXPLOSION TO A SEASHELL

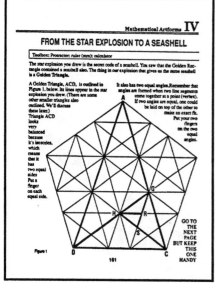

Student Page 161

## OVERVIEW OF THE ACTIVITY

The first concept developed here is the **isosceles triangle**. To discuss it in advance of handing out this sheet would be helpful. Mention that isosceles means any triangle with two equal sides and two equal angles. (Both have to be true if either is true.)

Have students draw several different-sized and different-shaped isosceles triangles. This way they can learn that isosceles is not a shape, but a statement of equality.

Students will also get to become familiar with the **protractor**, and get used to using it. Practice using it yourself (with the directions on the student page) before passing out the sheets.

## ANSWERS TO QUESTIONS ON PAGE 162

**1.** 72°, 72°,  36°

**2.** Yes, 72° is twice 36°.

**3.** 72°, 72°, 36°, which makes the small triangle *also* a Golden Triangle. Now this is an unusual feature—a triangle that *spawns* copies of itself. The last time we saw this was with the Golden Rectangle.

**4.** GCH is also Golden, though the angles may be hard to measure accurately.

**5.** It should seem that GSH and HRS are Golden Triangles also because they are obtained in the same way from a *parent* triangle. They **are** Golden.

**6.** The triangles your students can draw inside HRS would look something like this (see left). Since the child triangle can nestle at either base angle of the parent triangle, there will be some variations in how this can look. Theoretically, this Golden Triangle drawing can go on forever—there is an infinite number of Golden Triangles inside any Golden Triangle.

## Teacher's Guide to Student Pages 161-166

A class discussion of this fact would be stimulating. Help them make the distinction between what is **theoretically possible** and what is **physically possible.** The mathematical definition of what **infinite** is in this case is that no matter how many triangles you've drawn, you can always draw one more.

## THE SPIRAL FROM THE TRIANGLE

The three student pages describe how to proceed to make the seashell spiral from the Golden Triangle. This final spiral should be a surprise—a nice connection to the Golden Rectangle work they did in the last unit. The finished product should look like the spiral on page 166.

**NOTE FOR THE MATHEMATICALLY MINDED TEACHER ON DRAWING SPIRALS:** The arcs drawn on both the Golden Rectangle and the Golden Triangle are not the **exact** curvature of a shell. A shell's curvature is changing radius at every moment, not just at each new place where you move the compass point. A careful look at the spirals the student has drawn will reveal that there is a *pointed dip* where each arc joins the next one—a point of abrupt change of curvature. It's not necessary to get most students involved in this technicality. To get around it, one would have to use a French curve. No, thanks!

## REMEMBER THE PENTAGRAM

**Remind the students that this means the seashell spiral is subtly hidden in the pentagram, too. No wonder the pentagram used to be thought to have magic in it!**

## A GOOD REFERENCE

A good source of inspiration and further development of several concepts in this book is **The Divine Proportion** by Huntley, a low-priced paperback available in most good bookstores. Some parts are very technical, but other parts are poetic and informative.

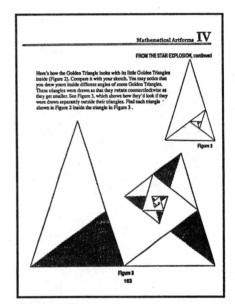

Student Page 163

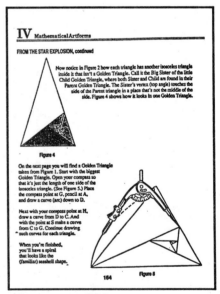

Student Page 164

## Teacher's Guide to Student Pages 161-166

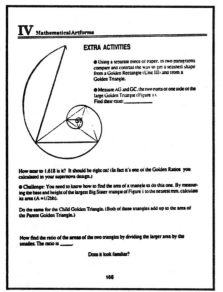

Student Page 166

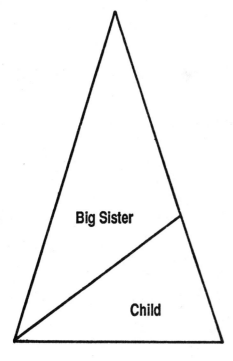

**Big Sister**

**Child**

**Parent Triangle**

### EXTRA ACTIVITIES

• This one is important if you wish to develop students' abilitiy to synthesize their two spiral experiences. It also helps them really recall and analyze the procedures.

Here's a comparison:

#### Similarities
Each larger shape gives birth to a smaller copy of the same shape, and the procedure spirals down infinitely to a point. Both result in the same spiral.

#### Differences
The *leftovers* inside are always a square in one case, and an isosceles triangle (larger than the Golden Triangle) in the other. In the Golden Rectangle arcs are drawn inside each leftover (square), whereas in the Golden Triangle arcs are drawn outside each leftover (isosceles triangle).

• If your students know about, or want to learn about, areas of triangles, you may want to have them try this. A basic simple procedure for finding the area of an isosceles triangle is as follows:

The **base** is the side that shares the two equal angles. The **altitude** is the height the triangle apex stands above this base when the base is horizontal—spin the triangle if necessary to get the base at the bottom. The area—the number of square cm—is found by multiplying base length (cm) by **half** the altitude (cm).

If this procedure is done on the Big Sister triangle and Child Golden Triangle, the ratio of

$$\frac{\textbf{Big Sister area}}{\textbf{Child area}}$$

should be exactly 1.618. Students' results will differ some because of measurement approximations that get multiplied. This reveals more of the Golden Ratio magic of the pentagram.

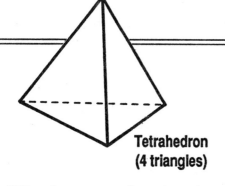

**Tetrahedron
(4 triangles)**

# PLATO'S BELOVED POLYHEDRA: OR, GOING 3-D WITH PENTAGONS AND TRIANGLES

What happens when the triangles and pentagons we've been working with go **3-D**? (That is, they don't just lie flat.) They make some very nice, very perfect solid shapes, which Plato thought were the loveliest things he had ever seen. There are only five such perfect shapes possible and they look like the shapes on this page.

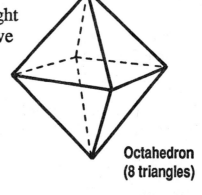

**Octahedron
(8 triangles)**

**Cube
(6 squares)**

This is a good place to stop and read more about the very famous Greek thinker Plato and how he thought these five solids had meanings hidden within them. Then we will go on to make these solids for ourselves and find a very important secret in them. Read "Plato Pulls New Surprises" in your *Tour Guide* newspaper.

**STOP**

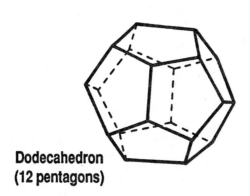

**Dodecahedron
(12 pentagons)**

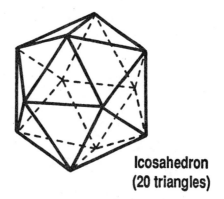

**Icosahedron
(20 triangles)**

There, you now know Plato's point of view. Back to the geometry of the five solids. What do you think they all have in common that makes them so special? Use a separate piece of paper.

## PLATO'S BELOVED POLYHEDRA, continued

These solids are special because:

First, each solid has faces that are all the same **shape**.

Second, all faces are shapes that have all **edges** the same length.

No other solid can be constructed that fulfills these two rules. Try to imagine one. Or, at the bottom of this page draw another one and see what you think would be wrong with it.

Plato thought of these solids as *perfect*. The Golden Ratio seems often to show up in things that are *perfect,* like Greek statues and faces and buildings as well as pentagrams and seashells. Wouldn't you also expect the Golden Ratio to show up in Plato's solids? Well, it does! But before you get to see how, you need to get more familiar with some solids by building them, which is what you will do next.

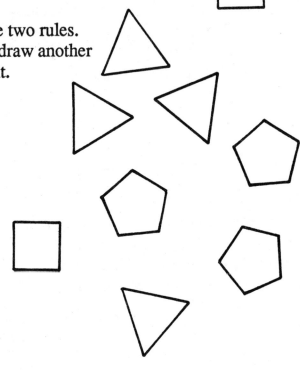

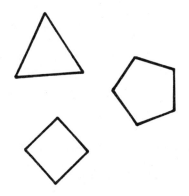

# HOW TO MAKE BIG JEWELS

**Toolbox:** Scissors; six sheets of triangles and four sheets of pentagons per group; stapler

It's time to make four of the five solids Plato loved. We won't bother with the cube because you have seen millions of them by now.

You and your companions will need **32** triangles and **12** pentagons cut out of the 10 sheets you have been given by your teacher. Be sure to cut around the curved parts rather than along the straight dashed lines!

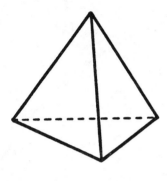

First we'll make the **tetrahedron** (four triangles). Join triangles by folding their tabs and stapling them together (see right). Fold up the three triangles that aren't in the center, like petals, until their tabs meet. Staple all tabs to get the solid.

For the **octahedron** (eight triangles), try to make it just by looking at its picture. (It's just two pyramids whose bottoms are stuck together.)

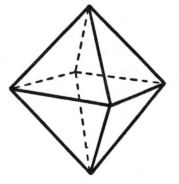

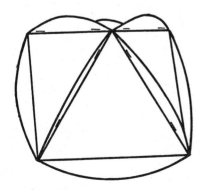

If you still have trouble, try sticking four of them together like this and then staple up the seam to make a pyramid. Have a partner make another pyramid, and then staple the pyramids together bottom to bottom.

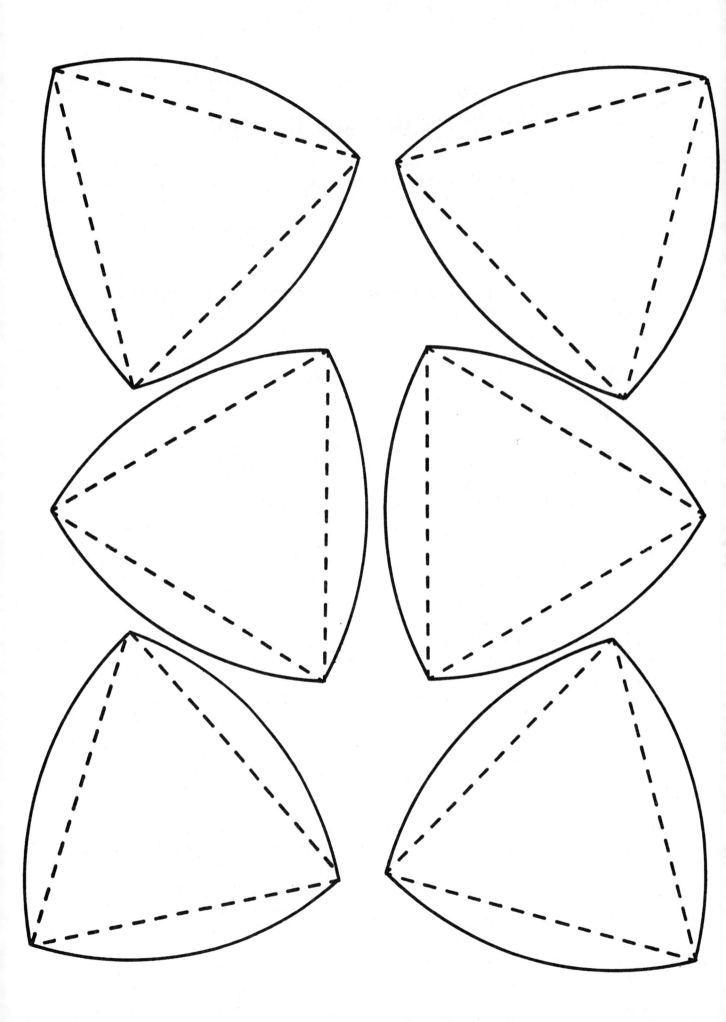

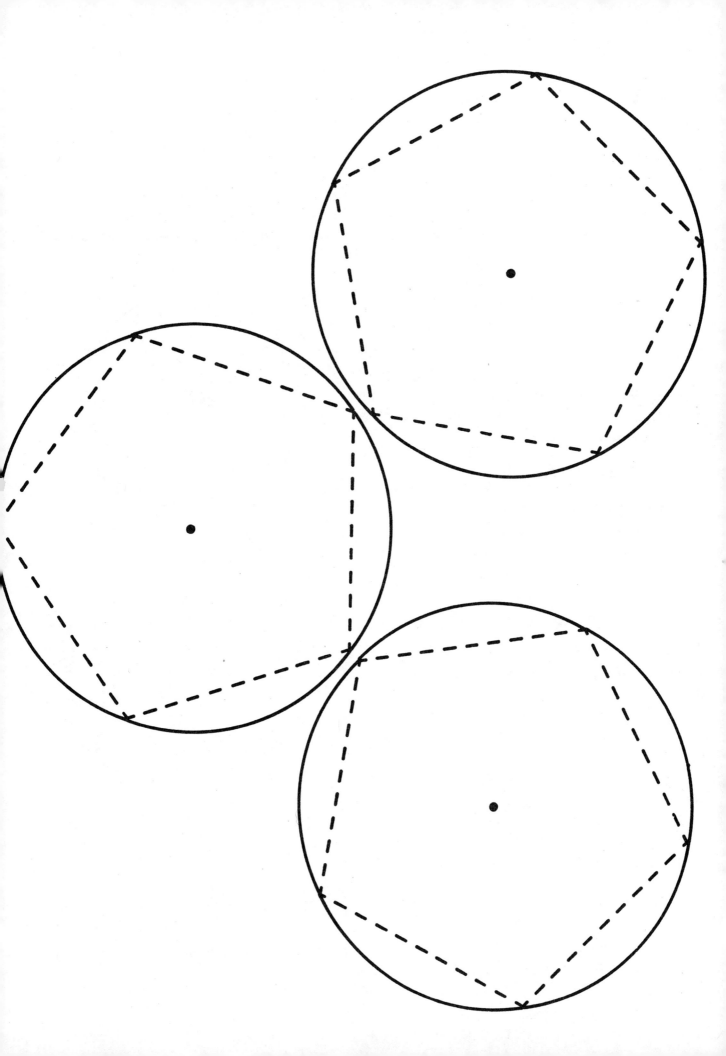

## HOW TO MAKE BIG JEWELS, continued

For the **icosahedron** (20 triangles), you have to follow the directions carefully because there are so many triangles to think about!

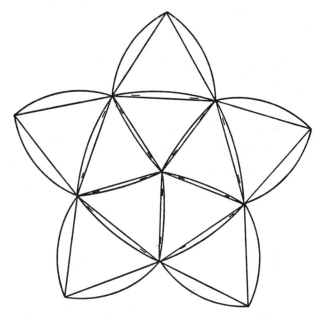

● Make a little tent by stapling *five* triangles together with their points touching at the center.

● Make another tent the same way.

● Put *petals on the flower* by stapling a triangle on each edge of a tent. Do it on the other tent, too.

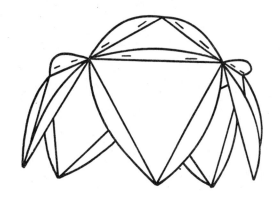

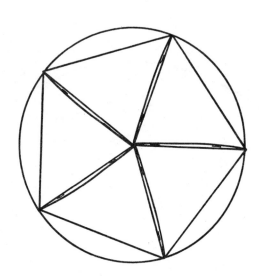

● Make each flower look like a tulip. Push the petals of one flower into the petals of the other until they nicely interlock. Staple tabs to make them stay that way.

**HOW TO MAKE BIG JEWELS, continued**

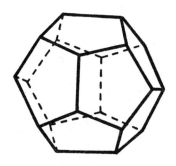

And finally, the **dodecahedron**. For this you need the 12 pentagons with dots in their centers. (Ignore the dots for now.)

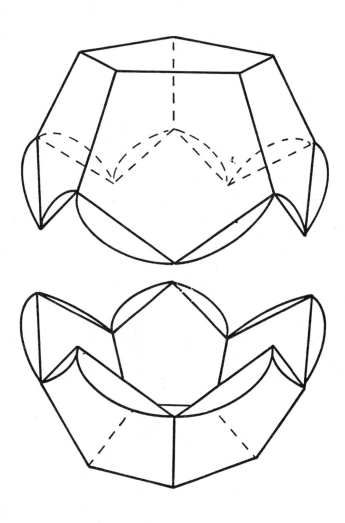

● Staple six pentagons together as follows: One pentagon will be the center. Each other pentagon shares **one edge** with the center pentagon. Staple these five pentagons to the center one to get a kind of flower again. There's still some space between each of the five pentagons.

● Lift the five pentagon *petals* up, join their edges, and staple to make a bowl with jagged edges.

● Make another bowl the same way.

●Turn one bowl upside down over the other and join them so that peaks go into valleys. Staple all tabs that hold them together.

You've made the dodecahedron! **Congratulations** on finishing a lot of complicated work. You now have four large jewels. Take time to admire them.

On the next page you'll find . . .

**THE GOLD IN THE JEWELS**

## Teacher's Guide to Student Pages 173-177

# HOW TO MAKE BIG JEWELS

### OVERVIEW OF THE ACTIVITIES

Give students only the first sheet to begin. The next sheet has the answer to the one question posed. Both activities connect well with each other, but should be given out one at a time. The first activity is more philosophical. The second activity is very "hands-on," which should please the more concrete students.

Note that in the first sheet, before they answer the questions, students will be exposed to some of the thought of the great Greek philosopher named Plato. He popularized and interpreted—but didn't discover—these solids around 350 B.C. Plato was not a great mathematician, but mathematicians flocked around him because he seemed to make their results meaningful. If you read the article in the *Tour Guide* newspaper first, you will be prepared to discuss Plato with the students.

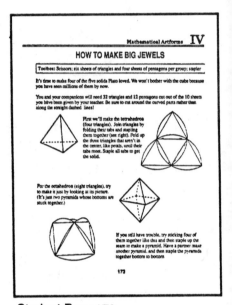

Student Page 173

### EXTENSIONS OF ALL FOUR ACTIVITIES

• Have one student do research on Plato and his times. Have another student research Einstein and his ideas in a general way, and another student restudy Leonardo Fibonacci. The three do a panel discussion, complete with costumes. They each know about who the others are, even though they lived in different times. They discuss these questions—or others:

1) What good are numbers and what is math for?
2) How do numbers give us information about the world?
3) Is the universe completely orderly?
4) What question do you wish you could really answer?

Give the panel the questions in advance, so they can be more prepared to be their character. Don't let it turn into an "Einstein-knows-more" session because each of these men had some important ideas. Just a couple of points to help you coach the panelists:

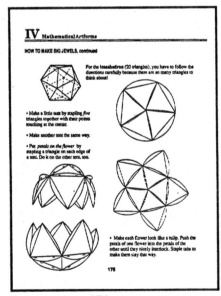

Student Page 176

**Plato** treated numbers as Qualities rather than quantities. He thought there was an Ideal Place where "pure number" and "ideal things" existed. On Earth we are just trying to find out about things by studying the ideas behind them. Modern times make room for idealists who speak of values. It might seem that Einstein could do

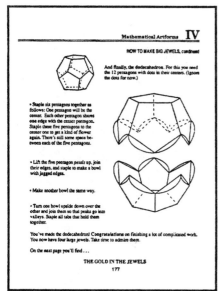

Student Page 177

more because of his knowledge of the scientific method, but Plato's point would be that "You helped invent the A-Bomb. Scientists should have been thinking about ideals instead."

**Einstein** represents the modern scientific point of view that numbers are tools of science and that we find out about the world by doing experiments with real things. He is like Plato in that he was an idealist about a lot of things. He also thought about things and how they seemed to be long before he put them into equations. But he based his thoughts on the scientific experiments of others. Plato thought Truth could be arrived at with no experiments, only deep reflection on meanings.

**Fibonacci** thought numbers were a kind of game. He was more interested in getting the solution of a puzzle than calculating something of useful value. He was a "pure mathematician" who explored number relations just for the enjoyment of it. He also didn't get philosophical about the meaning of his new decimal numbers; he just showed how they worked. But he probably knew that the new numbers would have great practical value to business in Europe, and wanted that to happen. Without these numbers, Einstein couldn't have done his science.

• Research the work of Buckminster Fuller, a sort of modern Plato who believed that the triangle is the best shape of all. He invented the Geodesic Dome made from triangles.

The Geodesic Dome is based on the icosahedron, but each triangle of that solid has been divided into four more triangles—not kept on a flat plane. The result is a half-"spherical" structure made of flat, smaller triangles. (A junior-high student of mine once asked me to help him design a full-sized dome he could live in. We did it and he built it.)

## Teacher's Guide to Student Pages 173-177

• This line of research can be continued with the "D-Stix" kit from Creative Publications. The kit is available in Junior size (down to 3rd grade), Apprentice size (intermediate), and Pre-engineering size (upper grades). Students can build the solids and the geodesic structure from sticks.

• Dungeons and Dragons dice (also sold as "Polyhedra Dice" from Creative Publications) come in these five shapes. A student may have them at home and can bring them to school. Have students evaluate which is best as a random die for which purposes. (One has only four faces with three numbers each; another has 20 faces available, and so forth.)

• All of these solids are great Christmas tree ornaments, classroom hangings, and the like, when they are colored. All lend themselves to group art projects because large triangles or pentagons can be artfully decorated with any medium, one by each student, then afterwards assembled to a solid. This is a nice way to group everyone's "Explosion of Stars" work with the pentagram—just make sure everyone leaves little staple-tabs on the pentagons they cut out.

# THE GOLD IN THE JEWELS

**Toolbox:** The icosahedron; dodecahedron; three rulers (mm); scissors; cardboard; paper punch; yarn or string; calculator

In the two most complicated jewels you made, there is a piece of **gold**. This gold is the Golden Rectangle, which has the Golden Ratio in it.

Follow these steps to find the Golden Rectangle in the dodecahedron:

● Pick one of the pentagon faces. Put a colored circle around its center dot.

● Find the pentagon exactly on the opposite side of the dodecahedron from the first pentagon you chose, and color a circle around its center dot as well.

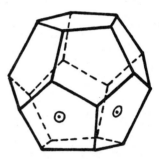

● Right next to the first pentagon you chose, find another pentagon and color a circle around *its* dot.

● Find the pentagon on the opposite side of the dodecahedron from the one you chose above and put a circle around the dot in its center.

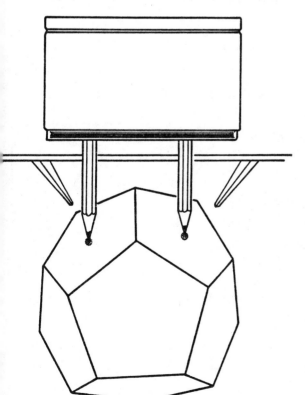

The four dots you chose should form a rectangle. To measure the **width** of it, put two pencils under a book at the edge of your desk so that the points stick out over the floor.

Adjust your pencil points so that one touches one circled dot on your dodecahedron and the other touches the neighboring circled dot that forms the rectangle width.

**181**

## THE GOLD IN THE JEWELS, continued

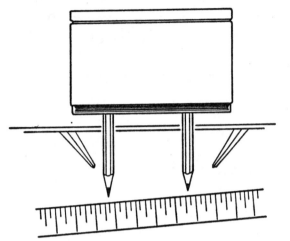

Then remove the solid and hold a ruler up to the pencil points. Measure how far apart they are.

The width of your rectangle is _____.\_\_\_\_ cm.
Find the length the same way: _____.\_\_\_\_cm.

**1.** The ratio of length-to-width of your rectangle is (to three decimal places): _____.\_\_\_\_
This should be close to **1.618**.

**2.** How far away from **1.618** is it? _____

**3.** Explain what might have caused your ratio to be a little different from **1.618**:

_____

_____

**4.** In one sentence explain where a Golden Rectangle can be found in a dodecahedron.

_____

_____

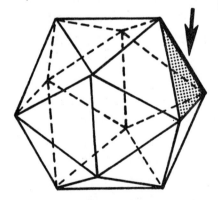

## GOLD IN THE ICOSAHEDRON

● On your icosahedron pick out a triangle **edge** segment.

● There's another triangle edge segment running the same direction but exactly on the **opposite** side of the icosahedron from the first one.

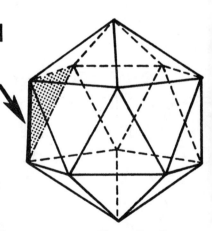

• These two segments are the ends of a Golden Rectangle. With the same pencil method used on the dodecahedron above, measure how long and how wide this rectangle is.

Length:_____.\_\_\_\_ cm    Width:_____.\_\_\_\_cm

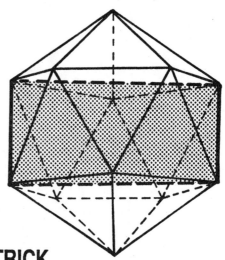

● The ratio of length-to-width for this rectangle is

_____._____ (to three decimal places).

How much does it differ from **1.618**? _____

● Estimate how many Golden Rectangles must be in your icosahedron.

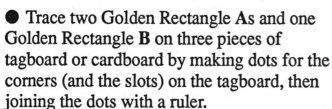

## A GOLDEN RECTANGLE TRICK

Here's how to make an icosahedron from Golden Rectangles.

● Cut out the copy of Golden Rectangle **A** given to you by your teacher, and cut along the slots.

● Cut out Golden Rectangle **B** that you've also been given, including the slot.

● Trace two Golden Rectangle **A**s and one Golden Rectangle **B** on three pieces of tagboard or cardboard by making dots for the corners (and the slots) on the tagboard, then joining the dots with a ruler.

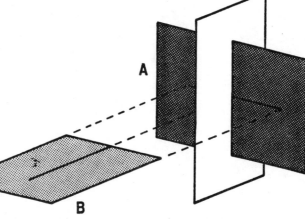

● Cut out the three rectangles, and cut the slots just wide enough to let a tagboard rectangle slip tightly through them.

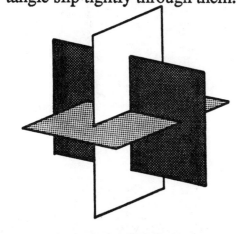

● Join them together as shown in the diagram.

● With a paper punch make a hole in each corner of each triangle.

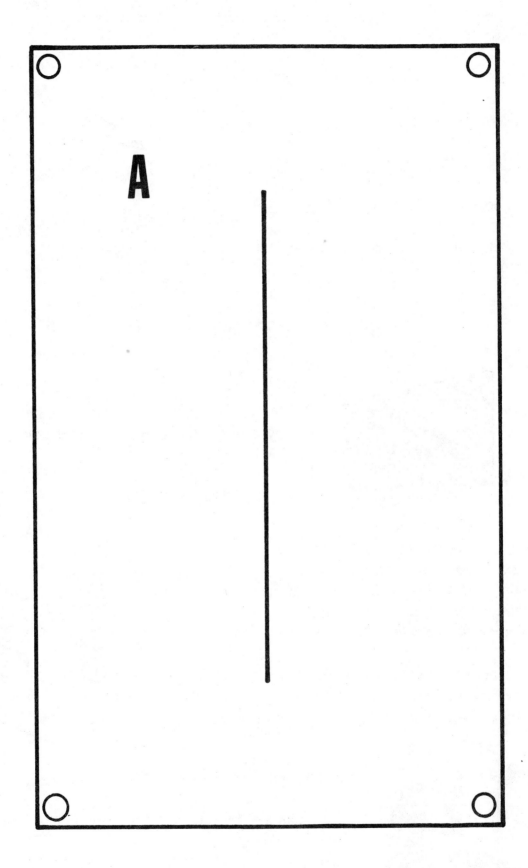

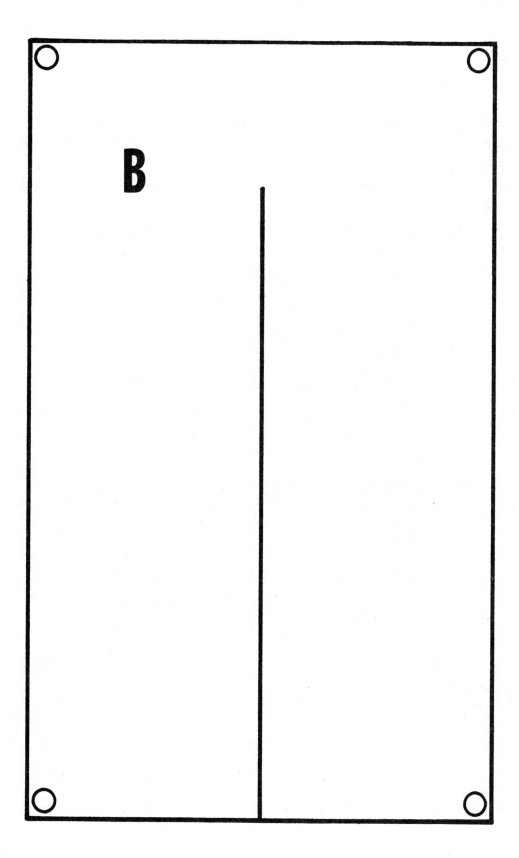

## THE GOLD IN THE JEWELS, continued

● Using yarn or string, *lace up a triangle* by putting string through three holes that form a triangle and then tying the string ends together (see figure below). Don't bend the rectangles while tying.

● Lace triangles until you have done 20 in all. As you get further along, you will find that one side of a triangle you are lacing already has string on it. You will need to lace only two sides of this one. You may also find that you can lace two or three triangles at a time before tying the ends.

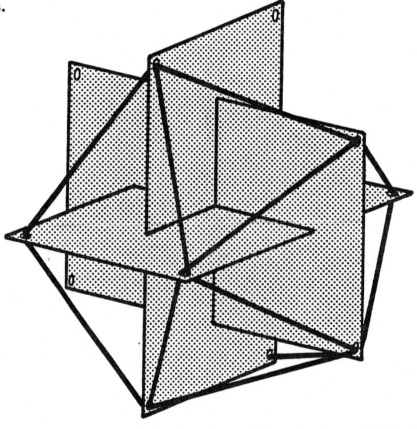

● You'll get a string icosahedron at the end, and you'll see its three Golden Rectangles (the cardboard ones) inside.

Now, in your own words, write one sentence describing where a Golden Rectangle is in an icosahedron. _____

_____

_____

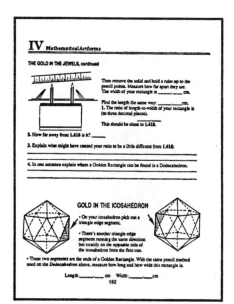

Student Page 181

Student Page 182

# THE GOLD IN THE JEWELS

## OVERVIEW OF THE ACTIVITY

The creation of the jewels has an aesthetic and geometrical learning payoff in itself. However, the major point for our **Tour** is that the two most complex Platonic Solids also have the Golden Rectangle (and therefore the Golden Ratio) in them. These solids are attractive **mathematical** designs that depend, as do the attractive designs of the human body and face, on the Golden Ratio for their structure.

The students also get a chance to explore the scientific method as they answer Question 3.

## ANSWERS TO QUESTIONS ON PAGE 182

**1.** Something around 1.618.

**2.** They should subtract their number from 1.618 (or subtract 1.618 from their number) to find this difference.

**3. There is a lot in this simple question.** It's a lead-in to a lesson on scientific method. Ask students to discuss in pairs or groups what factors might cause their final result to be inaccurate. (If it wasn't inaccurate at all, they may have taken *Plato's shortcut*—reason it out but don't experiment—or their errors happened to balance each other out.)

The ratio might be a bit different from the *ideal* 1.618 because:
  • The pencils were dull.
  • The dots were too big around and the actual centers of the pentagons were lost.
  • Ruler measurements were not accurate.
  • Ruler measurements could only be accurate to one decimal place.
  • The pencils got bumped.
  • The solid is off or crumpled.
  • "It shouldn't really be the Golden Ratio." (It should, say mathematicians all the way back to Pythagoras!)

Now ask students to list suggestions for each of the above that might increase the final result's accuracy. Send them back to recalculate the Golden Rectangle.

## Teacher's Guide to Student Pages 181-186

One of the more sophisticated solutions would be to average all the results in the room. Discuss this possibility *after* they remeasure. Discuss why it might be the best method (too-highs and too-lows should cancel each other's effect on the total used for the average). This is a good tie-in to the statistics concepts used with the body and face measurements of Unit III.

Discuss why the statistical method might have some inaccuracies, too (only one main reason): **Everyone's solid is somehow off the same way.** (Maybe all have faces slightly caved in.)

Calculate the average. (Let students organize the task and you observe and give feedback about the efficiency of their organization afterwards.) Draw conclusions from the size of this average.

**4.** Make sure they can generalize in one written sentence that states where a Golden Rectangle is in the dodecahedron. Something like: "The Golden Rectangle is made by joining four centers of faces, where two are next to each other and two on the opposite side are next each other." Hard! Introduce the word **adjacent** to mean *next to each other*. Have them try it with this word.

### THE GOLDEN RECTANGLE IN THE ICOSAHEDRON

Do the same activities and draw conclusions from the icosahedron measurement activity.

### A GOLDEN RECTANGLE TRICK

Be sure to distribute to each student or group a copy of Golden Rectangle A and Golden Rectangle B. Warn the students that the width of the slits they cut in each rectangle is determined by the thickness of the cardboard used. The slit should just rub the cardboard sliding through it. Some tape might steady the rectangles, too. Students should be able to verbalize something about the fact that in the icosahedron the two short sides of a Golden Rectangle coincide with edges of the triangular faces. These edges are on opposite sides of the icosahedron and run parallel to each other. The long sides of the Golden Rectangle are formed by joining the endpoints of the short sides.

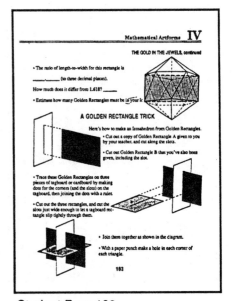

Student Page 183

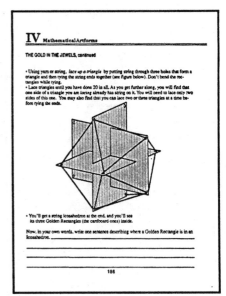

Student Page 186

# A LOOK AT THE TERRITORY: UNIT IV

● Once again, look at the section of the map where you have traveled. Discuss with another student the meaning of the arrows inside this piece and the arrows that go outside this piece to the Tour Map.

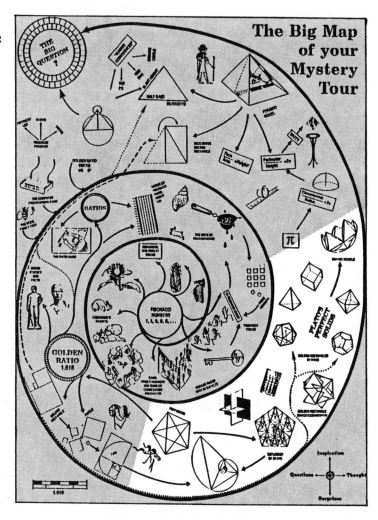

● As you've done before, look at this piece for three minutes and then draw it from memory (just making simple drawings in place of the complicated ones). Include the labels.

● Write a one-page description of the sights and action of this part of the **Tour**. Write down any questions you have and in a class discussion talk about anything that has amazed you.

● (Challenge) Work with other students to see who can draw the most complete map of the first four units' journey. Set up your rules in advance. For example, allow five minutes to study the Tour Map first, then put it away and draw for no more than 15 or 20 minutes. The map will be judged on the total number of topics shown, the number of arrows connecting things, general neatness, and so forth.

# LEARNING INVENTORY

> **Toolbox:** Calculator; ruler

This inventory will check which of the ideas of Unit IV are strong for you. If it shows that some of them are weak, confused, or missing from your memory, you should go back and study those. Then you can write something about them to show your teacher that you know them.

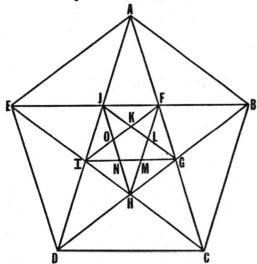

**1.** Here is a pentagram with Son of Star inside. Different places on it are lettered. List as many **Golden Ratios** as you can by naming the segment lengths that go on the top and bottom of the ratio.

Example: **AC/AB.**

(If you list fewer than three, it means you need review.)

_____   _____   _____

_____   _____   _____

**2.** On the diagram, if **FG** is 89 inches long, how long must **GC** be? _____

**3.** What is a Golden Triangle? _____

_____

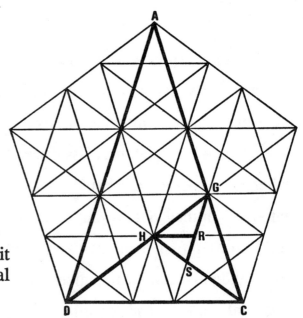

**4.** Find three Golden Triangles in this figure. They must have letters at all three of their points. Name them by their three letters.

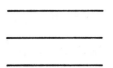

_____

_____

_____

**5.** Draw the beginning of a spiral in this pentagram. Place one more line segment so that it makes the next Golden Triangle that the spiral hits.

**6.** How is the Golden Triangle like the Golden Rectangle? Give two different ways.

_____

_____

**7.** Name the five perfect solids.

_____  _____  _____

_____  _____

Tell why they are called *perfect*.

_____

_____

_____

_____

**8.** What does the **Golden Ratio** have to do with these solids?_____

_____

What did Plato have to do with them?_____

_____

_____

**9.** In the space to the left, try to draw the solid that has four faces, then name it.

**10.** How is the Golden Ratio found in the 12-faced figure? _____

_____

_____

## Teacher's Guide to Student Pages 190-191

# LEARNING INVENTORY

## ABOUT THIS INVENTORY

The questions require a lot of thought and understanding. Here are some suggestions for insuring more success and learning with its use:

• Have students complete the Inventory in groups and award a group score for their final answers;

• Let students research their past papers while answering the questions (open book ); or

• Have students try it individually, then encourage them to research the answers afterwards to improve their scores.

The main purpose of the Inventory is to deepen by one more level the concepts they have learned by asking them to *apply* them.

## ANSWERS TO QUESTIONS ON PAGE 190-191

**1.** There are many possibilities for Golden Ratios here. Here are 6: AC/CD, FC/AF, AC/FC, GJ/GK, GF/LF, FH/FG, and some that may be between segments located farther from each other. Chances are good that a review of the first activity in Unit IV will help this concept sink in.

**2.** The students should know that the two segments named are in Golden Ratio to each other. This means they can calculate the longer from the shorter this way: 89 x 1.618 = 144. Some may realize that 89 is a Fibonacci Number and so it is in Golden Ratio to 144, the next Fibonacci, and have to do no calculating.

**3.** A Golden Triangle is an isosceles triangle with angles 36°, 72°, and 72°.

**4.** Possible answers are ADC, GDC, CGH, GHS, HSR. The criterion here is that **any** tall, narrow-shaped isosceles triangle in the pentagram is a Golden Triangle (angles 36°,72°,72°).

To be able to really *see* these, students may need to go back and see again the infinite chain of decreasing-sized Golden Triangles that spirals out of the large one.

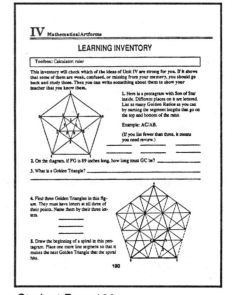

Student Page 190

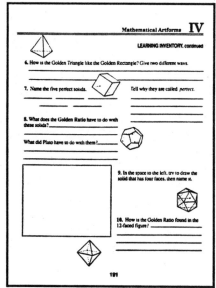

Student Page 191

**5.** The spiral can start at the top of any large Golden Triangle. Spirals can wind either way. Consult the illustration on page 166 for the exact location of the spiral on the triangles.

**6.** Both have an infinity of the same shape in them. These are spiraling down to a point. Thus the seashell can be found in both of them. Both, of course, have 1.618 . . . as the ratio of two of their segments.

**7.** Tetrahedron, cube, octahedron, dodecahedron, icosahedron. They are *perfect* because they are made totally from one kind of face, and the faces have all sides equal. Only these five are possible.

**8.** Two of the solids (dodecahedron and icosahedron) have the Golden Rectangle (with Golden Ratio) in them. Plato popularized them and gave them meanings in philosophy. They are often called the **Platonic Solids** because of this.

**9.** Any reasonable attempt at drawing the tetrahedron is good, but to let their right brains comprehend the solid it's wise to have them redraw it while looking at the solid.

**10.** The Golden Ratio is found in the dodecahedron by making a rectangle joining the center dots of faces. We pick center dots of two adjacent faces and centers of the two adjacent faces on the opposite side of the solid. (They may not say it this technically, of course, but encourage them to use "adjacent.")

# UNIT V: GEOMETRY, THE PYRAMID, AND THE MOON

## PACKING FOR EGYPT AND A MOON TRIP

**Toolbox:** Paper cup or glass; Ball (between softball and volleyball sized); three 1-ft rulers with metric scale; calculator

In this unit you will reach the climax of your **Mystery Tour**. It's the strangest and most exotic of the adventures we'll take. We'll travel to Egypt and to the moon to find more **Golden Ratios**. In the journey we'll also encounter another very famous number in a very unexpected place.

As you know, it's necessary to prepare for a long journey—to pack important things to take along. You're about to read of a fabulous ancient journey and how the travelers prepared for it. But you will also have to prepare **yourself** for **your** journey by packing in a few ideas that you'll need along the way. This first activity will help you dust off some old ideas and pack a few new ones.

First you'll need to be comfortable with **circles**. Here are a few useful facts you may have learned before.

The **circumference** of a circle is the distance around the circle, as measured along its curved edge. *Circum-* means **around** and *fer* means **carry** in Latin.

The **diameter** is the distance clear across a circle (that is, two radii). The diameter must be measured through the **center** of a circle.

The **radius** of a circle is the distance between the center and the edge. If we have more than one radius, we say **radii** ("ray-dee-eye").

Perhaps the first concern about the distance around a circle was to answer how far some person or animal had to carry something. Geometry has a lot of Latinized words because until about 300 years ago everyone studied geometry in Latin.

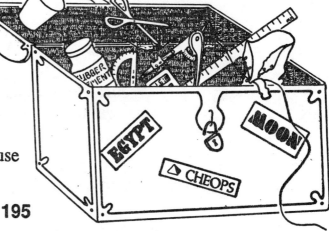

# MEASURING PROBLEM

● Take a paper cup or glass and measure the diameter of its top. Do this to an accuracy of a mm (.1 cm), and measure to the outside edges of the top:

_____.____cm.

Now, how will you accurately measure the **circumference** of the top? Your ruler doesn't bend! There's a way to do it *accurately* with an ordinary ruler. Can you figure out how?

Think about it and try it, then fill in your answer here:

_____.____ cm.

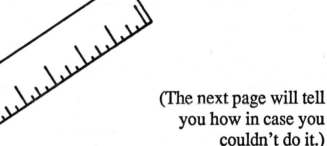

(The next page will tell you how in case you couldn't do it.)

**Here's a bigger challenge:**

● Take the ball and *accurately* measure its **diameter**. (**HINT:** You'll need some other things to go along with your ruler.)

Diameter = _____.____ cm.

Its radius is_____.____ cm.

**Accurately** measure its **circumference** by the same kind of trick that was needed for the cup:

_____.____ cm.

(Again, the next pages will tell you how to do this if you had trouble.)

# THE SOLUTION TO THE MEASURING PROBLEM

If you had trouble being accurate in measuring the circumferences of cup and ball and the diameter of the ball, follow these instructions and drawings. Otherwise go on to the next page.

To determine the **circumference** of the **cup:**

● Put a mark on the outside top edge.

● Lay the cup down with your mark touching the first line (or starting end) of the ruler.

● Roll and guide the cup's edge along the ruler until the mark comes back around to touch the ruler again.

● That point marks the length of the circumference.

● If you didn't do it this way, try again and record your answer on the previous page.

197

## THE SOLUTION TO THE MEASURING PROBLEM, continued

The most accurate way to measure the **circumference** of the **ball** is to get a long piece of paper (or the floor if it's ok to mark on it). Use the same method you used with the cup circumference—see figure at right.

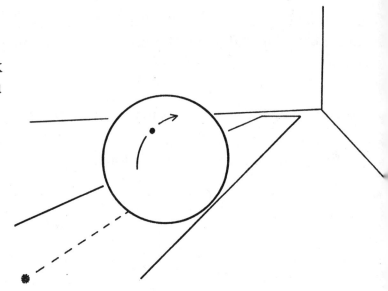

The most accurate way to measure the **diameter** of the **ball** is to use the three 1-ft. rulers.

● With a friend, stand the two rulers on the floor or table with their 1-cm marks visible at their bottoms.

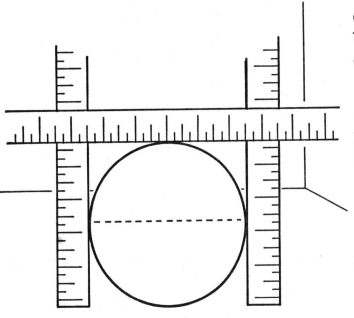

● Cross them with the third ruler, like the bar of an "H." Always make sure the bar crosses each ruler at the same number.

● Now, make the "H" wide enough and the bar just high enough to let the ball graze it as it rolls under.

● After you have checked that each end of the bar is at the same height on the ruler and the ball still just touches, note the height. This height is the diameter of the ball. Write it on page 196.

# FINDING THE CIRCLE NUMBER

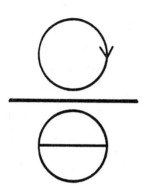

Use the measurements you finally found for the cup to calculate this ratio:

$$\frac{\text{Circumference}}{\text{Diameter}}$$

to two decimal places:_____

It should be very close to **3.14**. If it's not, recheck your measurements, make sure the cup isn't warped, and try it again.

If you could do the measurements and calculation to the finest precision, you would get this number: **3.1415926535. . . .** We usually just write **3.14**. It's the number called **Pi (π)**, which is a Greek letter *P*. It can be expressed almost exactly in fraction language as **3 1/7**. It tells

● How many diameters of a circle can be bent and laid around that circle's rim.

● That 3 1/7 diameters make one circumference no matter what size the circle.

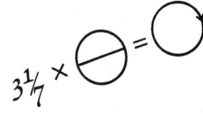

● That the diameter of a circle is *about* 1/3 the circumference in length.

● That 6 2/7 radii would fit around the edge of a circle.

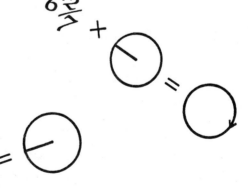

● That the radius of a circle is *about* 1/6 the rim's length.

## EXPERIMENTS

**1.** Find a shoelace or other piece of string. Measure it

_____.____ cm

and predict how large a circle (i.e., the diameter) it would make if it were laid in a circle shape on the floor.

_____.____ cm.

Then check and see.

**2.** Estimate how many times a piece of string that just reaches around your head could reach along the length of your body: _____ times.

Then try it with some string.
Answer: _____ times.

**3.** Find the ratio of the circumference of the ball to its diameter:

_____ Is it very near **3.14**? ____

If it's not, recheck your measurements and try again. (And check that the ball is really round.)

**4.** What should the ratio of the circumference to the radius be?
Predict it here._____

Now calculate this ratio using the measurements you wrote for the ball two pages ago. _____

In question **#4** above, you should recognize that the ratio of the circumference to the radius is 2 x $\pi$. Now, with the valuable concept of $\pi$ and the names of parts of circles, you are packed for your trip to Egypt and the moon—to begin on the next page! First, read the article called "The History of $\pi$" in your *Tour Guide* newspaper.

**STOP**

# UNIT V: GEOMETRY, THE PYRAMID, AND THE MOON

Student Page 195

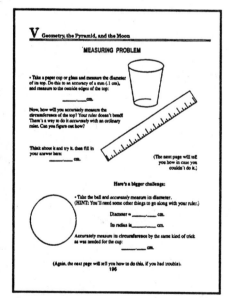

Student Page 196

## PACKING FOR EGYPT AND A MOON TRIP

### AN OVERVIEW OF UNIT V

Welcome to what I consider the most exciting unit! This is really the climax of the **Tour**. Students have traced the Fibonacci Numbers mathematically and in Nature, but then found that they *merge* with the versatile Golden Ratio, revered from antiquity. They have become more comfortable with searching for ratios. Here they'll unearth what I feel is one of the most *exciting* results that relate to two of the most *exotic* places—the **Great Pyramid** and the **Moon**.

### AN OVERVIEW OF THIS ACTIVITY

Because they'll need to understand the meaning of the Pyramid, we *pack for the journey* by first truly comprehending what $\pi$ (pi) is. (A ratio, of course.) Keep their eyes on the purpose of finding why the Pyramid was built and it'll add motivation for $\pi$. By the way, there are many high-school seniors who still haven't gained this simple tool! Instead, they fear and mystify it.

Now is the students' time to get crystal clear about $\pi$. They get to experimentally derive it as a ratio, conceptualize its role in circles in several ways, and learn about its history. The student pages will sequence these approaches.

### MEASURING THE CUP AND BALL

The answer to students' calculations of **Circumference/Diameter** should be about 3.14, though few will be this close. If below 3.1 or above 3.2, have them recheck the procedure. The cup or ball may be warped, or methods were sloppy.

This is another good chance to discuss scientific method. An average of everyone's findings should theoretically be very close to 3.14. If it's not, the methodology is suspect.

## Teacher's Guide to Student Pages 195-200

### DISCUSSION

Make sure the students discuss why each of the five statements about π are really saying the same thing. It will develop their number intuition.

### ANSWERS TO EXPERIMENTS ON PAGE 200

The students should use π = "about 3" to make the estimates in #1, #2, and #3.

In #4 the ratio should be 6.28, or *twice* π, since the radius is only *half* as big as a diameter. This is the basis for the usual formula for circumference: $C = 2\pi r$, meaning the circumference of any circle is twice π times the radius length.

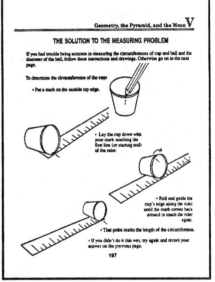

Student Page 197

### EXTENSION ACTIVITIES

If you wish to carry the theme of π even further, here are a few ways to do it:

• An earlier article in the *Tour Guide* newspaper gives the circumference of the Earth calculated by Eratosthenes as 25,000 miles. What would have been his calculated radius for the Earth? (Answer: $25,000 \div 2\pi = 3978$ miles, the real value being about 3962 miles.)

• Here is π to 50 decimal places:

3.1415926535 8979323846 2643383279 5028841971 6939937510

This is a good sample of the kind of random digits that π has. Any irrational number, and π is one, has unpredictable patterns in its digits. Take a poll of the digits and tabulate the number of 0s, 1s, 2s, etc. Draw conclusions about whether they seem really *random*, or whether a certain digit or digits are preferred. (3 is definitely preferred—nine occurrences so far—and its close relative 9—with eight occurrences—is too. Since the whole number part is 3, I'm not surprised!)

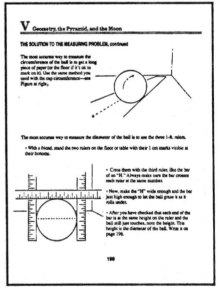

Student Page 200

Post Script: Random eventually wins, because there are only four 3s in the next 50 digits and four 3s in the 50 after that, and then my eyes start crossing.

# BUILDING AND EXPLORING A GREAT PYRAMID

I hope you find these next few activities some of the most mysterious and interesting ones you've done. You're going to take a fascinating trip to Egypt, where you'll search an awesome building for mathematical clues to why it was built. Then you'll bring the moon to Earth for a soft landing. And there are some other things besides.

One of the largest buildings in the world is the Great Pyramid of Cheops on the Giza Plateau, near the Nile River in Egypt. We'll go after some of our old number friends there.

**Khonsu, Egyptian god of the moon**

**Re⁰, the Egyptian sun god at noon**

To get in the mood for this mysterious trip, please read the large story/article in your *Tour Guide* newspaper called "Inside the Great Pyramid" and the short article called "Who Was Cheops, Anyway?" You'll find them very interesting. Then return here to begin building a Pyramid of your own. See you in a while!

**STOP**

# STEPS TO BUILDING A GREAT PYRAMID

**Toolbox:** A piece of flat posterboard about 1 ft. square; five pieces of 8 1/2 x 11 inch tagboard, or thin cardboard; a copy of triangle **A** and a copy of triangle **B**; metric ruler; scissors; tape; rubber cement

● Mark the triangles on tagboard this way:

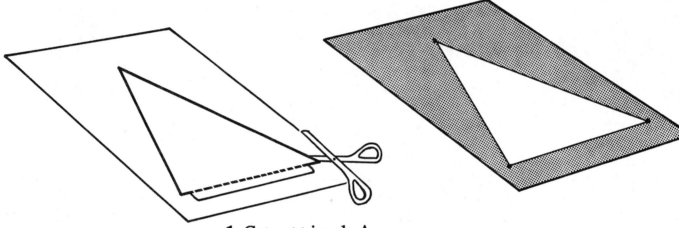

**1.** Cut out triangle **A**.

**2.** Lay it on your tagboard as shown.

**3.** Mark dots for each point of the triangle.

**4.** Join these dots with a ruler.

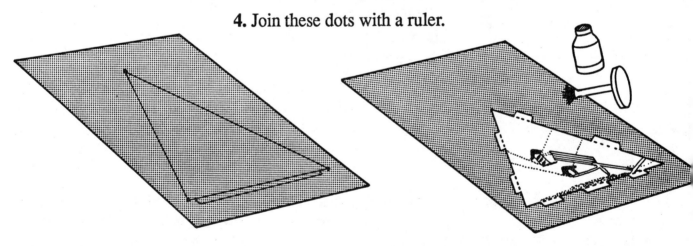

**5.** Trace the tab on the triangle.

**6.** Do this to three other pieces of tagboard.

**7.** Glue the page with triangle **B** onto a piece of tagboard with rubber cement and cut it out along the solid line (include tabs).

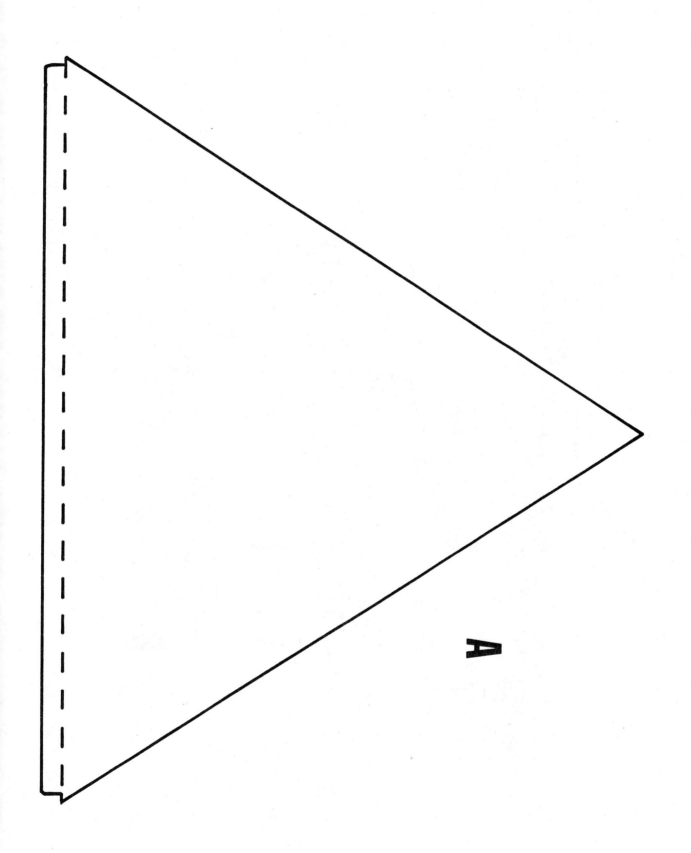

A

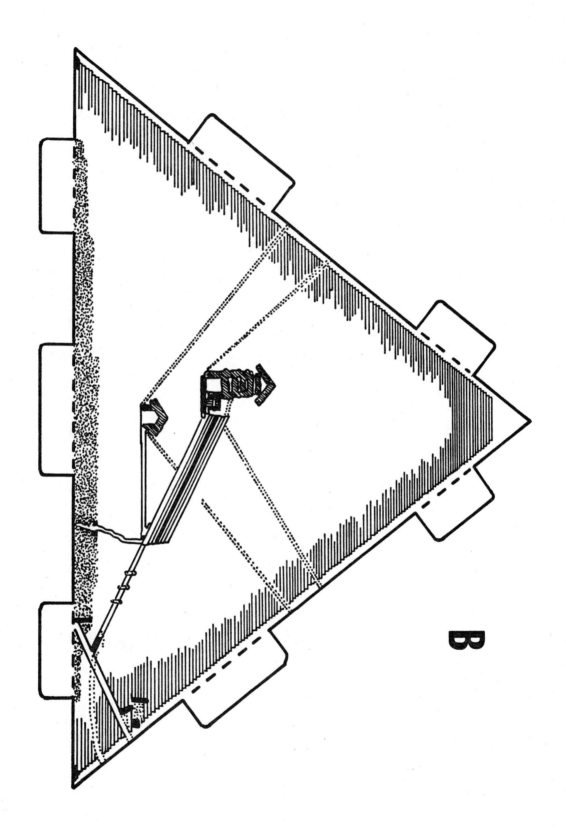

B

## MORE STEPS!

● Carefully cut out all triangles drawn on tagboard (include tabs).

● Lay the four triangle As on your desk like this, with long edges together, and tape the seams.

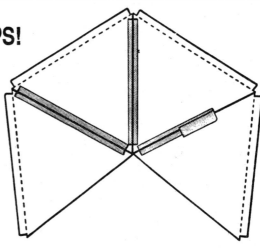

● Using your protractor and ruler, draw a perfect square, 20 cm to a side, in the middle of the posterboard. Make sure the four corners are 90°. Do it lightly in pencil first!

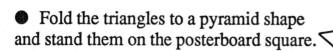

● Fold the triangles to a pyramid shape and stand them on the posterboard square.

● When you have "squared up the pyramid," tape the tabs to the posterboard. One triangle should be left as a swinging door you can open.

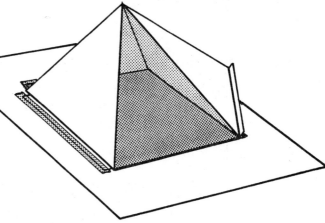

● Open the door and fold the tabs on triangle **B** so they come forward. Slip triangle **B** into the middle of the pyramid. Its point should be right in the point of the pyramid, and its edges should be cutting the pyramid's sides in half. Tape the tabs to the pyramid sides.

● Now you have a pyramid that shows its inside view. Put marks on the outside where the secret entrance to the pyramid is and where Al Mamun broke in.

# PYRAMID EXPERIMENTS

## Experiment 1

● Measure the height of the pyramid's point (**vertex**) above the center of the base to the nearest .1 cm:
_____.____ cm.

**Vertex**

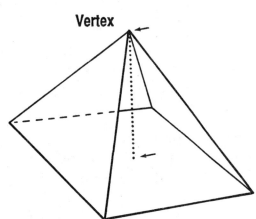

● Measure the length of the bottom (**base**) of one of the triangles:
_____.____ cm.

● Measure the length from bottom center to top on one of the side triangles of the pyramid. (This is called the **altitude** of the triangle and the **apothegm** of the pyramid):
_____.____ cm.

● The area, in square cm, of a triangle is found by multiplying **half** the base length times the altitude. Calculate the area of one **face** (one of the side triangles):

_____.____square cm.

**Base**

● Multiply the **height** of the pyramid (from the first step on this page) times **itself** (that is, "square the height"):

_____.____ square cm.

● Compare your last two answers (the face area and square of the height). If they are *very* different, check your measurements and calculations because on the Great Pyramid they are known to be the same.

This is a strange property of the Great Pyramid of Cheops, namely, that **the square of its height equals the area of its face. (Remember** *square* **means to take something times itself.)**

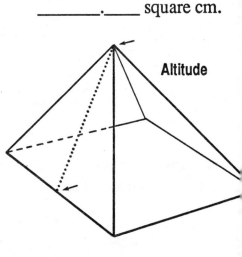

**Altitude**

## Experiment 2

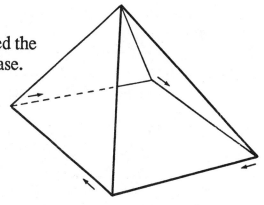

● Find the **length** around the **base** of the pyramid, called the **perimeter** ("pe-<u>rim</u>-iter" measures the <u>rim</u>) of the base. (Do you need to measure all four sides?)

The perimeter = _____.____ cm

● Measure the **height** (to the vertex) of the pyramid :

_____.____ cm.

● Find the ratio of the perimeter of the base to the height by dividing:

perimeter ÷ height = _____.____

The answer *should* look *familiar*! If it doesn't, divide it by 2 and check for familiarity:

_____.____ What is it? _____ Right!

This is a very famous number the Egyptians wanted to make sure was in their most famous building!

**The Hidden Meaning of Experiment 2:** Experiment 2 helps give us a clue about what the Egyptians may have had in mind when they built the Pyramid. Remember, a few pages ago you divided the circumference of a ball by its radius, and got $2\pi$. On a half-ball (called a half-sphere), the circumference divided by its height (radius) must be $2\pi$ also.

You've divided the perimeter of the pyramid by its height and obtained $2\pi$. The Pyramid is acting mathematically like a half-ball or half-sphere!

# A MIND TRIP

**Toolbox:** A wild imagination

Let a classmate or your teacher read the following paragraphs s-l-o-w-l-y to you while you relax and close your eyes. It's best to have a world globe in the room before starting.

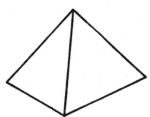

"Relax. . . . . Relax. . . . You see the Great Pyramid, majestic on the desert. Suddenly it starts to shimmer and it's almost transparent so you can see the far sides. It looks hollow and light, like a feather. . . .

"It lifts into the air. It's hovering like a spacecraft in the air. Focus on this as clearly as you can. Then you notice that the base is slowly getting rounded at the corners, and the sides are bulging out a bit.

"The point of the Pyramid stays the same height, but the triangle sides are puffing out until there's a smooth roundness instead of a point. The edges are getting rounded—the Pyramid is slowly becoming a half-sphere shape, like a sliced bubble!

"This huge half-bubble shrinks until it's the size of the world globe in the room and settles onto the top half (without hanging up on the globe's brackets and supports). The Pyramid bubble disappears and only the globe is there.

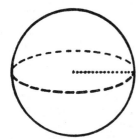

"Then something really strange happens. The globe splits into a top half and a bottom half! The two rise into the air. They go through a reverse of what happened before. A point forms on top of each while four sides flatten to triangles and the bottom gets more square.

"They're becoming two pyramids! They still have the countries and ocean printed on their sides! They join together and float back to be in the globe stand. But now the globe has points, a diamond shape, kind of like the octahedron.

"Now you can come back to the room . . . ."

Discuss your experience with your classmates.

## LET'S TALK ABOUT THE MEANING OF THIS TRIP

There's a lot of evidence that the Egyptians knew the Earth is round, that they even knew its size, and that they wanted the Pyramid to be *tuned* to that size.

For instance, they made the Pyramid large enough that *Exactly* **480** of them (a nice round number) could lie end to end along **one degree** of longitude at the equator. On your globe move your fingernail this distance. (How many Pyramids would go clear around the equator?)

_____

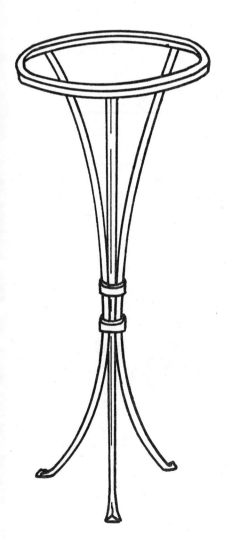

There's other evidence that the Egyptians wanted the Pyramid to be somehow like *half* the Earth. One example is found in the article in the *Tour Guide* newspaper called "More Half-Earth Evidence for the Pyramid." Read that article and return here.

**STOP**

What you found out from the article and your measuring is evidence that the Egyptians were trying to make a **scale model** of half the Earth, but there was no way they could make it *round*. The next best thing was to make it have π, the circle number, in the same way that a half-sphere has π.

Give your evaluation of what you think about the *tuned* theory and the half-Earth theory so far: _____

_____

_____

_____

In the next lesson you'll see that the Egyptians also wanted to make the Great Pyramid imitate natural growing things as well!

## Teacher's Guide to Student Pages 203-211

# BUILDING AND EXPLORING A GREAT PYRAMID

### ABOUT THIS ACTIVITY

On to the **Great Pyramid**! This building holds a lot of fascination for youngsters and adults alike. It offers opportunities for fantasy, drama, art, research, and of course, math.

Students will spend quite a bit of time reading about the Pyramid in the *Tour Guide* newspaper before they actually start this activity. If you want, you can simply request that they start on the articles indicated. Pass out the activity pages afterwards. That way students won't get antsy to start the Pyramid construction.

### REFERENCES FOR INTERDISCIPLINARY CURRICULUM

This is a golden opportunity for interdisciplinary curriculum. You may get *stuck* here doing exciting things for a week! These are some references that may help broaden the possibilities for you. They are available from **Zephyr Press** (see bibliography).

**Architexture** by Patton and Maxon. For intermediate students, exploring the architecture of many eras.

**Ancient Egypt** by Clements, et al. Research projects for grades 2-8.

**Archeology** by Tanner. Helps students dig into archeology.

**Dig 2.** An archaeological simulation game about reconstructing a lost culture. Intermediate grades and up.

**Mummy's Message.** A simulation of tomb and pyramid exploration. Grade 5-12.

**The Timetables of History** by Grun. Ties together many periods of history. Grades 5-adult.

A good hardbound reference book that is the source of several ideas in this section is **Secrets of the Great Pyramid** by Thompkins. It's chock full of stories, pictures, lore, math, and more. It's written for the interested adult reader, but many youngsters would enjoy parts of it,

Student Page 203

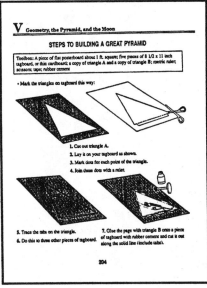

Student Page 204

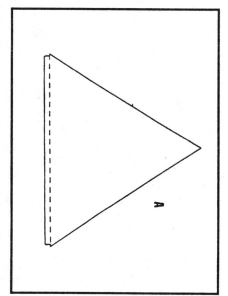

Student Page 205

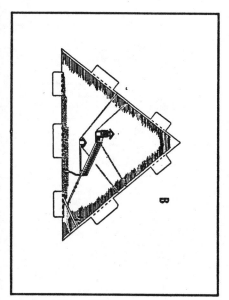

Student Page 206

especially the pictures. It gets a lot of credit for my interest in this whole subject.

## EXTENSION ACTIVITIES RELATED TO THE GREAT PYRAMID'S HISTORY

• Bring the class to a location (or ask each student to visit that location on the weekend) where they can see the amount of acreage the Pyramid covers. It takes up 13 acres!

Call the City or County Parks Department and ask what parks or empty tracts are 13 acres or more, and what their exact acreage is. (A confident student can do this, too. I always encourage students to do telephone research.) Have the students estimate what part of the park or land is the size of the Pyramid base. Only by viewing it, though, will they get the sense of size.

• As an alternative, do this excellent spatial estimation activity. Take the class outside and have them figure out in any way they can how far 755 feet is. A yardstick or short tape measure is all that is needed. They need to develop a pacing system, then figure out the length of a city block. Then tally how many blocks long this is.

This is the length of the base of the Pyramid! From their block tally, they will know how far 610 feet is. This is how far up the slope of one triangle face goes (the **apothegm**, it's called technically). Imagine those 610 feet (2+ city blocks) tilted up in the air and your trying to find a doorway in them!

A refinement: The slant of the pyramid side is about 52°. Ask someone to mark a piece of posterboard with a line making a 52° angle with the bottom. Then cut off the whole piece at that angle. Presto! You have a good suggestion of the slope to have outside with you. Now picture the 610 ft.—as 2+ blocks—slanted this angle and your trying to walk up it to search!

• Preferably after either extension above, encourage students to close their eyes and relax. (A good book to help you feel secure with visualization exercises is **200 Ways of Using Imagery in the Classroom** by Bagley and Hess). Re-read **slowly** all or part of the selection "Inside the Great Pyramid" from the *Tour Guide* newspaper as they visualize the adventures and the sizes of things. It will have a dramatic effect.

• Give them a writing assignment: "Describe some strong visualization or feeling that arose during the visualization activity. Write from the viewpoint of someone who was with Al Mamun." Students may also wish to describe Prince Al Mamun's activities as seen by an observer.

• Many young people come up with compelling pictures during a visualization. Encourage them to draw, whether realistically or abstractly, the image or impression that struck them the most. Ask those who feel courageous to describe the meaning of the picture to the class.

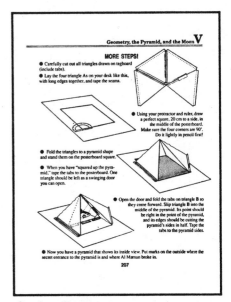

Student Page 207

## THE PYRAMID CONSTRUCTION

The purpose of the Pyramid construction is to gain hands-on experience of the various measurements and ratios of it. It also gives a sense of the relative size of the passages and chambers.

You can save students time if you photocopy the five necessary construction triangles (found on pages 205-206) right onto tagboard. I hope it's possible on your photocopier.

An enthusiastic student may want to cover the Pyramid with a texture like sandpaper, brown-painted paper, or brown lined paper. (**Do this after measurements are done.**) Placing it in a sandbox with dunes around makes an effective model. There are some smaller pyramids with the Great one on the Giza Plateau, and the Sphinx is there too, as mentioned in the *Tour Guide* newspaper story. Some students may enjoy working together to make a full model of the Plateau from pictures common to many reference books.

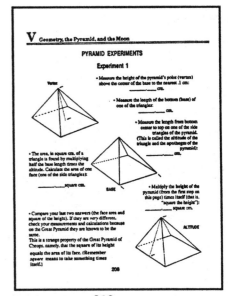

Student Page 208

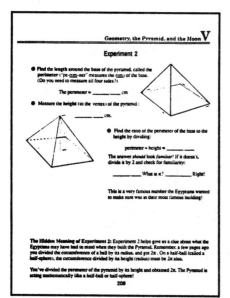

Student Page 209

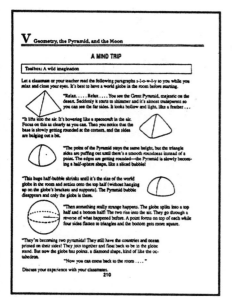

Student Page 210

## EXPERIMENT 1

This is a curious mathematical fact. It's true but too hard to mathematically prove here that the square of the height equaling the area of a face is directly related to the fact that the Golden Ratio is in the Pyramid. How the Ratio's in there, though, will be highlighted in the next activity.

So this experiment is left as a curiosity. Just make sure students can state that it is a mathematical characteristic of the Great Pyramid only. And it's not a coincidence—the Egyptians wanted it that way.

## EXPERIMENT 2

This finding is more interesting because it reveals that $\pi$ is definitely in the Pyramid. The really fascinating fact, though, is that $\pi$ is in there *exactly* the way it is in a half-sphere! This and several other pieces of evidence coincide to strongly hint that the Pyramid was meant to be a model (a **scale model**) of half the Earth! The discussion of Experiment 2 on the student page brings this out.

Scale model means that if you magnify the Pyramid a certain number of times, it will be as big as the Earth. Usually the scale chosen is a nice round number. That's the case with the Pyramid. The discussion with the globe and the article in the *Tour Guide* newspaper "More Half-Earth Evidence for the Pyramid" help develop this idea.

## A NOTE ON LONGITUDE

If your students are vague on what **longitude** means, have a discussion of this concept with the help of a globe and a reference book. Clarify the fact that longitude is in **degrees** (because it expresses an **angle** whose point or vertex is at the center of the Earth).

Yet it expresses **distance** on the Earth, too, because a navigator can travel so many degrees of longitude on the equator. If the navigator travels the same number of degrees near Alaska, the actual **distance** meant by these degrees is not the same. The Egyptians were interested in equator degrees and their distance apart.

In your discussion bring students back to the relationship of the Pyramid's size to equator degrees of longitude discussed on their sheets.

## ABOUT THE MIND TRIP

The fantasy that students are asked to imagine about the Pyramid shape transforming into a half-sphere and the globe to two Pyramids would be best led by you or they can lead each other in pairs. It's good for them to be guided to relax well first. This helps to firm up the concept of the lesson and paves the way for the discussion afterwards. Young people are always enthusiastic about sharing their experiences after a Mind Trip.

## THE "LET'S TALK" SECTION

Exactly 172,800 Great Pyramids would reach around the equator. This is a nice, fairly round number. The really astounding thing, though, is that the Pyramid extends exactly 1/8 of a minute of degree of length at the equator. Probabilistically, it's impossible for this to be a coincidence.

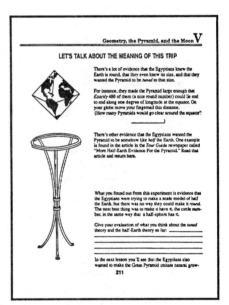

Student Page 211

# FINDING THE GOLD IN THE PYRAMID

> **Toolbox:** Protractor; calculator; scissors; ruler; copies of triangle **A** and triangle **B** of Pyramid model

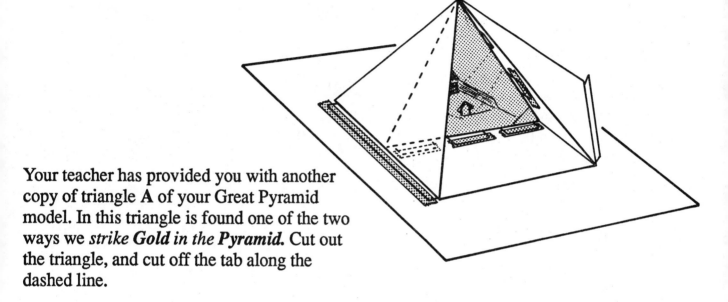

Your teacher has provided you with another copy of triangle **A** of your Great Pyramid model. In this triangle is found one of the two ways we *strike Gold in the Pyramid.* Cut out the triangle, and cut off the tab along the dashed line.

No, this triangle is not a Golden Triangle. Remember that a Golden Triangle has a top (apex) angle of 72°. What apex angle does this triangle have? (Use your protractor.)

_____°

Let's explore further. What are the usual ways you have learned to explore things during this **Mystery Tour**? With numbers, of course. We turn things into numbers, whether they be pinecones, pentagram stars, or Fibonacci Numbers (which we turned into ratio numbers). We then look for a pattern or familiarity in the numbers.

There are two usual ways to turn this triangle into numbers. Either measure angles or measure sides and related things like the height (altitude). Do all these things and look for patterns. Any luck?

Probably not. It took mathematicians a long time to find this out, too. On the next page are the clues you need.

## FINDING THE GOLD IN THE PYRAMID, continued

### CLUES

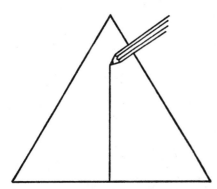 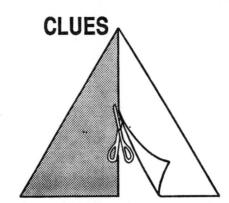 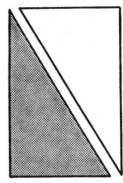

● Draw the altitude line in the triangle—from the top to the center of the base. **Don't guess!** Use your tools and make it exact.

● Cut the triangle in half along the line you just drew.

● Put the pieces together to form a rectangle. Measure the length and width of this rectangle (to the nearest .1 cm):

l:\_\_\_\_\_.\_\_\_\_cm

w:\_\_\_\_\_.\_\_\_\_cm

**1.** What is the ratio of length to width of this rectangle?

\_\_\_\_\_.\_\_\_\_

Draw a conclusion about this number and the rectangle. Write it here: _____
_____
_____

**2.** Make a statement about what parts of the *original* triangle make this ratio with each other: _____
_____
_____

**3.** Why do you think the Egyptians did these mathematical things with their greatest pyramid? _____
_____
_____

● **Remember that the Golden Ratio number is one that arises from Nature.** We found it in the human body and face, we found it in seashells and horns, and we found it in the Fibonacci Numbers, which also came from pinecones and sunflowers. **Is it possible that the Egyptians were trying to make the Pyramid somehow like a natural, living object?** Describe your point of view on this on a separate piece of paper.

**FINDING THE GOLD IN THE PYRAMID, continued**

● Here's another interesting viewpoint on the Pyramid. When travelers approached the Pyramid in the desert, they first saw it as a **silhouette,** just an outline that looked like a flatter triangle than one of the triangle sides.

Look down on your pyramid model and then slowly move down to where you are at the desert level looking at the pyramid. Describe how the triangle face changes:

This silhouette triangle is the same as triangle **B** of your model. Your teacher will give you another copy of that triangle to work with.

     **4.** Measure its angles: _____°, _____°, _____°.
     **5.** Measure its sides: _____._____ cm, _____._____cm, _____._____cm.
     **6.** Calculate **half** the bottom side: _____._____ cm.
     **7.** Calculate the **ratio** of a slant side to half the bottom side:

**Surprise!** But is it a surprise? If you think about it carefully, and look at the numbers, you have really just found the same ratio you found on triangle **A.** Check it on your model and explain why:

**Remember this Silhouette Triangle! We'll meet it again in a strange place!**

## Teacher's Guide to Student Pages 217-219

# FINDING THE GOLD IN THE PYRAMID

## AN OVERVIEW OF THIS ACTIVITY

What is truly remarkable about the Egyptian Pyramid designers is that they did all this with π and managed to get the Golden Ratio into the Pyramid in a prominent place. It resides in the fact that each triangle face is made of two halves of a Golden Rectangle! The illustrations on the student page show how this works.

Make sure students realize that this close interplay of several key concepts at once on a scale the size of the Pyramid is a powerful intellectual feat. These things don't just accidentally happen.

All may not agree with the above statement. Some may feel that if you search any building long enough you'll find the numbers you want. It's good to entertain differences about what all this means concerning the Egyptians. If there are strong points of view, set up a debate between the sides. Or ask them to write an opinion piece for the *Tour Guide* newspaper "Dear Goldie" column and mail it in.

Room is also provided on the sheet for opinions about why Egyptians chose the Golden Ratio to be in the Pyramid. We already mulled over why they chose π. The Golden Ratio reason is left even more in the realm of speculation because we know only a little of what it meant to the Egyptians. The article "The Golden Ratio through the Ages" gives more about its meaning to them.

## ANSWERS TO QUESTIONS ON PAGES 218-219

**1.** 16.2 cm; 10 cm
**2.** 1.62. The rectangle is a Golden Rectangle.
**3.** The **altitude** and **half-base** of the original triangle face make the Golden Ratio.
**4.** 52°, 52°, 76° to the nearest degree.
**5.** 16.0 cm; 16.0 cm; 19.8 cm
**6.** 9.9 cm
**7.** 1.62

Thus, the silhouette of the Pyramid as seen on the horizon also has the Golden Ratio in it. This may seem like another occurrence of the Golden Ratio in the Pyramid, but it's totally a result of the fact that the face triangle is two halves of a Golden Rectangle. In fact, the ratio

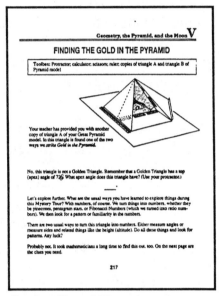

Student Page 217

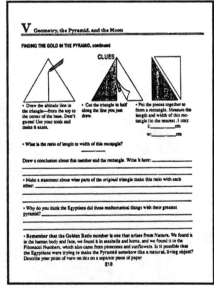

Student Page 218

## Teacher's Guide to Student Pages 217-219

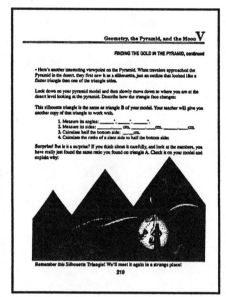

Student Page 219

found in the silhouette is really of the same measurements on the Pyramid, but somewhat in disguise.

If you look at a model, the slanted side of the silhouette is seen to be the same length as the altitude of a face triangle. The half-base line is the same length as half the base of the face triangle.

So the silhouette is just another way to appreciate the Golden Ratio in the Pyramid. But, the silhouette turns out to be the important way to see the Golden Ratio when we go to the moon!

# AND NOW THE MOON . . .

> **Toolbox:** Compass, ruler, protractor, calculator

The moon is a wonderful companion to the sun and Earth in space. It's well suited to both in size. The sun is very far away (91,423,000 miles) and very large (864,000 miles in diameter). The moon is "close" (250,000 miles) and small (2160 miles in diameter). It is remarkable that their distances and sizes are such that from Earth they both look exactly the same size.

The figure shows an exaggeration of the true situation with distances made smaller and the moon made bigger. It shows why the moon and sun look the same size to us.

But that's only the beginning. We're going to involve the Earth and moon in a more striking diagram that will reveal some very surprising mathematical realities.

Imagine that the moon came down from space and just sat on the Earth. If the Earth were the size of a basketball, how big would the moon be? A basketball, a soccer ball, a softball, an orange, a golf ball, a cherry, or a pea? Make a sketch that shows what you think. Save your sketch and answer to be checked as you draw the true picture.

**On the following pages is enough information to make the drawing accurately.**

It will take some thinking to turn this information into a drawing. You'll need the equipment listed above.

If you have trouble, there will be more instructions at the beginning of the next page . . . but give it your best shot on a clean sheet of paper. Do your thinking before you start drawing.

The Earth has a radius of 3960 miles.

The moon has a radius of 1080 miles.

# HINTS ON DRAWING THE EARTH AND MOON

A good way to draw the picture is to cut everything down to an easy scale. The metric system (cm, mm) is the easiest to use because it's based on 10, and the miles of the Earth and moon are given in the 10s system. Here's a nice conversion to centimeters:

3960 miles . . . 39.6 cm
1080 miles . . . 10.8 cm

The only problem here is that a page is only about 28 cm long. Even half the Earth won't fit on one page!

Here's the way out. As long as we multiply or divide both numbers by the same amount, they'll stay in the same **ratio** to each other.

(Do you understand this principle? To see it, suppose that in a large photograph a tree is five times as tall as you are. Then suppose you got the photograph reduced to 1/4 its size. In the new photo the tree is still five times as tall as you are, because you've both shrunk proportionally. That's what we're doing to the Earth and moon measurements.)

So, let's divide each of the cm radius measurements above by 4 to make them proportionally smaller:

39.6 cm . . . 9.9 cm
10.8 cm . . . 2.7 cm

## HINTS ON DRAWING THE EARTH AND MOON, continued

Twice these (a **diameter**) will still fit on the 28 cm page. Now to draw them. Remember, a compass draws circles when you set it to a certain **radius**; the numbers above are radii.

So, set your compass to these settings and draw the circles so that they touch (with the Earth on the bottom).

To set the compass to 9.9, lay it on your ruler and adjust it so that the point is at 0 and the pencil is at 9.9. When drawing a circle, it's better to hold the compass steady and turn the paper slowly.

**GO TO IT!**

Your drawing will be used in the next activity.

## Teacher's Guide to Student Pages 222-224

# AND NOW THE MOON . . . .

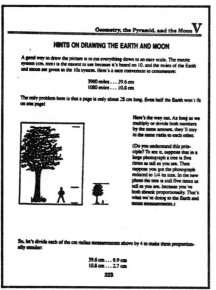

Student Page 222

Student Page 223

## PREPARING STUDENTS FOR THIS ACTIVITY

Another big chance for interdisciplinary education! The moon, like the Pyramid, is an object of fascination. What is called for in this activity is that there be some appreciation of how the Earth and moon (and the sun as well) do their cosmic dance together.

Any lessons on this in advance will make the mathematical result we find more meaningful. Here are some ways to set the stage.

## A SCALE MODEL IS GOOD PREPARATION

It's always valuable to set up a scale model of the Earth and moon (to say nothing of the planets!). The information on the first activity page is enough for students to be able to do this.

The first question asks students how large the moon would be if the Earth were a basketball. Make sure students reason out the relationships. The moon's radius is about 1/4 the Earth's radius. A large orange is about the right size.

To continue the scale model, the moon is about 240,000 miles from Earth. Students should decide how to position the two objects outdoors somewhere. (240,000 + 7920 = 30, which says that 30 basketball diameters are between the basketball and the orange.)

Mark the orbit of the orange with chalk or rocks. One student walks with the orange at a speed of about 7 basketball diameters every time another student rotates the basketball once (a day). It works out that the moon goes around the Earth about once every 28 days—hence the name "month."

Meanwhile, the sun is a mega-monster whose diameter is about 109 basketball diameters, or 100 feet. Two students stand this far apart some distance away from the moon orbit to show how big the sun is. How far away would they have to go so that the orange would cover the sun as viewed from the basketball? This happens when the sun hides behind the moon during a solar eclipse.

(It turns out that the sun is 11,500 basketball diameters away. How far is this? A basketball is just under a foot, and there are 5280 feet in a mile. Can the students calculate it? The sun would be roughly two miles away!)

This is a good start. There are other nuances like phases of the moon, winter-summer, and the lunar eclipse. There are many references the students can consult and facts they can enact with these models if you wish to pursue the astronomy lesson. There are films, maps of the moon, and moon-watches to continue the themes started here.

### THE SCALE DRAWING OF MOON AND EARTH

Students should now be thoroughly prepared to try to make the requested scale drawing. Let them mull it over, trying things and discussing. If they bog down, give them the page of hints that follows (p. 223). Page 227 has an illustration you can look at to see if theirs look right.

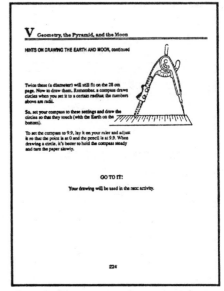

Student Page 224

# THE GOLDEN PYRAMID PAYOFF

You are about to see one of the most amazing sights on your **Tour.** To start with, your drawing should look something like the figure below.

We're going to add a few more lines, **carefully, slowly,** and **accurately!** First, *lightly* draw a line that connects the center of the moon and the center of the Earth.

Use your ruler! (This is called a **line of centers.**)

Now we need a line that goes through the center of the Earth and is at a right (90°) angle to the line of centers you just drew. That is, we are making a line **perpendicular** to the line of centers through Earth's center. We need the protractor's 90° mark for this.

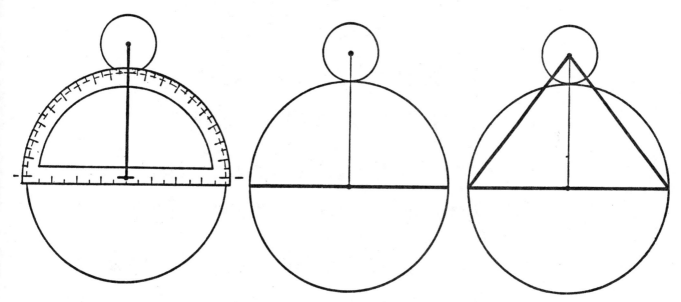

Here's how:
● Place the protractor bull's eye on Earth's center so that the 90° mark lies on the line of centers.
● Make a mark at the 0° and 180° lines of the protractor.
● Connect these with a line segment that stops at the edges of the circle.

● Now draw a segment from the **center** *of* the moon to each end of the Earth diameter. You've made a triangle. And *what* a triangle! Measure its three angles carefully:

_____°,

_____°,

_____°

Compare these numbers to the three angles you measured on the Pyramid **silhouette** triangle on the page 219. The angles should be identical.

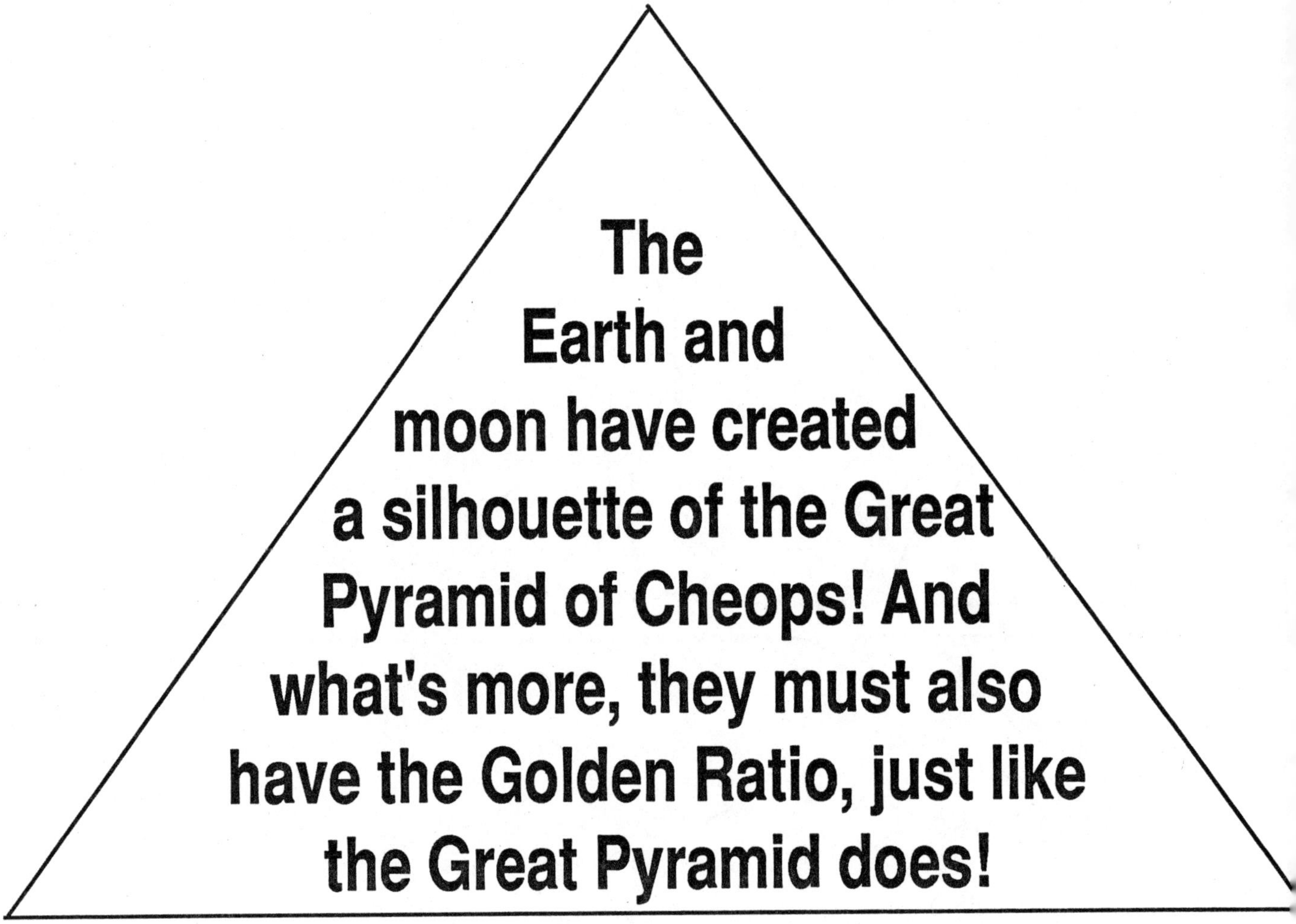

# The Earth and moon have created a silhouette of the Great Pyramid of Cheops! And what's more, they must also have the Golden Ratio, just like the Great Pyramid does!

Check it by finding the ratio of the slant line (moon to end of Earth diameter) to half of Earth's diameter. Write what you get here:

_____·_____

Is it the Golden Ratio? It should be!

228

# A MOON'S-EYE VIEW OF OUR MYSTERY TOUR

While we're on the moon, which is standing on the Earth, we have a magnificent view of the whole path of our **Tour**. The detailed map of our voyage is on  page 241. Let's now, though, just try to see the general path we've traveled in Nature, history, and thought to reach this moon-pyramid we're now standing on.

We started with a spiral form in Nature—on sunflowers, pinecones, and the like—and found some marvelous (Fibonacci) numbers that march in a very orderly way with each other. We saw how they do number tricks and put prime numbers in predictable places.

We learned about ratios; we then looked at Greek statues and found the wonderful Golden Ratio throughout the body and face. From this Golden body Ratio we made a Golden Rectangle, which produced for us a seashell and a ram's horn. We also found that the Golden Rectangle has an infinity of Golden Rectangles spiraling inside it. We found the Golden Ratio in the ancient magic Pentagram and in the perfect solids of the Greeks.

We reached a major crossing of paths when we discovered that the Golden Ratio could be found right inside the Fibonacci Numbers! (The ratios of consecutive Fibonaccis approach the Golden Ratio more and more accurately as the numbers get larger.) So we then were on a **Golden Fibo-Ratio Journey!**

Finally came a trip to the Great Pyramid and even to the moon, where we're now standing. In these exotic things we find the Golden Fibo-Ratio (with the ever-present π) controlling shapes and distances.

# BIG QUESTION

**"How come so many amazing things (like pineapples, pyramids, prime numbers, and planets) march to the same mathematically amazing number?**

The following questions are all related to the **BIG ONE** above:

**1.** Why is the Fibo-Ratio both mathematically *nice* and very *natural* at the same time?

**2.** Why does the Golden Fibo-Ratio appear in the Great Pyramid? And how did the Egyptians manage to get π *and* the Golden Fibo-Ratio to work out in the same Pyramid measurements at the same time?

**3.** Why does the Great Pyramid connect to the Earth-moon relationship? Did the Egyptians know this, and if so, how?

**4.** How do natural things *know* about mathematics?

**5.** The Pythagoreans say, *All is number*. Do you agree?

**Nobody really knows the answers to these questions—
or if they do they're not telling!**

**But you are about to be asked to answer them!**

If you just *think* about it, your mind may not give very interesting answers. So first try this to get the more creative part of your brain going.

Choose two of the three activities below and take sufficient time to do them well. They will cause another part of your mind, besides the *Thinker*, to wake up.

● On a separate sheet of paper, write *at least* a one-page fantasy story (get **way-out** and **sci-fi** with it!) showing how these strange coincidences came to be.

● Write a poem about the Golden Ratio and Mother Nature. The poem can be silly or serious.

If you're stuck for ideas, start your poem by thinking of the Golden Ratio as a person. Talk to it in your mind.

Then list 15 words that describe this "person" that's the Golden Ratio.

Then use these words in your poem. And don't worry about rhyme.

● Using water-color or acrylic paints, or crayons, or pens, create a picture that shows some of the relationships in the questions above.

Don't try to make it *realistic*. Make it more like a fantasy.

Now, get more serious, and write on a separate page at least 1/2 page on *your* answer to the Big Question. You can include answers to any part of questions 1-5, which might help you get started.

But *don't* just answer questions 1-5 without joining your remarks into a Big Answer to the Big Question. Remember . . . there's no "right" answer to this in an answer book somewhere, so just write what you think.

## Teacher's Guide to Student Pages 227-231

# THE GOLDEN PYRAMID PAYOFF

## AN OVERVIEW OF THE PYRAMID PAYOFF

Students are about to discover a truly astounding coincidence. I'm indebted to the writings of John Michel for calling it to my attention.

If students pursue the construction carefully, they will end up with an exact silhouette of the **Great Pyramid of Cheops** created by the Earth-moon size relationship. The angles are off by only about 2 minutes of degree or an error of about 5 in 1000.

Make sure students recheck the silhouette angles of the Great Pyramid. They can also confirm that the Earth-moon triangle is the same as the Pyramid silhouette by finding the Golden Ratio in it the same way.

This lesson represents a grand unification of many different themes of the **Mystery Tour** and so is a kind of climax. The meaning of it all may be elusive to the left-brained, logical mind. But the interconnections take on a kind of appropriateness and generate in me a sense of relief that there is an underlying order in the world. These sensibilities fade under the harsh light of logic, which is, fortunately, not the only referee of reality.

Now it's time to try to bring your students to a Grand Synthesis of what it's all been about.

## MEASUREMENTS OF THE EARTH-MOON TRIANGLE

The three angles are 52°, 52°, and 76°. (The two really are closer to 51°51', but protractors can't discriminate that finely.) These are exactly the angles (within 2 minutes of degree) of the silhouette triangle of the Great Pyramid. The ratio of the side to the Earth's radius is 1.62, the Golden Ratio.

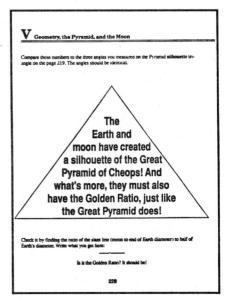

Student Page 228

Student Page 229

## Teacher's Guide to Student Pages 227-231

# A MOON'S-EYE VIEW OF OUR MYSTERY TOUR

Student Page 231

### THE MOON'S-EYE VIEW

This is a review of the journey before popping "The Big Question."

### THE BIG QUESTION

This is a reflective activity. It poses the Big Question. You and your students must have felt some kind of question trying to bubble its way up to the surface during these later activities. I've written down for the students a few that strike me.

A discussion is probably in order, either as a whole class or in groups. Ask students to just raise questions that are still unanswered at this point on the **Tour**. Then choose some of the *juiciest* for class discussion.

But then the logical left brain has to be told to wait. It's the right brain's turn to comment. Students are being prepared to go more into their right brains by the series of activities suggested on the next page—poems, drawings, and stories. These would make good homework assignments or class projects. Encourage students to share them with the whole group or class before they attempt to write the answers.

Then, finally, a class or group discussion of answers would be very lively indeed.

# SOME TASTY EARTH-MOON TIDBITS

**Toolbox:** Calculator; Earth-moon diagram; ruler; compass; protractor

The best dessert was finding the Great Pyramid in the moon-Earth drawing. But there are a few more tidbits I find tasty that I can't resist giving to you. There are three main ones:

**1.** Get out your Moon-Touching-Earth diagram.

Mark 7920 miles on the diameter of the Earth.

Mark **1080** miles on the half-diameter (radius) of the moon.

Mark 3960 miles on the radius of the Earth.

Notice that the line joining the center of the Earth with the center of the moon is 3960 + 1080 = 5040 miles long. Put this number on that line.

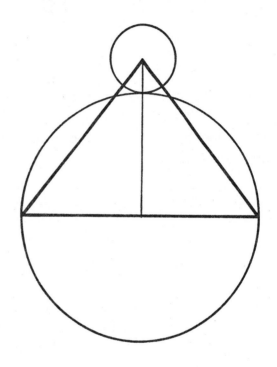

Let's explore these numbers. On your calculator, find these answers:

$$1 \times 2 \times 3 \times 4 \times 5 \times 6 \times 7 = \underline{\qquad}$$

$$8 \times 9 \times 10 \times 11 = \underline{\qquad}$$

Compare your answers to numbers above. Surprised? Why is this remarkable?

_____

_____

_____

**2.** This is the **Squaring-the-Circle** Tidbit. Continue using your diagram from Tidbit 1.

Imagine that the radius of the Earth were just 8 miles shorter (**3952** miles) than the **3960** figure we've been using.*  Use **3952 + 1080 = 5042** as the moon-center to Earth-center length.

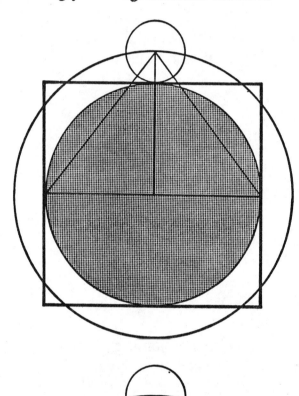

Imagine this new radius length turning like the hand on a clock and tracing a circle bigger than the Earth—the circle passes through the moon's center (see diagram). Now use your compass and draw this circle.

Calculate the **circumference** (= $2\pi r$) of the big circle:

_____ miles
(round to nearest mile).

Now with your ruler make a square that just holds the Earth inside. (See diagram.) Make top and bottom parallel to the Earth diameter you drew earlier, and make the corners 90°. Figure out what the **perimeter** of this square is (sum of the sides):

_____ miles.

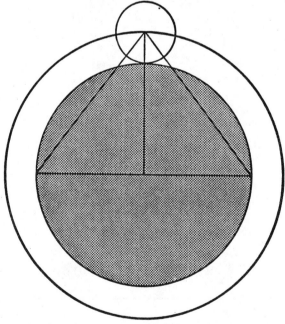

Compare answers. The ancient mathematicians of Greece called this "Squaring the Circle." This means making a square that has a perimeter equal to the circumference of a circle. The Earth and moon know how to do this.

*The radius of 3952 miles is a real radius of the Earth at about Northern Egypt—the radius gets shorter as you go toward the pole because the spinning Earth has a slightly fat *belly*. The 3960 figure is the radius at the Equator.

**3.** Some research seems to say that the mile is a measurement from very ancient times, way before Greece and the Roman Empire. Tidbit 1 showed you that mile numbers for the Earth and moon make remarkable number *coincidences*. It makes me wonder whether the people who invented the mile somehow knew it was *tuned* to the Earth and moon.

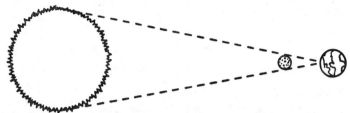

To add more evidence, this third tidbit shows even more coincidences with mile numbers of Earth, moon, and sun. There are no such coincidences with distances expressed in kilometers (which were invented just 200 years ago).

This is the **Dance of the Sixes.** To within just a few miles, here are some measurements in space. Multiply them out:

Diameter of the moon: 6 x 6 x 60 miles _____

Diameter of the Earth: 2 x 6 x 660 miles _____

Diameter of the sun: 2 x 2 x 6 x 6 x 6000 miles _____

Distance of Earth to moon: 6 x 60 x 660 miles _____

The speed of the Earth as it goes around the sun: 66,600 miles per hour

The number of radii of the Earth that would reach to the moon: 60

What is your opinion about the *coincidences* in all three Tidbits? _____

_____

_____

_____

_____

## Teacher's Guide to Student Pages 235-237

# SOME TASTY EARTH-MOON TIDBITS

### TIDBIT 1

This tidbit is surprising. 1x2x3x4x5x6x7 = 5040, which is the sum of the Earth and moon radii, when they are measured in miles. This too was pointed out by John Michel.

The number 5040 has some other importance. It has more numbers (factors, divisors) that will divide into it than any other number its size. The *Tour Guide* newspaper article on Plato points out his statement that the population of the *ideal city* would be 5040 because of its many possible groupings.

A good class activity would be to log, using calculators, all the divisors of 5040. Without calculators, it becomes good long-division practice.

The Earth's diameter being 7920 = 8x9x10x11 adds to the mystery. It seems either beyond coincidence or a highly improbable coincidence.

There's an issue here. If these lengths weren't measured in miles, the numbers wouldn't do this. Kilometers don't work out nicely here. How come the mile measure seems to make such nice Earth and moon numbers? Wasn't it invented by a king or something? There's mounting evidence that the mile was part of a very ancient and very coherent system of measure. A good discussion question, or sci-fi question, is "Where do you think the mile came from?"

### TIDBIT 2

The first calculated answer is 31617 miles and the second, the perimeter, is 31616 miles, essentially the same number.

The radius had to be *fudged* a bit, you say? Well, the Earth is fatter one way than the other. The **polar** radius is about 120 miles shorter.

The earth radius measured from somewhere *above* the equator (Egypt?) straight to the center of the earth would be 3952. Maybe this is still fudging?

Student Page 235

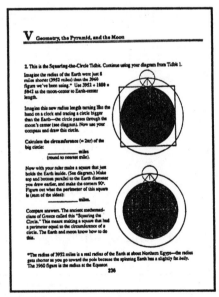

Student Page 236

## Teacher's Guide to Student Pages 235-237

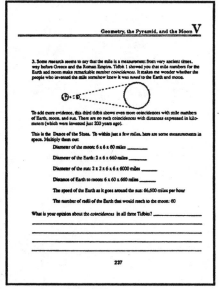

Student Page 237

But we can still say that the circle drawn with the Earth-moon radius has a circumference essentially equal to the perimeter of the square around the Earth. And this equality doesn't depend on the use of miles—it would exist in any system of measure.

### TIDBIT 3

Moon: 2160
Earth: 7920
Sun: 864,000
Earth-moon: 237,600

The mile numbers are doing it again! They are creating sixes way beyond probability. And by the way, there are many other coincidences with the mile numbers, but these take more mathematics than I can show you at this time.

What do **you** think about all of these coincidences? Be sure to share your opinion with the students while leaving them room for theirs.

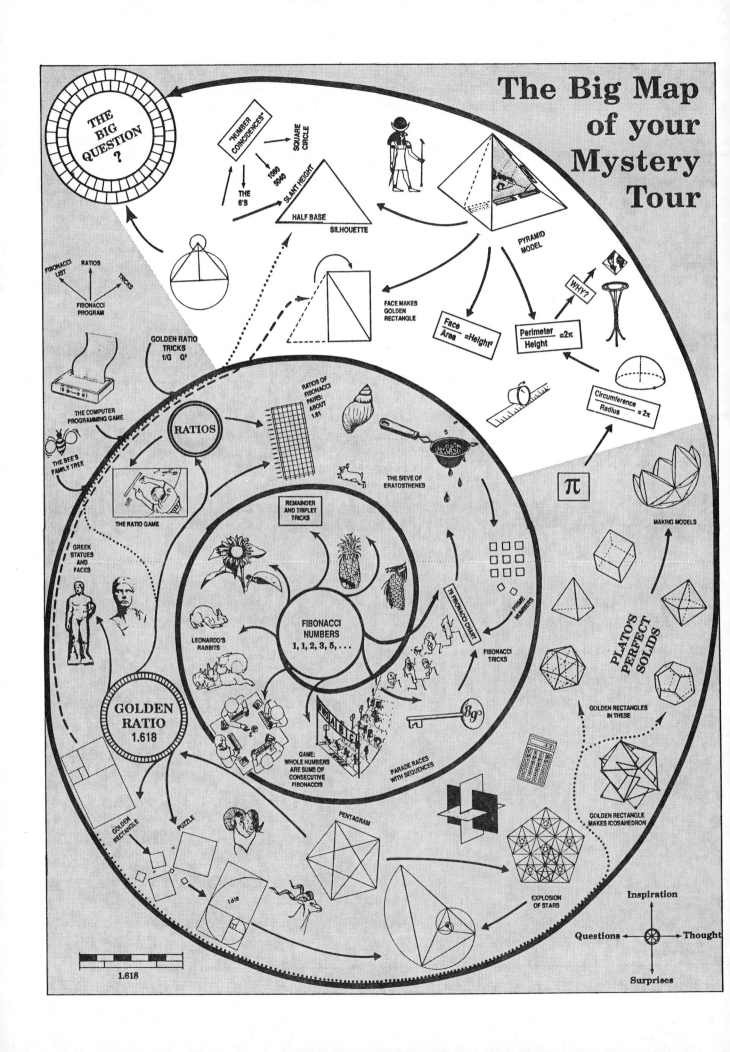

# A LOOK AT THE TERRITORY: UNIT V

Here we are again at the section of map you just covered. You made some of the longest voyages of the whole **Tour** here.

● Discuss with someone else the parts of this section of the map and all arrows that relate to these (even those that come from the Tour Map).

● Study this map for three minutes and draw it from memory (no exact pictures necessary).

● Write a one-page letter to Leonardo Fibonacci about the whole journey of this unit, raising questions you have thought about and telling him some exciting connections to his rabbit-numbers he would have enjoyed knowing. (Leonardo Fibonacci knew nothing about these connections.)

# LEARNING INVENTORY

**Toolbox:** Calculator

Get out your calculator. Here are some questions to see how well you can use or say what you have learned. Again, if you have trouble with some, go back and restudy the material. Your teacher will tell you what to do from there.

**1.** What is the circumference of a circle with **radius** 2.5 cm?

Your Estimation:_____
Your Calculation:_____

**2.** What is the radius of a circle with **circumference** 31.4 cm?

Your Estimation:_____
Your Calculation:_____

**3.** What is $\pi$? Give your best answer without using the decimal or fraction number:

_____

_____

_____

**4.** What does $\pi$ have to do with the Great Pyramid? _____

_____

_____

_____

**5.** (Challenge) The Pyramid is 755 feet along one side of its base. Use the relationship you wrote in #4 to figure how tall the Pyramid is.

_____

**6.** What does the Golden Ratio have to do with the Pyramid? _____

_____

_____

**7.** (Challenge) Calculate the slant height (**apothegm**) of the Pyramid from the relationship you wrote in **#6** and the number given you in **#5**. **HINT:** Start with the half-base length.

**8.** What is a theory as to why π is in the Pyramid?

_____

_____

_____

● What is a theory as to why the Golden Ratio is in the Pyramid? _____

_____

_____

**9.** How does the length of the Pyramid relate to the Equator? _____

_____

**10.** Moon and Earth:

● How does the Pyramid shape relate to the moon and Earth? _____

_____

● What does 5040 have to do with the moon and Earth? _____

_____

● What is interesting mathematically about 5040? _____

_____

## Teacher's Guide to Student Pages 242-243

# LEARNING INVENTORY

### DESCRIPTION OF THE INVENTORY

The questions here invite comprehension and application. There are two *challenging* calculation questions that invite some analytical thinking. Again, group work on the inventory may be more beneficial. Or an *open book* might be of value, depending on students' comfort with the material.

Be sure there's some accountability for any answers missed by having students write up a more descriptive account of the concept they failed to retain.

### ANSWERS TO QUESTIONS ON PAGES 242-243

**1.** 2.5 x 2 x 3.14 = 15.7 cm. It's important to have them write *cm*. The unit of the answer is the same unit the radius has.

**2.** 31.4 ÷ 3.14 = 10, the diameter. The radius is half this, or 5.

**3.** Something like "the number of diameters that go around a circle" or "a ratio of circumference to diameter." It's important that they always have a *concept* of π as well as a number for it.

**4.** The perimeter of the base of the Pyramid divided by its height is 2π, which is also true of a half-sphere.

**5.** The perimeter of the base is 755 x 4 = 3020. If this is divided by the height we get 2π, or 6.28. So if 3020 is divided by 6.28, we get the height, 481 to the nearest foot.

**6.** Two things: The face is a triangle made from two halves of the Golden Rectangle. This means that the ratio of the altitude of that face to half the base is 1.618. The other is that on the silhouette triangle, the ratio of the slant side to half the base is 1.618.

**7.** Half the base is 377.5 ft. The other side is 1.618 as big, or 1.618 x 377.5 = 611 feet to the nearest foot.

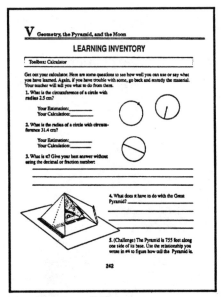

Student Page 242

Student Page 243

**8.** A theory is that the Egyptians were trying to represent a half-sphere, in fact half an Earth sphere, with the Pyramid. They couldn't build a *dome* so they built in the spherical/circular number π instead.

A theory as to why the Golden Ratio is in the Pyramid is that the Egyptians felt it was an important number related to living things, especially the human body, and they wanted the Pyramid to imitate Nature's design. (The important thing here is that students know how to state a theory whether it's theirs or not.)

**9.** The Pyramid is 1/8 the length of a minute of longitude at the Equator.

**10.** The Pyramid shape can be constructed from moon+Earth radii, and Earth diameter.

5040 is the moon+Earth radii together.

5040 is 1x2x3x4x5x6x7 and it has more divisors than any number less than or equal to its size.

Optional Activity 3:
# GOLDEN RATIO TRICKS

**Toolbox:** Calculator

The Golden Ratio number is 1.618034 . . . . You have seen this number perform its tricks in the Golden Rectangle, Golden Triangle, spirals, human bodies, heavenly bodies (Earth, moon), and the Great Pyramid. But like the Fibonaccis it has a few mathematical tricks of its own. To show you these tricks, I'll write "G" when I mean 1.618034 . . . just to make things look simpler.

## Trick 1

How much is 1/G? (Find out by dividing 1 ÷ 1.616034.)

Answer: _____

Does it look familiar? _____ How does it relate to G?

_____

Now calculate:
1 divided by the answer you got above.

Your answer: _____.

Surprised? Why should this be no surprise?

_____

_____

Express your finding using the letter G and a nondecimal number:

1/G = _____

## Trick 2

Find, as a decimal, $G^2$. (That is, multiply G x G.)

_____

Look familiar? If your calculator didn't round off any decimal places and you weren't using rounded-off numbers to start with, you would get exactly the decimal it looks like it's trying to be.

Use only G, and a simple nondecimal to fill in this statement:

$G^2 =$ _____

## Teacher's Guide to Student Page 247

Optional Activity 3:

# GOLDEN RATIO TRICKS

### TRICK 1

The Golden Ratio is not without its mathematical tricks, so we end the **Tour** with a couple of them. After all, this ratio has really been our **Tour Guide** for a major part of the journey.

The essence of this first trick is the surprising fact that

$$\frac{1}{G} = G - 1$$

That is, if you take the reciprocal (the one-over) of G, by **dividing** 1 by G, your decimal is as though you just **subtracted** 1 from G! You get the identical decimal part again. Now if you divide

$$1 \div .618034,$$

which is the reciprocal of *that* reciprocal, you get 1.618034 again. This reciprocal just adds 1 to the decimal.

Students can appreciate more the uniqueness of this trick by trying it with 1.3, 1.5, or 1.8, for instance. None will reproduce its decimal part even closely. Example:

$$1/1.5 = .6666667, \text{ not } .5$$

If they try several examples with other numbers, the significance of this trick will begin to dawn on them.

### TRICK 2

$G^2$ turns out to be 2.618034! This is simply G + 1. With G, taking it times itself is equivalent to simply adding 1 to it! This is very strange and simple behavior for a complicated-looking decimal.

Again I recommend that students try squaring other decimals to see if they get anything resembling 1 more than the decimal. The sharper

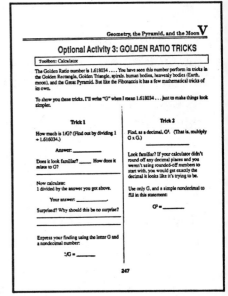

Student Page 247

researchers will begin to realize that the closer they get to 1.61804, the more the squaring is like adding 1 to the decimal.

In both tricks we see that G has the ability to turn division into simple subtraction, and multiplication into simple addition. An extension of this into algebra leads to a dynamite conclusion. Even if you don't like algebra, you might appreciate the concluding line of . . .

### G'S SUPER TRICK FOR ANY ALGEBRA-ORIENTED STUDENT

G has its own algebra. We saw that $G^2 = G + 1$, so what is $G^3$?

By simple substitution and use of distributivity,

$G^3 = G(G^2) = G(G+1) = G^2 + G = (G+1) + G = 2G + 1$; that is, to **cube G**, simply **double G and add 1!**

$G^4 = G(G^3) = G(2G+1) = 2G^2 + G = 2(G+1) + G = 2G + 2 + G = 3G + 2$; that is, $G^4$ is obtained by **tripling G and adding 2.**

Now speculate what $G^5$ would be. $4G + 3$, you say?

$G^5 = G(G^4) = G(3G+2) = 3G^2 + 2G = 3(G+1) + 2G = 3G +3 + 2G = 5G + 3$! Not quite what was expected! We seem to be going to the Fibonacci numbers instead! Indeed, $G^6 = 8G + 5$, and so on!

Recall that G can be obtained from **ratios** of successive Fibonaccis. Well, now we see that the Fibonaccis can be obtained from **powers** of G. Voilá!

# A FINAL LOOK AT THE MAP: THE MAP GAME

**CONGRATULATIONS!** You've just completed the **Magical Mystery Tour!**

The whole map of the **Tour** is now understandable to you. You are capable of pointing to any object on the map and explaining how it connects through all its arrows to the other places in the map.

### To prove it, play the MAP GAME.

| | |
|---|---|
| **Players:** | Two or more |
| **Materials:** | Scissors, thick paper, pens, die |
| **Preparation:** | Cut out 24 slips of paper and divide them up among the players so that each person has the same number. Put aside any extras. Each player takes charge of a section of the map, until the whole map is spoken for. All players write on their pieces of paper some key ideas or objects from their section of the map. |
| **Play:** | All slips are mixed up and dealt back to the players, who spread them out **face-down** in front of them. Players throw the die. Highest number starts. |

(Players who throw a tie throw again.)

The Tour Map is kept out of sight during play. Player 1 picks one card from his hand and one (without seeing it) from the person to his left. He must describe a clear relationship between the two ideas on the cards (if there is one). He must be able to trace the relationship along arrows on the map, if challenged.

If he can't describe one, someone else can try. (Challengers take turns, starting with the first to Player 1's left.) The first person to describe the connection keeps the card. If nobody can, the Tour Map is consulted to make sure there is no set of arrow connections. If there is none Player 1 returns the cards to where he got them. If there is a connection, he keeps the cards. The next player to the left plays the same way, and so on.

The game ends when a player has eight more cards than the number she started with. If a player runs out of cards, he must drop out of the game.

**And remember, all games have some ways they can be improved. If the whole group agrees on a way to change the rules to make play go better, try it!**

## Teacher's Guide to Student Page 251

# A FINAL LOOK AT THE MAP: THE MAP GAME

**The Map Game** is a good way to really challenge the students to go after the multiple interconnections of the material in the **Tour**. It further familiarizes them with the map as well. If they can take this mind map away with them from the **Tour**, they will always be able to pull out a great deal of it from their memories.

Another good wrap-up activity for the **Tour** is to produce a **time-line** from it. On the time-line go names of people and places as well as discoveries spoken of on the **Tour**. The Pythagorean Community has a place on it. So does the Mayan zero and the start of the Fibonacci Society. If small groups pool their gleanings from past notes and the *Tour Guide* newspaper, then join together as a class to make one big time-line, most ideas will be hit.

Another possibility is to make an exhibit for the school halls. Students pick different topics from the Tour Map. They make models, charts, drawings, and explanations for their particular exhibit idea.

A final ending idea is to have a *Mystery Tour Costume Party and Performance*. Students dress up as either main or supporting characters encountered on the **Tour**. The title song of the Beatles' *Magical Mystery Tour* album plays in the background. Refreshments have little mathematical twists like fraction cookies, Golden Rectangle bread slices, Pyramid cake, or the like. Performances involve a spoof on the characters' contributions, like Pythagoras plunking a string, Plato **thinking** of an ideal performance, Leonardo pulling Fibonacci rabbits out of a hat, and so forth.

**And now this Tour comes to an end. And yet this is only one more turn of an unending spiral journey we all take through the mysteries of this universe.**

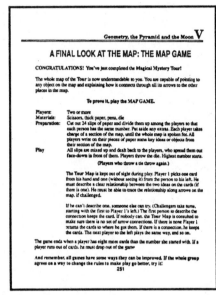

Student Page 251

# KEY TO THE TOUR GUIDE NEWSPAPER

## Bees Form Labor Union and University

1. Varies—any town with 35,000 to 50,000 inhabitants.

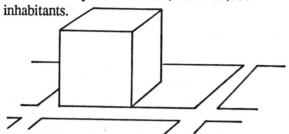

3. 40,000 1/2-inch bees = 20,000 inches of bees. In 1 block there are 300 ft. x 12 in. = 3600 in. 20,000 ÷ 3600 = 5.56, or about 5 1/2 blocks of bees.
4. 1500 feedings ÷ 24 hours = 62.5 feedings per hour, or about 1 feeding per minute.
5. 18 hrs. x 60 min. = 1080 minutes of egg-laying per day.
   1700 eggs ÷ 1080 = 1.57 or about 1 1/2 eggs per minute.
6. 3 yrs. x 52 wks./yr = 156 wks. for average queen's life.
   Workers live 6 wks. 156 ÷ 6 = 26 worker lives/queen.

**Brain Bender:** Plant the cabbages at these points of a pentagram star:

## Eratosthenes Measures the Earth!

1. 1988 + 231 = 2219 years ago (for present year 1988).
2. One stade = 1/10 mile.
3.a. The most familiar countries are Mexico, Taiwan, China, Burma, India, Saudi Arabia, Egypt, Libya, and Algeria.
   b. The Tropic of Capricorn is 23° *below* the equator and passes through Australia, Africa, and South America.
   c. The sun is directly over the Tropic of Capricorn on the first day of winter (Dec. 21), shortest day of the year (but longest day of the year in the Southern Hemisphere).
4. Midway between the horizon and overhead.
5. 7.2°

6. The sun moves from overhead down to the horizon, continuing to straight below the finger's "feet," and back up from the opposite horizon to be straight overhead again.
7. Pacific: Somewhat under half the equator—11,500 miles.
   Atlantic: About 1/6 of equator—4000 miles.

## Fibonaccium Discovered

1. The ratio starts at 0, gets bigger, and approaches the Golden Ratio.
2. 147 ÷ 90 = 1.633, which differs from 1.618 by only .015, so we call it the Golden Ratio.
3. Answers will vary. Scientists don't know.

## The Golden Ratio Has Been in Style For Years

1. Mr. Schwaller is saying that if a style of art is developed by a society for many generations, and an artist in that style makes something perfectly pleasing, then it will probably have the Golden Ratio in it. This is just an opinion.
2. Answers vary.
3. 8.9 cm, 5.5 cm, 14.4 cm; 14.4 ÷ 8.9 = 1.618 and 8.9 ÷ 5.5 = 1.618.
4. In the illustration of the vase, the following ratios are Golden: b/a, g/h, f/c, e/d, f/e, and a/f. The whole length of the bird head divided by the outside length of the eye oval is the Golden Ratio.
5. Perhaps the Greek, because the Golden Ratio was well known by the ancient Greeks. Probably the Indian artist was just intuitively aware of good proportion.
6. In the U.N. Building, the large Secretariat Tower is a Golden Rectangle, and the grill work division of the tower creates a Golden Rectangle at the top.

## The History of π

Note: Information here is obtained from Petr Beckmann's book, **A History of π.**

1. 3.1416 - 3 = .1416 off.
2. 256 is their value, and 254.47 is the value using π, giving a difference of 1.53 unit.
3. (64 + 81) x 4 = 3.1604, a bit too high.
4. 3.1416000 is exactly equal to modern π to four decimal places. It differs by .0000074 from π if decimal places are continued.

5. 3 10/71 = 3.140845 and 3 1/7 = 3.142857. The first is below π by .00075 and the second is above π by .0012645.
6. Very close.
7. 3.1255, differing from π by .01605.
8. 3 1/7 = 3.1428571.
9. √10 = 3.1623.
10. Exactly the modern value to 5 decimal places.

## Inside the Great Pyramid of Cheops

1. Answers vary.
2. 2 1/2 dozen centuries = 3000 years.
   1988 - 820 A.D. = 1168 years to Al Mamun's time. Add 3000 years to that and get 4168 years old for the Great Pyramid.
3. 340 ft., 40 ft. longer than a small city block.
4. Answers will vary.
5. Probably more than a month, anyway, with severe dust and smoke conditions in their cramped work area.
6. Five days? Answers will vary.
7. 6300 times their estimate in #6.
8. On the average the block could be considered 6 feet (6 mosque stones) wide, 5 ft. (5 mosque stones) high, and 12 ft. (6 mosque stones) long so there are 6 x 5 x 6 = 180 mosque stones in one Pyramid stone. Answers may vary a bit.
9. East is sunrise and the Egyptians worshipped the sun.
   The obelisk may have been intended to cast a shadow on a special place on the sphinx on certain special days of the year. What the sphinx means is "The Riddle of the Sphinx."

## The Magical Pentagram of Old

1. 13.
2. 1776.
3. 13.
4.

## Mega-Spiral

1. About 7 light-years thick.
2. 186,000 x number of seconds in a year x 80,000 light-years = about 469,260,000,000,000,000 miles. This problem is best done by leaving off

zeros during the calculation, then putting all omitted zeros onto answer at end.

## More Evidence for the Half-Earth Theory

43,200 seconds in a half day; Yes; 43,200 Pyramid heights = 1 Earth radius; Same.
Since the number of Pyramid heights in an Earth radius = the number of seconds it takes the sun to move over half the Earth, it seems that once again the Pyramid height is strongly related to the Earth radius, and that the Pyramid is related to half the Earth-sphere.

## New Book By Leonardo Fibonacci Released!

1. 1988 + 800 = 2788 A.D.*
2. 212 yrs. old; almost 4 U.S. histories; Leonardo lived about 304 years even before Columbus.*
3. Red mark on Pisa; dotted line Pisa to Bugia; Southern Spain, Northern Africa, Middle East, and Turkey are colored in.
4. 1988 - 800 - 600 = 588 A.D. near the time of the Fall of Rome (576 A.D.)*
5. Arrows come from India, through the middle East to Northern Africa and southern Spain.
6. a. Green dot at Alexandria; purple dot at Baghdad.
   b. Green arrow from Alexandria to Baghdad.
   c. 300 B.C.- 600 A.D. next to Alexandria.
   d. 800 A.D. - 1450 A.D. next to Baghdad.
*Note that these answers depend on current year being 1988.

## Postage Stamps

Longer postage stamps are about 40 mm x 25 mm, ratio 1.6, the Golden Rectangle.

## The Pyramid at the Center

The Great Pyramid is at the center of the circle which contains the arc of the Nile Delta—something amazingly "coincidental."

## The Pyramid on the Globe

Measurements will vary with globe size. The 30° latitude circle through the Great Pyramid crosses more land than any latitude circle. The 31° longitude half-circle crosses more land than any other longitude half-circle. In a way, then, the Great Pyramid is in the middle of the land mass of the Earth's surface.

**Pythagorean Puzzle**
    Advanced Insight: 3-4-5 "jumps"; yes.

**Scientists Vote Ratio Most Useful Tool**
    a. 36 boys/20 girls = 9/5 boys/girl or 1.8 boys/girl.
    b. 88 cm/102 cm = .863  (no units—they canceled out.)
    c. 64 balloons/16 balloons = 4  (no units).

**Secrets of Pythagoras's Community Exposed**
    1. A sphere is a perfect round-ball-shaped solid.
    2. Sun, moon, Mercury, Venus, Mars, Jupiter, Saturn.
    3. Sunday, Monday, Saturday.
    4. 28 is perfect because 1,2,4,7 and 14 divide into it and the sum of these numbers *is* 28.
    5. 1.4142136 . . .; √3 is irrational; √3 = 1.7320508

**Tower in Pisa Leans 5°**
    1. 176 years.
    2. 19 stories, approximately.

**Weird Fractions with Ones**
    3/5. Continuing the pattern then simplifying the fraction always gives a ratio of Fibonacci Numbers: 5/8, 8/13, etc.

**Who Was Cheops Anyway?**
    1. 2600 +1988 = 4588 (Answer depends on current year.)
    2. Answers will vary.

Answer to the student crossword puzzle:

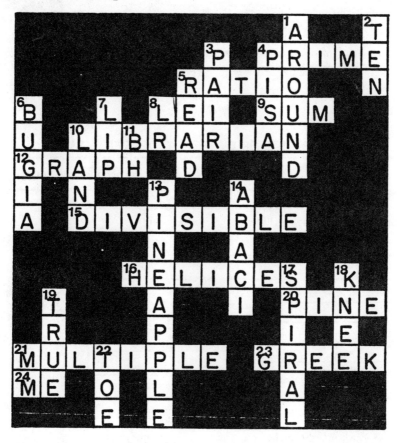

# Help students apply what they learn in school to their lives outside the classroom.

## TURNING LEARNING INSIDE OUT
### A Guide for Using Any Subject to Enrich Life and Creativity
by Herbert L. Leff and Ann Nevin

Grades K–12

Help your students gain a new sense of purpose, excitement, and value for learning. Teach them how to develop cognitive bridges that link academic and real-world problem solving.

Have fun with dozens of "minds-on" activities. Apply flexible strategies to all content areas and educational settings. Your students will—
- Find academic content more involving and relevant
- Combine metacognitive skills and content learning
- Develop a self-directed and cooperative approach to learning

256 pages, 8 ½" x 11", softbound.
**ZB48–W . . . $29**

## DOORWAYS TO LEARNING
### A Model for Developing the Brain's Full Potential
by Peter Majoy

Grades K–12

Use this model to traverse ability groups, age groups, and socioeconomic boundaries effectively. Capitalize on the real experiences of students by respecting each individual learning style.

Find the theory behind each doorway of learning. You'll also have lots of activities you can adapt to any curricular area. You'll find methods to—
- Promote a blend of challenge and calm
- Produce firsthand experiences, the most effective way to learn
- Encourage the exchange of information among all learners
- Incorporate movement into special settings, such as exams
- And much more

256 pages, 7" x 9", softbound
**ZB41-W . . . $25**

---

## CALL, WRITE, OR FAX FOR YOUR FREE CATALOG!